IN DARKEST HOLLYWOOD

IN DARKEST HOLLYWOOD
Exploring the jungles of cinema's South Africa

PETER DAVIS

Ravan Press

OHIO UNIVERSITY PRESS
Athens

Published by Ravan Press (Pty) Ltd, P O Box 145, Randburg 2125
South Africa

ISBN: 0 86975 443 2

Published in the United States of America by Ohio University Press,
Scott Quadrangle, Athens, Ohio 45701

ISBN: 0 8214 1162 4

Library of Congress Cataloguing-in-Publication Data available

First published 1996

Cover design, Ingrid Obery and Centre Court Studio
DTP setting and design, Luisa Potenza & Associates

Printed by Creda Press, Cape Town

CONTENTS

Dedicated to author Mary Benson, a friend deeply cherished

Much of this book is the outcome of research undertaken by Daniel Riesenfeld and myself as co-producers of the two-part television programme *In Darkest Hollywood: Cinema and Apartheid*, a five-year project. I would like to extend special thanks to the personnel of the National Film Archives, Pretoria, and to Madeline F Matz of the Motion Picture Division of the Library of Congress, Washington, DC.

A note on spelling:
In the discussions of films, the names of historical characters are spelled as they appear in the particular film's cast-list. So, for example, Cetshwayo is spelled Cetewayo in the credits for *Zulu*, and Cetswayo in those for *Shaka Zulu*.

Introduction

The nineteenth century, spilling over into the early years of the twentieth, saw the European conquest of Africa. This was justified in terms like 'civilising', 'Christianising', 'enlightenment', but basically it was a sordid grab for land and resources. Colonial conquest was firmly embedded in a racism that gave superhuman pre-eminence to white people. The fact that small European armies could prevail, and prevail so decisively, seemed in itself to be Darwinian proof of racial superiority. There were few who would openly admit to the real reason, revealed in Hilaire Belloc's trenchant couplet:

> *'Whatever happens, we have got*
> *the Maxim gun, and they have not.'*

In a romantic age, when the function of romance seems in large degree to have been to varnish over the desperation and degradation of masses of people, not least in Europe itself, the preference was for emotional invocation of 'heroism', of 'patriotism' and of 'national destiny'.

Around the apex of the age of empire there occurred a phenomenon that seemingly had nothing to do with massive land-theft and subordination of native populations. It was, however, part of the technological advancement and industrial development – which had also produced the Maxim gun – that characterised the Western powers at that time. The invention of motion pictures towards the end of the nineteenth century had an impact more subtle, but arguably no less profound, than imperialism itself, since the impact of cinema – followed by television – is ongoing, and, moreover, the numbers touched by these mass media in a single day can be compared with the numbers of those touched by imperialism over three centuries. The movie camera opened up the world in a way that no other medium had ever done. Oral and written descriptions of faraway places left much to the imagination; and even still photography, because it was linked to printing, was not easily accessible to the masses of people who could not read. But films, rapidly established as popular entertainment, displayed other people, other customs, other places in a way so lifelike that it seemed undeniable. Films gave the illusion of reality. Just like freebooting imperialists in their quest for plunder, motion picture photographers scurried all over the globe, frenetically gathering images – exotic, arcane, bizarre, sensational, revelatory – which became 'the reality' about the world for millions of people.

From the beginning, these images were 'property': pictures did not belong to the people they portrayed, but to the person who took them. There is even a kind of rapacity lurking in the very phrase 'to take' a picture. Image control – which meant choices in selection of subject, of camera angle, in editing, in dramatic effect, in distribution – existed from the very beginning. Greatest of all was the image control (as yet unsensed by the beholder) exercised by the cameraperson, usually unconsciously, that was dictated by his or her culture.

The invention of the movie camera began a second conquest of Africa, not merely in the acquisition of images, but in the way these images were presented. The bloody safari of the former American president Teddy Roosevelt through Africa during the early years of the twentieth century was documented on film, and the pictures of the native people are scarcely distinguishable from those of the animal trophies. Africa was a vast hunting-ground for the white man, and when Hollywood seized on Africa, this was the Africa it offered.

The literature of empire that had come into being during the nineteenth century found its second wind in the cinema – *King Solomon's Mines, Prester John, Stanley and Livingstone, Rhodes of Africa, Trader Horn, Symbol of Sacrifice, Sanders of the River, Untamed, Zulu, Zulu Dawn* and *Out of Africa,* to name but a few, from the earliest years of the century to the latest. Hollywood made this literature even more vivid and accessible to many more people. Evidence of the direct link between the literature of empire and the film-making imagination is epitomised in Michael Korda's description of the young Alexander Korda reading to his little brother Zoltan from Henry Morton Stanley's *In Darkest Africa* – and this in Hungary, in the early years of this century. Michael Korda points out that Zoltan Korda went on to make *Sanders of the River, Elephant Boy, Four Feathers* and *Sahara,* all of them celebrating heavily romanticised aspects of white rule.

Dozens of similar films, as late as *The Power of One* (1992), emphasised the supremacy of the white race, directly and indirectly justifying conquest. Imperial and racist images, messages, codes, cyphers, attitudes and behaviour were copied indiscriminately. Up to the present time, Hollywood perpetuates the ethos of empire.

In this new geography revealed by the movie camera, what was shown specifically about South Africa around 1900, when motion pictures were fast becoming an industry? The era coincided with a great struggle for power among competing white groups at the tip of the continent, a struggle that became known as the Anglo-Boer War. It was one of the earliest wars to be recorded by the movie camera. A handful of snippets remains, mostly of columns of troops filing past the camera. One of these shows mounted troops fording a river, a vast array of cavalry with baggage trains. Near the end of this very short film, an ox-driver carrying a whip moves lower right frame to control his ox-cart. In the military mass, his is the only African figure, one of the very few to be recorded by the movie-camera in this war. In his solitariness, he takes on symbolic significance. The war, after all, was *about* the soil of southern Africa, but in it the principal inhabitants of the land have been reduced to worse than irrelevance – if they participate at all, they do so as servants of the white combatants, on both sides. The camera casually reveals a significant fact: by 1900, the political decisions about South Africa were being made exclusively by whites, shutting out the African majority.

What happened in South Africa happened all over Africa. The placing of Africans on the cinema screen reflected their dispossession, for their loss of political power on the field of battle determined their siting in the field of focus: they forfeited the right to appear centre-screen. That position was reserved for white heroes and heroines. When Africans did appear on the screen, it was as adjuncts to whites; in that role, they told us more about whites – how whites saw themselves, how they reinvented and re-enacted mythologies of white supremacy – than they ever revealed about African lives. Africans in the cinema were but as dark shadows affixed to white foreground figures. Throughout Africa, in countries ruled by French or English or Portuguese colonial powers, Africans were deliberately blocked from access to the technology of cinema. This was a political decision on the part of the colonial authorities, who recognised the enormous power of cinema to influence and propagandise, and who wanted to retain that power for themselves.

As African countries, from the 1950s on, became liberated from European colonialism, many started to make their own films, with African heroes. Francophone Africa (albeit with considerable help from France, which now wanted to retain influence over a newly liberated people) has produced hundreds of films, and directors of the stature of Gaston Kaboré (Burkina Faso) and Ousmane Sembène (Senegal). Western fables about Africa continue to be repeated. But there now exists a considerable canon of African cinema to offset these fables – if the distribution system would allow free access to them, which it seldom does. Cornelius Moore, of California Newsreel, probably the leading distributor of African films in North America, points out that no more than twenty cinemas throughout the entire USA have ever shown an African film, and that this situation is worsening as art theatres continue to close down.[1]

---

1   *Africa Film & TV*, 1994.

Where South African film is concerned, even though Africans have begun to move out of the shadows, the arc light is still controlled by whites. One hundred years after the birth of motion pictures, there is still no authentic black cinema coming out of the African country that, almost from the beginning, was the best equipped technically to produce one. This is so despite the fact that South Africa has been consistently popular in the cinema, perhaps the most popular African locale. Its appeal came from the raw material of fable that it had to offer – its wealth of gold and diamonds, intrepid pioneer history, and savage Zulus.

In studios inside and outside South Africa, these elements, often woven together into the same plot, were spooled in celluloid throughout most of this century. I do not think that it is an altogether fantastic hypothesis that the persistent presentation of South Africa in cinema as a country appropriately ruled by whites, to whom all the wealth of the country rightfully belonged, and in which the only Africans depicted were marauding savages, was a massive propaganda gift to the forces of racism and apartheid. This may go a long way in explaining why it took the world community over forty years, after the United Nations' Declaration of Human Rights to mobilise sufficient pressure to bring about effective change in South Africa.

This book is about the power of cinema, and about the devastating impact of a generic 'Hollywood' that is constantly protesting that it is apolitical, even while it stamps stereotypes and projects behaviour that is as profoundly political as it is influential. At the same time, I shy away from the accusation of 'cultural imperialism'; people everywhere were not coerced into going to the cinema (quite the opposite in South Africa, where there were few cinemas available for blacks). On the contrary, they eagerly allowed themselves to be seduced into an addiction that is well-nigh incurable. For decades, Native Americans, Africans, women, went to see films that seemed to demean them, and were apparently entertained by what they saw. Nowadays, when most national cinemas are in decline, the cry of 'cultural imperialism' levelled against American films reaches an hysterical pitch; but the plain fact is that in France, Sweden, Germany and all over the globe, people prefer to see American films above their own indigenous cinema. And that is their choice. This does not stop me from believing that American films have had a devastating effect on human behaviour.

Although I draw from the entire range of South Africa in cinema during this century, this does not attempt to be a comprehensive history of cinema depicting that country. My concern is with selected genre films, and other exemplars fall outside my area of interest. I do not touch on Afrikaans cinema, nor on the considerable canon of African-language films. Both these categories are relatively narrowcast. A film like *Ohm Paul* (1941), made in Nazi Germany for a very specific propaganda purpose, is fascinating, but not relevant to the study. An oddity like *Diamond Safari* (1958), which stitches together plots from what were intended to be two different films, one about diamond theft, another about lion-hunting, reveals something about rag-trade aspects of film-making, but does not fit into my overall plan. My principal concern is with an image-bank relating to South Africa, especially the way that black South Africans have been presented on film, how the image-bank changed (or significantly failed to change) during this century, what impact this may be presumed to have had, and what it reveals about those who created, and continue to create, the images. Because of what has happened in South Africa during this century, this has had implications that are profoundly political.

I have identified a number of themes, which I have separated into different chapters; inevitably, several themes may be discernible in the same film – for example, the theme of the Faithful Servant existing together with the theme of South Africa's wealth. One I have not dealt with is that of Sisterhood. Cinema about South Africa up until most recent times has been about the doings of men, with women in largely submissive sub-roles. In the 1980s this began to change, with *A World Apart* and *Mapantsula*, and into the 1990s with *Sarafina!* and *Friends*. The women in these films mark the beginning of a new sensibility, coinciding with a new South Africa, not the South Africa of apartheid and before.

Peter Davis
Johannesburg 1996

The Savage Other and the
Faithful Servant:
The Zulu's Heart

There is, in the Paper Print Collection, Motion Picture Division, of the Library of Congress in Washington, an old film from the Biograph Studio. It is from the pioneer years of film-making, and would not attract much attention were it not for the signature it bears: D W Griffith. It dates from 1908, the year that Griffith signed on with Biograph. This film, *The Zulu's Heart*, was made when Griffith was learning his trade as a film-director. About seven minutes long, it is a melodrama of the kind that Griffith was cranking out at the rate of one a week. Today, the acting looks histrionic, even for the silent era; but it comes out of a different tradition, and one should not infer that it was not taken seriously by the people who saw it then. However, at first glance it does not seem to hold much merit, other than what we can glean from it about the evolution of Griffith's art. In the history of film-making, it is a curiosity, because of its director, and because it has the great comic director, Mack Sennett, in the leading role, and was shot by Griffith's great cameraman, Billy Bitzer.

But motion pictures can have social implications that transcend their value as art. And this early little pot-boiler by Griffith carries more than its weight in cultural baggage. It may well be the first fiction film set in South Africa, and the first on a subject to which the cinema would return again and again – Zulu. Shot in New Jersey, across the Hudson River from Biograph's New York headquarters, with white actors playing the Zulu roles (Griffith would not use blacks because he thought they could not act), this primitive film demands a considerable suspension of belief. The story is as follows (each scene is shot by a camera in one position only. I omit one or two connecting scenes):

> Scene I: In a Zulu village, a Zulu chief and his wife are performing a funeral ritual for their dead child. A warrior dashes in to report something he has seen. The Zulu chief and his band rush off.

> Scene II: In a rocky landscape, we see a covered wagon with a Boer pioneer family: man, woman, and child. They are attacked by the Zulus. The woman and child run off, while the man tries to hold off the attackers. He is killed by a spear, and the Zulu chief exults, in savage triumph, with his men. They rush off in pursuit of the woman and child.

> Scene III: The white woman hides the little girl before she herself is captured by the Zulu band. The Zulu chief finds the little girl. He is about to kill her when he is reminded of his own dead child. He hides her amid the rocks, and returns to the village.

> Scene IV: Back at the village, he rescues the woman from the other Zulus, reminding them that he is their chief. He and the woman go off to collect the child.

Scene V: Other warriors find the little girl, and drag her off. They are about to cut her throat when the Zulu chief intervenes, and fights them for the child, defeating them all.

Scene VI: The Zulu chief releases the woman and child. Before the little girl leaves, she gives him her doll as a present. This affects him deeply.

It is a melodramatic story, and Griffith made scores of such films. But it establishes something remarkable. Drawing on colonial experience with its ingrained biases and distortions, absorbed second-hand, Griffith unwittingly projected, in a few clumsy and ludicrous frames, an image of black Africa that would dominate the screen for most of the twentieth century. It is a Janus-faced image. Griffith's Zulus either threaten whites, or serve them. The Zulu chief, who does both in turn, is a Noble Savage – but his nobility lies in his good deed towards the white woman and child. After this, in film after film, Africans would be defined as either good or bad by their actions towards whites, which determined whether they were the Faithful Servant or the Savage Other. These stereotypes, which block the perception of Africans as existing in their own right – and not merely as adjuncts of white society – obstinately and harmfully persist up to the present day.

More will be written about the Savage Other in a later section which deals with the image of the Zulu in cinema. Suffice to say at this point that the conversion of the Savage Other into the Faithful Servant (which parallels the metamorphosis of the archetypal enemy, like Sitting Bull, into a Tonto in Hollywood Westerns) is a fictional analogue of the taming of the indigenous peoples of South Africa. Establishment cinema appeared to have no interest in changing this formula, and exploited it shamelessly for half a century. The majority of films about South Africa present at least one African in the role of Faithful Servant, even in the context of a Zulu war. The formula had other uses than that intended for a white audience, where it both confirmed the white man in the role of master, and flattered him as being the worthy recipient of black fidelity. Mark Beittel gleans the following from a book by a missionary in Johannesburg, Ray Phillips, entitled *The Bantu in the City*, published by Lovedale Press in 1938. Observing that 'In South Africa, cinema has long been considered a valuable instrument of social control', Beittel writes that Ray Phillips

> *spent years devising a 'Social Gospel' that would solve 'the whole great problem of moralising the leisure time of natives', and most particularly of the 200 000 African men who worked on the gold mines and were housed in huge single-sex compounds. When he finally came up with movies as a solution, the Chamber of Mines*

was so enthusiastic that it agreed to finance – to the tune of 5 000 pounds annually – a scheme run by Phillips's mission. Within a year, 'clean, wholesome pictures were being shown regularly in each of the great compounds', including an early South African production called **A Zulu's Devotion** *(1916). This circuit of distribution soon grew to include not only the sixty mine compounds, but an additional eighty exhibiting centres for Africans living in towns. Phillips spent fifteen years personally selecting and editing these movies – 'every foot of film', he proudly claimed, was 'carefully censored'. As for the controlling effects of the films, Phillips maintained that during the great 1922 strike by white miners – the so-called Rand Revolt – a violent clash between white and black miners was averted when he rushed out to the New Primrose mine and showed Charlie Chaplin films.*[2]

There can be little doubt that films on the mines came about less from the desire of mine-owners to see their workers entertained than to see them distracted from their very real grievances: it was an opiate made in mine-owners' heaven. This real reason for 'the moralising of leisure time of workers' (in the missionary expression of Ray Phillips) may not have been so obvious to the workers, who may well have interpreted it as a gesture of magnanimity on the part of the mine-owners in a landscape desperately devoid of such gestures. In the case of a film like *A Zulu's Devotion*, there was the added bonus of teaching the Africans how to be 'good kaffirs'. Phillips, in his book *The Bantu in the City*, quotes the 'sober conclusion' of a 'group of educational experts which investigated Native Education in South Africa' in 1936:

If Plato was right in saying that he who makes a nation's songs exerts a greater influence than he who makes a nation's laws, then it will certainly not be far wrong to say that he who controls a people's films exerts a greater influence for good or ill, than he who makes the country's laws. [3]

Phillips acted with the full weight of this responsibility in choosing films for the miners. As much as anything, he – together with white authorities throughout Africa – was concerned that Africans should not be confronted with images that showed whites in a demeaning fashion. Nothing should be shown that would depict whites as morally corrupt, because this would undermine their authority in the eyes of those over whom they ruled. The censorship that Phillips exercised,

---

2 Mark Beittel, '*Mapantsula*: Cinema, Crime and Politics on the Witwatersrand', *Journal of Southern African Studies*, Vol. 16, No. 4, December 1990.

3 R.E. Phillips, *The Bantu in the City*, Lovedale Press, Alice, 1938.

although it extended over sexual matters, was inherently political. Explaining why certain films were banned to Africans, he commented:

> *... while they may not have contained scenes which were vulgar or suggestive, they did not convey an elevating or ennobling picture of Western Civilised Life to the spectators many of whom had had scant experience of the ordinary home life of the European ... The African ... does not see enough of the finer side of the life of the White man to enable him to form a true estimate of his Western civilisation and standard of morals and conduct. Care should be taken to present programmes which reflect, as far as possible, the whole life of Europeans of an exemplary type.*[4]

But especially in the South Africa of 1938, at the height of the Depression, the reality of cinema distribution could not be ignored. One cinema owner remarked: 'This censorship is a farce. We don't exclude anybody. The educated Native is a better patron than many Coloured or Poor Whites.'[5] Phillips conceded: 'It is expecting a good deal of exhibitors that they shall turn customers away who come with money in their hands asking for admission.'[6]

Ray Phillips recognised that 'Africans are enthusiastic about motion pictures. It is not lack of interest, but lack of money which keeps Native people from demanding and patronising the cinema in their hundreds of thousands to-day.'[7] Yet simple economics of the entertainment market-place, both before and during the apartheid period, would not be allowed to interfere with the controlled production and distribution of films in South Africa. This dynamic for censorship only became more imperative with apartheid. Right up to the period of the dissolution of apartheid, the role of cinema – as interpreted by those who made the laws – was to ensure that Africans continued as Faithful Servants, and did not become Savage Others.

---

4   *Ibid*, p. 322.

5   *Ibid*, p. 323

6   *Ibid*.

7   *Ibid*, p. 324.

The Taming of the Savage: *The Zulu's Heart*, 1908

Savage with a human face: the Zulu chief mourns the death of his child.

A family of peaceful Boers in a covered wagon.

Zulus mount an unprovoked attack on the Voortrekkers.

The noble Zulu chief fights his own men to rescue the mother and daughter. As a reward he is given a doll, a reminder both of the child he lost and the one he saved.

The Image Makers

Left: I W Schlesinger, head of
African Film Productions, which
dominated film production in South
Africa for almost half a century.
Below: The all-white production
crew for *They Built a Nation*, 1938.

Producer Eric Rutherford and director Donald Swanson filming *Jim comes to Jo'burg*, 1949.

Lionel Rogosin, director of *Come Back, Africa*, filming in the streets of Sophiatown.

Director of *Zulu*, Cy Endfield.

Zoltan Korda and Alan Paton, director and writer of *Cry, the Beloved Country*.

Richard Attenborough, director of *Cry Freedom*.

Jamie Uys (left), director of *Dingaka* and *The Gods must be crazy*. William C Faure (right), director of *Shaka Zulu*.

Oliver Schmitz (left) and Thomas Mogotlane, co-directors of *Mapantsula*.

Fabulous Wealth

There are similarities between the men who exploited the mineral riches of the Rand and the men who pioneered the film industry in America. Neither area of human endeavour was for the fastidious. A character like Barney Barnato would surely have been as much at home in Hollywood as he was in Johannesburg. The vision of empire of a Cecil Rhodes is not far removed from the epic sensibility of a D W Griffith. Isadore William Schlesinger, who can claim to be the father of South African cinema, actually emigrated from the United States to South Africa, and was a successful financier before he became a successful film tycoon. What was needed was a determination to turn a dream into some kind of reality, whether it was a mine two thousand feet deep or an image on a thin strip of celluloid.

In the case of South Africa, there was an added audacity, which impelled Schlesinger and a handful of others to create a film industry where there were few amenities and trained technicians, and precious few actors, and where the rest of the film-producing world had a ten-year jump on them. They also lacked that which gave American cinema a huge advantage – a substantial home audience. But Schlesinger and African Film Productions set out to make dramas that would compete in the world market. As did the mine magnates, they imported the equipment and the necessary skills from thousands of miles away.

South Africa had only existed as a united country for about five years when, in the second decade of the twentieth century, African Film Productions began to make films that celebrated it; or, more precisely, celebrated its white inhabitants. The favourite ingredients – conquest of the native population and exploitation of the natural resources – have proved remarkably enduring. They were eagerly adopted by foreign film-makers as well, and they have lasted from the earliest years of the new art form up to the present. This section deals with the impact of the wealth of South Africa on cinema's story-prospectors. (A random search of titles listed at the National Archives in Pretoria reveals how South Africa's riches are a perennial source of inspiration for the cinema: *Call a Spade a Diamond, City of Diamonds, City of Gold, Diamond Beach, Diamond Detectives, Diamond Hunters, Land of Diamonds, High Diamonds, Dick Donald the Diamond Detective, Diamonds and Dust, Diamond Mercenaries* – and so on.)

The first fiction film recorded as being made in South Africa was *The Great Kimberley Diamond Robbery* (aka *The Star of the South*) (1910). *The Star* (12 December 1911) described the plot as follows:

> *(it) shows the finding of a big diamond – 'The Star of the South' – by a native and its purchase by two prospectors who in turn dispose of it for 1 000 pounds. The final purchaser decides to trek for the Cape but he is soon pursued by a couple of desperados who get wind of the big stone and decide to get it. They (recruit) a small patrol of native warriors to assist them in an attack on the owner of 'The Star' whose (camp) is overwhelmed after a fight. Failure to locate the diamond (which has been hidden on her person by the owner's wife) rouses the anger of the would-be robbers and their decision to torture the woman is frustrated by the native chief. A band of mounted police arrive on the scene and after a stiff fight, the biters are bitten and are hauled off to the Kimberley gaol.*

Notice how, in *The Great Kimberley Diamond Robbery*, the native chief is cast in much the same role as in D W Griffith's *The Zulu's Heart*: first as villain, and then as protector of the white heroine. This and other South African films like *A*

Story of the Rand (1916), about illicit gold-buying; *Gloria* (1916), whose plot involves the discovery of a diamond mine; *The Adventures of a Diamond* (1919); and *Prester John* (1920), in which a young adventurer foils a native uprising and gets rich off diamonds in the process, have been lost, and we have no way of judging them, other than from some surviving stills and contemporary reviews. These were all stories about white heroes and heroines, and it would have been instructive to see how Africans were portrayed in them. During this same period, several thousand miles away, Hollywood became aware of South Africa, and made a short film, *The Kaffir's Gratitude* (1916).[8]

> Synopsis: An English farmer in the Cape Colony has been sufficiently successful in his farming to bring a young woman out from England to be his bride. Prior to her departure, she meets a 'social parasite' who has designs on her. She sails to South Africa, and marries the farmer. On their way to the farm, his 'kaffir' servant is attacked by a lion, and the farmer saves his life.
>
> The farmer runs into bad times. Concerned about his stock, he neglects his wife – 'He thinks more about his old cows than he does about me' reads one of the silent film inter-texts. But she receives good news – the cad from England is coming to pay a visit.
>
> Meanwhile, the gang of the farmer's neighbour is planning to steal a piece of the farmer's land which unknown to him contains a diamond mine. But the 'kaffir' sees them moving the boundary marker. When he tells his master, the farmer rides off to save his land. Back at the ranch, the cad makes his move, is rejected by the wife, and forcibly abducts her. The 'kaffir' sees all this, and rides off to report to the farmer.
>
> In a showdown, there is a shoot-out with the gang, which restores the farmer's land, with the bonus of the diamond mine, and he gets his wife back. There is probably a short fragment missing at the end, where the cad would get his come-uppance and the 'kaffir' be duly thanked.

Thus, *The Kaffir's Gratitude* is about that which belongs to the farmer: the farm and its stock, and the diamond mine it contains; his servant, the 'kaffir'[9]; and his

---

8   'Kaffir' is a South African word approximating to 'nigger', and could be used in the same derogatory sense.

9   *The Kaffir's Gratitude* gives a leading role to a black man; and yet, unlike the other actors in the film, he is not dignified with a name among the credits. (He is the same actor who appears as a black diamond thief in *Sins of Rosanne* – there, his name is given as James Smith.)

wife. All are threatened in some way, and all are restored to their rightful owner. (In The Great Kimberley Diamond Robbery, the distinction between wife-as-possession and diamond-as-possession is blurred when the wife hides the diamond on her person; it seems that when it is her womanhood that is about to be violated, the native chief acts to protect her.)

From exactly the same time, one of the first fiction films produced in South Africa, *A Zulu's Devotion* (1916), has the same themes of fidelity and protection of property. A white farmer comes upon a Zulu with a wounded foot, and looks after him. In gratitude, the Zulu becomes his faithful servant. When cattle thieves kidnap the farmer's daughter, the Zulu, Goba, rescues her and brings about the capture of the thieves.

Unfortunately, nothing survives of this film but a few stills. In a review from the South African publication *Stage & Cinema* dated 3 June 1916 the writer complains that the characters are not clear: '(in the film) there has been some talk about a Zulu herdboy being allowed to arrest a white man. The stock thieves in this picture are not supposed to be white men, but half-castes – a fact which might have been explained to the audience ...' It would have been a major affront for an African to arrest a white man, even a crook; similarly, the 'kaffir' in *The Kaffir's Gratitude* cannot himself intervene when the cad abducts his mistress – that is a matter between whites. In *Symbol of Sacrifice*, when a black servant does intervene to rescue his mistress from a white man, he is filled with remorse at having broken the social code.

Another Hollywood film, *Desert Nights* (1929), starring the great heart-throb of the period, John Gilbert, and the tantalising fragment that survives of *Sins of Rosanne* (1920), also deal with diamond thieves. In *Desert Nights* and *Sins of Rosanne* the focus of interest is on the doings of the white protagonists, with the mine compound as exotic background – there are authentic-seeming shots of regimented workers, miners being searched as they come off shift, barbed wire fences, and armed guards.

The Gene Autry vehicle *Round-up Time in Texas* (1936), although an undistinguished piece of film-making, is remarkable for many things, not least for its completely nonchalant representation of South Africa. Although almost the entire action takes place in 'South Africa', not even the title identifies the locale.

The link between Texas and South Africa is tenuous in the extreme – Gene Autry is summoned to South Africa by a cable from his brother Tex: '... discovered a rich diamond mine in the Valley of Superstition. Need horses badly, but impossible to buy. Bring at once as many as you can round up.' To which Gene's response is, 'We're riding, fellas, it's South Africa or bust!' But Gene could probably have saved himself the trouble. The South African town of Dunbar in which he and his sidekick Smiley Burnette find themselves looks remarkably like a set for the standard Hollywood Western, complete with men in cowboy dress and a saloon. The concessions to some kind of South African reality include African buffalo horns and an African shield and spear hanging on the walls of the saloon. Everyone speaks either with an American accent or an American imitation of Cockney – except the 'natives', who speak injun:

> *Gene Autry: Where did you get that belt?*
>
> *Namba: Me trade-um knife to native boy for belt, baas … Two, three, four moons. Meet-um boy on the river. Like-um belt, make-um quick trade.*

Gene Autry comments that 'the rhythm of that tom-tom is very much like the American Indian', and again, 'That was a drum-signal of some kind. The Indians back in Texas use the same method to send their messages.' In one scene, director Joseph Kane has a tribe dancing around what appears to be an African totem-pole, preparing for a human sacrifice. There are of course lions, and an amorous gorilla. (Amorous or not, gorillas are not native to South Africa.) The newly-discovered diamond mine serves as the excuse for the villainy, and part of the plot involves Gene Autry being framed as an illicit diamond-buyer.

It is hard to find a story that more clearly reveals the link between colonialism and Hollywood than *King Solomon's Mines*. Originally, it was a highly popular novel from the age of empire, written by H Rider Haggard, a former colonial functionary in South Africa.[10] The story is set in southern Africa, and Haggard naturally drew on his own experience in writing the book. He lived in South Africa during the first years after the discovery of diamonds, at a time when there was a feverish rush to exploit them, and when the promise of the wealth to be gained thereby was dazzling.

There have been at least five versions of this adventure story, including one from the early days of South African cinema (unfortunately lost), but the one I deal with here is the 1937 Gaumont British version directed by Robert Stevenson. This version gave top billing to a black actor, Paul Robeson, the most popular black actor the cinema had hitherto produced. Robeson's leading role in the film is enhanced by the addition of a number of songs to show off his voice.

The essential elements of Haggard's story are retained in the film. A group of whites, partly led by a mysterious African, Umbopa (Paul Robeson), are on an expedition to seek the lost land of Ophir, with its fabulous riches, the diamond mines of King Solomon. After many adventures, they arrive in the land of the Kukuanas, ruled over by the tyrant Twala. It transpires that Umbopa is the rightful king of this land, and Umbopa offers the wealth of the diamond mines to the white men if they will help him defeat Twala. During the battle, the tyrant is killed. When

---

10   In his time, Haggard was the most popular writer in England.

the group goes to the mine, they are trapped by a volcanic eruption, but they escape with their lives – and sufficient diamonds to make them all rich men.

All these stories derive from the awe and covetousness aroused in the European soul by the prospect of South Africa's mineral wealth. The gold and diamond fields of South Africa attracted the scum of the earth, men who would cheerfully lie, cheat and kill. In no-one, from the lowliest digger through the claim-owners up to the colonial administrators, and on to the government in the metropolis seven thousand miles away, did there appear to be any doubt that whatever they could seize belonged to them, and not to the people whose land they seized it from.

It never crosses the minds of the adventurers in *King Solomon's Mines* that the diamonds they are seeking belong to anyone. Indeed, the very title dispossesses the Kukuana: even though they are on Kukuana land, the mines 'belong' to King Solomon, who of course is long-since dead, and cannot claim ownership. Therefore, the diamonds are up for grabs. When they are being led to the mine for the first time, before they even have the diamonds in their hands, one white man asks another, 'What are you going to do with your share of the money?' Umbopa, the rightful king, remarks contemptuously at one point, 'White man care for diamonds.' It was a cliché well established in colonial literature that natives did not value mineral wealth, thereby furnishing a rationale for stealing it from them. The heroine of *Untamed* (1955) restores her shattered fortunes by buying a huge diamond far below value from a native. An earlier film, *Diamond City* (1949), has a candid interchange between the prospector Parker and Jan Blum, a Coloured owner of land found to hold diamonds:

> *Parker: When news of this find gets abroad, they'll flock into Klippdrift from all over the world. You'll need a man like me to keep law and order.*
>
> *Blum: Maybe. But you ask me to hand over full control of these fields, in return for what?*
>
> *Parker: Loyal service. And wealth beyond your wildest dreams.*
>
> *Blum: I'd be richer if I controlled them myself.*
>
> *Parker: You couldn't do it, Jan Blum. White men take orders from white. Otherwise the British and the Boers will step in and you'll lose everything.*

The films all present diamonds as the property of whites, even in the matter of theft. In *Sins of Rosanne* and in *Diamond City*, blacks are lower echelon accomplices, and in the latter film the white miners constantly battle each other for the spoils, even though the diamond fields belong to Jan Blum. In the end, the opposing sets of miners both give way to *force majeure*, when Her Britannic Majesty's government, the biggest freebooter of all, announces annexation.

Reflecting recognition of a deeper geopolitical complexity, *Gold!* (1974) and *The Wilby Conspiracy* (1975) are no longer about simple theft. *Gold!* involves an international plot to manipulate mining shares, and the villains are suave and sophisticated. The top villain even goes unpunished, although his plot is foiled.

In *The Wilby Conspiracy*, a black resistance movement (based loosely on the African National Congress) is trying to smuggle diamonds out of South Africa in order to buy weapons. The agent for the Bureau for State Security, Major Horn, follows the path of the diamonds to the Black Congress leader, Wilby, whom he then arrests. Shack Twala, Wilby's right-hand man, tries to buy off Major Horn with the diamonds. Horn thereupon embarks on one of his characteristic tirades, this time directed at a crowd of Africans who dare not retaliate because there is a gun to Wilby's head.

> *Horn: No, no, no. Wilby has to stand trial in South Africa for all the world to see. Fair and legal. For incitement to treason! ... (Horn takes a handful of diamonds and scatters them before the crowd of Africans.) Conspiracy to commit sabotage! (Horn scatters another handful of diamonds.) Responsibility for armed incursions ... (another handful) with intent to commit murder! The diamonds (holding one up for the onlookers to see) for the ears ... (He tosses the remaining diamonds to one of the Africans in the crowd, who angrily throws them to the ground.) ... the fingers. Oh, man, you dom swarte ... For the nose! (He laughs mockingly.) Get Wilby on board.*
>
> *Van Heerden (Horn's sidekick): Don't worry about those diamonds. They're not real. They are paste.*

Horn had long ago substituted imitation diamonds for the real ones. In his moment of triumph, he taunts the defeated Africans by conjuring up the enduring image of the native who cannot tell the difference in value between real and imitation diamonds. Since Africans do not value mineral wealth, they do not deserve to own it. It belongs, by some kind of Darwinian right, to those who both know its value and are bold enough to seize it.

In *The Kaffir's Gratitude*, as in *King Solomon's Mines*, the riches of Africa accrue to the brave – the white farmer fights to get his land back, the adventurers overcome perils to reach the mines. In reality, the mineral wealth of South Africa went not so much to the brave as to the most unscrupulous – and in the process Africans lost their land.

The colonial farmer in *The Kaffir's Gratitude* owns a farm, but how he got the land is never broached. The 'kaffir' owes the white farmer a double debt – the farmer gives him work, and saves his life as well. The lion is the perennial metaphor for the 'savagery' of Africa, from which the master, by his presence and by the technological superiority of his gun, saves his servant. The farmer is thus both saviour and civiliser, whose godlike status is recognised by the servant when he genuflects before him in a gesture that is both grateful and adoring, and even sexually suggestive. The scene is a distortion of reality, for the indigenous Africans who now work as farm labour must have prior claim to ownership of the land.

In taking the land, the white farmers took the Africans' livelihood, and compounded the outrage by establishing the master/servant relationship, a relationship of dependency, of vassalhood. Historically, the natives had nothing to be grateful to the white invaders for. But, fashioned by the victor's view of history, the film has the dispossessed's, the 'kaffir's', gratitude extend to the conquering hero, the man who has just symbolically defeated Africa in killing the lion.

Those Africans who managed to hold on to land in the tribal reserves, where they could work as subsistence farmers, were burdened with a 'hut tax'. In order to find the cash to pay it, they had to seek work in the mines. In this fashion, they were forced into an alien economy, the white economy, and once this happened, their own agricultural economy and the culture based on it were doomed. This devastating fact of life for African labour would not be touched on in fiction cinema until the late 1950s. In *Sins of Rosanne* (1920), a black mineworker steals some diamonds, and then crawls through a tunnel to push them up through a hole on the other side of the compound fence. Rosanne, his unknown white accomplice, strolls along outside the fence, and when she sees a stick pushed up through the ground, bends over – her parasol shielding what she is doing from the armed guard in the watchtower – and plucks the diamonds from the ground as casually as one might pick a flower. It is a powerful, if completely unconscious, metaphor for the mining industry of South Africa itself, where almost all the manual labour has been performed by Africans burrowing ant-like underground, with the white managers and mine-owners and stockholders reaping the profits in the light of the sun.

The role of 'good' Africans in these films is to help whites in their exploitation of the mineral wealth, either in protecting that wealth from marauders, or in digging it out of the ground. Unlike the Zulu films (see later), the Africans portrayed are domesticated: they serve whites, even when they are helping them to steal, as in *Sins of Rosanne* and *Diamond City*. It is not until *The Wilby Conspiracy* that blacks, in the name of the freedom struggle, become in a sense rivals for possession of diamond wealth. Here, interestingly, the provenance of the diamonds that are to purchase weapons for the liberation movement is never discussed.

Africans as Property

Left: The "kaffir" finds that the boundary marker has been moved in an attempt to steal his master's land.
Below: The "kaffir" is rescued from a lion. Thus he *owes* his life to his *master*. *The Kaffir's Gratitude*, 1916.

Umbopa, the rightful king (Paul Robeson, centre), despises the diamonds which the whites covet. *King Solomon's Mines*, 1937.

'How much (land) is mine?' – the fiction that South Africa was empty land, up for grabs. *Untamed*, 1955.

Towards a Black Cinema in South Africa: The Promise of the 1950s

Non-Europeans Impress in First Full-Length Entertainment Film

By a Staff Reporter

SO RARELY ARE THE WORDS JUSTIFIED that writers treat with care and handle sparingly the phrase "History was made." History was made at the Rio non-European cinema, Market Street, last night when "South Africa's first full-length entertainment film featuring non-European South Africans" had its world premiere.

After a graceful appearance on stage with other members of the cast, Dolly Rathebe, the leading lady, who has earned the right to be called South Africa's Lena Horn, leaned

NON EUROPEAN

CRY, THE BELOVED COUNTRY

JIM COMES TO JO'BURG (aka AFRICAN JIM) (1949)

Whites always feel that we, the blacks – our minds are black, our breath is black, everything is black. Now, they never gave us a chance. People who really gave us chances are people from overseas who come in here and feel that these people have got talent. (Dolly Rathebe, singer and actress, interview, 1990)

In the late 1940s, two Britons happened to be in South Africa. They were the scriptwriter Donald Swanson and the actor Eric Rutherford. After the film was made, they stayed on in South Africa, the young, handsome Rutherford marrying Gloria Green, daughter of a wealthy Johannesburg family. Gloria Green was an artist, and wanted something more adventurous than she could expect from Johannesburg social life. Rutherford was of Scottish stock, restless and experimental by nature, and what came out of this union was a quirk in film history, an unpretentious little film that nowadays, in a sceptical audience, can provoke the accusation of paternalism, if not worse. But such a facile response obscures the film's merits as cultural history, which far outweigh its value as cinema art. It is in fact unique, and should be treasured for preserving a flavour of personalities who otherwise would have gone unrecorded. For the established all-white South African film industry, which controlled the money, the equipment, the studios and the technicians, was not interested in black subjects – and that is precisely what Rutherford, Green and Swanson wanted to put on film.

Rutherford, Green and Swanson came up with the daring idea of making their own film outside the monopoly control that existed. Swanson was a scriptwriter who wanted a crack at directing, Rutherford had considerable acting experience, and the Green family could provide a not insubstantial amount of money to indulge this whim of Gloria's. (Rutherford speculates that the family was so willing to put up the money because they wanted to make sure that Rutherford would stay on to marry Gloria.) Gloria's interest perhaps lay through Rutherford, but she was also involved as set- and dress-designer on the project.

These were all 'outsiders' – Rutherford and Swanson because they were not South African, and Green perhaps because she was Jewish, and Jews have historically played an 'outsider' role. It is certain that the film they made, *Jim Comes to Jo'burg*, was made with a particular kind of liberal sensibility, a kind that today is sometimes despised.[11] It is equally certain that without it, an important part of South Africa's black heritage would be totally lost to succeeding generations. So homage is due, and it should not be given grudgingly.

---

11   When the film was shown again after 40 years in South Africa, at the *Weekly Mail* Film Festival of 1990, Karen Rutter, reviewing in *The Daily Mail*, called it uncharitably 'perhaps the most extreme example of patronising propaganda'.

It was already a leap of the imagination to think of putting Africans into the foreground. 'Why not a feature film, why not, you know, really having a feature film, a full-length entertainment film, with African actors?'[12] So they debated what kind of film they should make. Now, they had already made this tremendous – for the times – leap of the imagination by even conceiving that Africans could be the central characters in a movie. But they were still trapped in a time and a social context that dictated certain responses, certain formulas. That Africans themselves were also trapped by the same circumstances meant that there were restrictions on what the film-makers could do, how far they could go.

I am not here talking about a racial situation that separated black from white but about a common culture that had developed that transcended race. Cultural cross-fertilisation is as explosive as it is unpredictable. In a peculiar sense, in the rough scrimmage of cultural confrontation, subject people have a distinct advantage over their oppressors – they have a measure of access to the dominant culture that is denied in reverse. That is to say, while a Zulu may have to learn English in order to survive economically, his employer has no incentive to learn Zulu. So the master, in his conviction of racial superiority, remains culturally limited, even if the limitation is voluntary. By having to deal with European culture in all its aspects on a daily basis, the African has a sophistication automatically denied to whites, an extra dimension.[13] The importance of *Jim Comes to Jo'burg* is that the film-makers, while still trapped by many of the conventions of the time, were nonetheless able to recognise the value of a despised culture.

During the great industrial expansion of the late 1940s, millions of Africans for the first time were forced into the urban experience, a cultural shock of the first magnitude, with much the same upheaval and massive poverty as had affected Europe and America during the preceding century. But at the same time, all kinds of new opportunities, new experiences and frenetic excitement arose. Africans could observe close up, if seldom participate in, the culture of white South Africa. But the pervasive culture, I think, came from outside South Africa itself – a culture overwhelmingly white, but one designed to appeal to a world audience.

Specifically, I speak of the mass-produced culture of Hollywood. And one of the most intriguing aspects of this Hollywood culture was that its effects were felt by black and white alike. American music, American fashions of dress, of behaviour, speech patterns – all were imprinted on South Africans of all colours. If this was cultural imperialism, whites as well as blacks were its willing subjects. (Even if among conservative Afrikaners, Hollywood was considered the work of the Devil.)

---

12 Rutherford, interview, 1990, reflecting on their feelings in 1949. The original suggestion came from none other than Orson Welles, at a chance encounter with Rutherford and Green in Harry's Bar in Florence.

13 For the most brilliant exposition of this see Jean Rouch's *Les Maîtres Fous.*

Naturally, films were available from sources other than Hollywood. There was the very modest local industry, and there was the not inconsiderable British production of post-war days, which was undoubtedly popular with South African whites, because of the close links between Britain and South Africa. But even the British industry was influenced by Hollywood and, for a number of reasons, the hegemony of American films worldwide had been established for some time, as far back as the First World War, and as direct consequence of that war.

Hollywood films had that heady mixture of Americanness – a contempt for convention, a freedom of action and of movement, an egalitarian ethos, a disingenuous charm, a self-assuredness, all packaged with a glamorous and glossy facade:

> *Just to sit in this dark place, and magic takes place on the wall. For a moment, we forgot apartheid, we forgot there was another world that wasn't good, we sat there and were carried away by the dream of these American movies. (John Kani, actor, interview, 1990)*

Itself a major industry, product of industrialised society, cinema was nevertheless almost by definition an escapist art-form. It transcended reality, yet, anchored in the photographic, it was deceptively lifelike, and to that extent, comprehensible to the masses. Also, being commercial, it was almost as accessible to the black thruppence as to the white shilling. The limitation to that access was censorship, which placed adult black South Africans on the level of a twelve-year-old white child.

When it came to making films, the very ubiquity of the American products made it virtually impossible to escape their influence. *Jim Comes to Jo'burg*, which was made by men who came out of the British tradition, has elements of post-war British film of the *Hue and Cry* genre, but it is saturated with things Hollywood. When Swanson and Rutherford came up with a plot, they placed it in an African nightclub of a kind that never existed.

The origin of the nightclub setting, where smartly groomed men and women came to wine and dine and listen to the best in entertainment, was of course Hollywood films. By the late 1940s, there was a well-established genre of films offering the audience the impression of being in a nightclub and watching the acts. There were also dozens of *films noirs* that revolved around nightclubs, casinos, and female singers.

Rutherford and Swanson transplanted this glamour, with disarming incongruity, to an African township. Gloria Green 'Africanised' the decor with tribal designs – which may well themselves have had their origin in Hollywood presentations of 'primitive Africa'. Although the camera does go outside the nightclub from time to time to depict other elements of the flimsy plot, it is the nightclub that constitutes the arena for the main action – the entertainment.

In that, it differed not at all from Hollywood movies of the same genre. What is astonishing, and what makes the focus on the nightclub a fortunate decision, is the type and quality of the entertainment depicted. Apart from traditional dancers, the film offers a wealth of musicians and singers who can hardly be distinguished from their American prototypes.

If you listen to the words, you can make out a South African accent. If you listen to the music, I think it would be virtually impossible to say that these musicians came from South Africa. Their very attitudes in performance, down to the cigarette dangling from the lips of Sam Maile as he tickles the piano keys, speak of an influence so seductive that they have given themselves to it body and soul.

Here was a cadre of entertainers accomplished beyond anything that existed in white South Africa. Where did they come from? None of them had been outside South Africa. Their only teacher was American films and American record albums, and they absorbed them so completely that their own cultural baggage seems to have been thrown out. At this stage, there does not seem to have been a synthesis of African and American in the music, where, of all the arts, it might have seemed most likely and possible. The African element is suppressed, and American jazz and swing reign supreme.

For white as well as black, there was rejection of the authentically African. It seemed impossible to think beyond the standards, traditions and clichés imposed by Hollywood. Yet, oddly enough, there was something of an anti-Hollywood crusade behind the impetus to make a black film.

> *We saw this situation where the African population were being fed these miserable films, I mean, they were full of violence, they were full of trivial lives, as I say, they were the cheapest kind of film you could get out of Hollywood, gangster films, stupid kind of cowboy films. The image that Africans were being given is the worst that you could possibly give them. (Rutherford)*

Rutherford was not alone in inculpating cinema. Mark Beittel writes, referring to 'a government commission appointed to investigate political violence that erupted in townships on the Rand during 1949 and 1950' (i.e. the same time that *Jim Comes to Jo'burg* was made):

> *In their account ... the members of the commission rolled out the usual litany of 'causes' of unrest in South Africa – outside agitators, intimidation, irresponsible press reports – and added*

to it a tsotsi 'reign of terror' and the evil effects of 'bioscope films'
...14

Rutherford describes the revelation of finding the talent for the film by going to the townships: 'Nobody in the white world really knew about this, it was a whole sort of subculture which they really weren't aware of.' That whites as a group were ignorant of the talent that existed is surely true, but it is misleading to label it a subculture, because the level of performance is evidence of a demanding, broad, and appreciative audience.

The films that followed in the path that *Jim Comes to Jo'burg* had beaten, like *Zonk* and *Song of Africa*, only confirmed the massive pool of talent that existed, a vast culture unknown only in the sense that it was unrecognised by a white overclass interested only in admiring its own image.

When they were auditioning for the female lead, which was a singing role, Swanson, the director, favoured a light-skinned woman whose manner was altogether too sophisticated for Rutherford's vision of the role. Rutherford wanted someone more authentically African. It was Dan Twala, their mentor in the townships, who brought another young woman to audition for the part.

> *And she was very nervous, quite hesitant, she was very unprepossessingly dressed, you know, we just took one look at her at first, we said, 'Oh, well, she's a nice-looking girl, but what can we do with that?' And then her turn came to sing, she got in front of a camera, and it was like something out of a movie, I mean, suddenly this woman took on a whole new personality, her eyes sparkled, her face broke into a smile, she had a sort of swing to her body, I mean she was just absolutely wonderful. And we immediately said, 'This, this is the woman!' (Rutherford)*

The young woman they had discovered was Dolly Rathebe, who in the 1950s would become known as 'the South African Billie Holliday', or, alternatively, 'the South African Lena Horne'. But at that time, in the late 1940s, she was very young, and had not yet made a name for herself. She was known as a singer at St Cyprian's, but popular music she got at the cinema – 'the songs we'd heard on the screen, we'd go about singing them in Sophiatown'. At her audition, she sang a song from *Cabin in the Sky*, which was rendered in that film by Lena Horne. The song was 'Salt Lake City Blues', which Dolly adapted to Johannesburg:

> *Oh, I came to Jo'burg, the Golden City,*
> *Oh, what did I go there for?*

---

14   *'Mapantsula*: Cinema, Crime and Politics on the Witwatersrand', *Journal of South African Studies*, Vol. 16, No. 4, December 1990.

> *I should have stayed down in New Orleans,*
> *And never gone nowhere.*

Rutherford found Dolly Rathebe a delight to work with, unpretentious and modest, qualities she has not lost with the years. These qualities in no way diminished her sense of fun and joy in life.

Rutherford's revealing phrase about Dolly's discovery – 'it was like something out of a movie'– shows how life was dominated by Hollywood stories of stars discovered in the most unlikely personalities, and in fact the plot of *Jim Comes to Jo'burg* is of that nature.

Jim, the country bumpkin, comes to the city to find work, proves incompetent at everything, but is accidentally discovered to have a fine singing voice. He is invited to sing in the nightclub, then goes on to make a record, finding fame and romance. The fairytale quality of it all is unintentionally revealed in the almost magical way that the symbol of his labour and station in life, the broom with which he is sweeping out the nightclub, is quickly superseded by a microphone.

The kind of transformation used in numerous American films, it is the essence of the American dream – that all of us have talents that are waiting only to be revealed, and the passage from rags to riches is a birthright. The caterpillar to butterfly syndrome.

Of course, in South Africa, for blacks this was a fantasy far beyond what it was in America. Even for African-Americans, there were certain channels open – notably sports and entertainment – to an albeit still-limited stardom that included recognition by the white world. In South Africa, these did not exist.

Through *Jim Comes to Jo'burg*, Dolly Rathebe and Daniel Adnewmah became movie stars – but only for Africans. Black audiences in South Africa had certainly seen black heroes on the screen – they had seen *Cabin in the Sky* and *Stormy Weather* (both made in 1943), they had seen Lena Horne, Rochester, Billie Holliday, the Ink Spots, and hundreds of other black entertainers. Cab Calloway was so popular that he had donated a word that now seems quintessentially township African – '*tsotsi*', from 'zoot-suit', Calloway's trademark dress. But there were no *African* screen heroes to transcend the Faithful Servant kind of role until *Jim Comes to Jo'burg*.

John Kani says that it was Dolly Rathebe's success in *Jim Comes to Jo'burg* that inspired him to try acting, and that convinced his father, a great fan of Dolly's, that it was not only possible, but respectable. 'It was like a miracle, we saw black people in this movie, we saw black people talking ... we could scream, "That's Dolly!" ' The quality of delighted recognition extended to the locales where the film was shot: 'A film shot with people you recognised, on streets that you knew, you know, sometimes it was difficult to hear the dialogue because people were

shouting, ... "Hey, that's my street, I live down that street!"... They became like –
home movies' (Arthur Maimane, writer).

Dolly Rathebe and Daniel Adnewmah[15] (Jim) were stars, but of a special
homegrown variety – they could never be 'shimmering stars in the Hollywood
firmament' (as it is described in *Singin' in the Rain*). Despite the film's success,
Adnewmah never appeared in another film. Dolly Rathebe was the female lead in
Donald Swanson's next film, *The Magic Garden*; she was given a tiny walk-on role
in *Cry, the Beloved Country*, and then she did not appear in another film until her
performance in *Mapantsula*, almost thirty years after *Jim Comes to Jo'burg*.

The choice of title, *Jim Comes to Jo'burg* (the film was also known as *African
Jim*) was unfortunate. 'Jim' was a generic name given by whites to blacks,
especially servants. Quite possibly it derives from 'Jim Crow', a phrase imported
from the United States in the early nineteenth century, and readily adopted to avoid
having to resort to the (for lazy Europeans) tongue-contortions necessary to
pronounce African names. In African societies, one's name had more significance
than in European, since it had to bear the weight of tradition, as well as defining the
owner. Depriving someone of his own name was reductive. Since the name Jim
could be applied to anyone, it also deprived an African of his personality, making
him indistinguishable from the next man. With customary white myopia, the
film-makers were not aware that this might be offensive to blacks. At the same
time, it should be recognised that the offence was unconscious, and for the most
part the film-makers appear to have been remarkably free of the prejudices of the
society that was currently hosting them.

The film is introduced by a text intended to disarm criticism:

> *The first full length entertainment film to be made in South Africa
> with an all native cast. It is a simple film , and its quaint mixture of
> the naive and the sophisticated is a true reflection of the African
> native in the modern city.*

Like most of the films about black life that were to follow during the 1950s, the
story involves a journey to the city from the countryside. Jim's life in the country
is idyllic, but he leaves it to earn money to pay for a bride. There is no sense at
all of socio-economic pressures beyond his control forcing him off the land.
Arriving in Johannesburg, ingenuous as he is, he is quickly taken in by a
conman, and taken to a spot where he is mugged and left unconscious.

He is discovered by a kindly nightwatchman (Dan Twala) who looks after him
and finds him a job. But he is baffled by even the simple technology of a garden
hose, and his inclination to day-dream gets him fired. However, this is a Lucky Jim.
He gets into a street dice game, and wins. He is found another job, this time as a

---

15   Adnewmah in real life was a schoolteacher.

waiter in the nightclub. There, the thieves who robbed him earlier happen to drop in, and Jim overhears them planning a robbery. He and the nightwatchman ambush and capture the criminals, Jim and the nightclub singer (Dolly Rathebe) fall in love and Jim's singing voice is 'discovered' by a white musical agent, who engages the two of them to make a record. Fade out as they cut a record in the sound studio, their future success and happiness assured ...

This is a world where jobs, albeit menial, are easy to come by. Crime there is, but it is an aberration, not pervasive, as it was in real township life – the kind of reaction to crime depicted in *Jim*, where a handful of righteous individuals could prevail over *tsotsis*, could not happen in real life, where there was no challenging the gangs. Most of the people in *Jim* are kindly and well-intentioned.

The only white character (apart from a sit-in role played by Rutherford) is the employer who fires Jim for incompetence – and he turns into a good fairy at the end, when it transpires he is a talent agent. Police there are, who break up the street gambling, but they are not threatening, just figures of fun for Jim to mock. It is a picture of black life that is quite palatable to whites, designed not to cause disquiet. Although the exteriors of *Jim Comes to Jo'burg* were shot in authentic township locales, the plot avoids or softens the harsh realities of urban African life.[16]

Meanwhile, the stories connected with the shooting of *Jim Comes to Jo'burg* resonate with township vibrations. Many seem to revolve around Dolly Rathebe. ('I led a terrible, terrible life,' sighed Dolly during our 1990 interview, without a shadow of regret.) Filming was delayed one day because Dolly, the star, showed up without her false teeth. On another occasion, she was away for two weeks, because she had been stabbed by a friend who was jealous of her success. And then, while filming was going on, she stayed part of the time with Gloria Green at her house in the white suburb of Houghton.

> *I thought I'd take a walk down the road one evening – I was arrested for pass. The film had to stop again – (Dolly giggles). They just took me, and I slept in jail. (Dolly Rathebe)*

The film company seized the opportunity for publicity, and reported the incident to the newspapers:

ARREST OF RAND NATIVE FILM STAR

*Johannesburg – Dolly Rathebe, the Native star in the film **Jim Comes to Jo'burg** was arrested in Yeoville yesterday for not*

---

16   *Zonk* Magazine (August 1949) points out, for example: 'In one sequence Dan (Adnewmah) is beaten up and robbed outside the railway station. A strange coincidence is that Dan actually was beaten and robbed of his money one night on his way home from the film studio.' Coincidence it may have been, but this was by no means an unusual occurrence.

carrying a special pass.

She was fined 15 shillings (or three weeks) in the Native Commissioner's Court, in Fordsburg, yesterday. Dolly did not tell any of the Court officials of her fame in the film world, and she was described on the Court docket as a domestic servant.

She was arrested at 1:20 a.m. in Hendon Street, and told the Magistrate that she had been 'with friends'.

All Native women who are in the streets between 11 p.m. and 4 a.m. must carry 'night specials', unless they are with a husband who can produce a Union exemption pass.

The newspaper clipping is heavy with nuance. There is surely mockery in the reporter's 'Native star' and 'fame in the film world'; the description of Dolly as 'domestic servant' sounds like a policeman's inability to comprehend that she might be anything else; her explanation that she had been 'with friends' is presented as a vague excuse, when it was nothing but the truth – it is just that her friends were white (she was almost certainly suspected of being a prostitute – why else would a young African woman be in a white area in the early hours of the morning?); and then there is the final affront of status before the law – that women were subject to male responsibility.

The film is free of such gender inequality. Dolly balances the male hero, Jim, and the film ends with a duet between the two. Their love affair is subdued and decorous, a movie formality. Lewis Nkosi's quarrel with the film is that it constricts Dolly's temperament:

The one thing you recognise immediately about a singer like Dolly Rathebe, that she was much more explosive as a person in real life than she is made to behave in the film. It is as if you needed to tame those energies … (Interview, 1992)

Nkosi is perhaps being somewhat anachronistic, in that Dolly Rathebe's stellar quality, launched on its way by *Jim Comes to Jo'burg*, did not become apparent until the next decade, when she would be celebrated in *Drum* magazine and become the supreme prize for lustful township gangsters. It would take an entirely different kind of film to do justice to a life as full of incident as Dolly's. In those days, with Mae West past her prime, no-one anywhere was making films of that kind about women. So we have to make do with what is left, which is the treasure of Dolly in performance, all the sweeter because it is a unique record of Dolly Rathebe in the full flower of her youth.

The cast and crew of *Jim Comes to Jo'burg* were paid, but neither the white producer nor director took any salary. Rutherford and Swanson owed money for filmstock and processing, and for equipment rental. They expected to get their income from the sale of the film. They were too naive to understand that they were, in Rutherford's words, 'treading on the toes of the commercial organisations', which meant Schlesinger's African Film Productions.

Rutherford negotiated with Schlesinger's distribution arm, African Theatres, for distribution of *Jim Comes to Jo'burg*, but when he found out that once African Theatres had bought the film they had no obligation to distribute and might just bury it, he backed out.

This put him in dispute with Swanson, and angered African Theatres. Rutherford describes a phone call from the head of African Theatres, threatening that unless he signed a contract by 5 p.m. that day, 'this is the end of your career in Africa, and all your friends!' Eventually they went with the smaller rival organisation, United Artists. They had a premiere – some kind of benefit show – in a white cinema. Returns were miserable. Nevertheless, the film did achieve a *succès d'estime*. Under the headline 'NON-EUROPEANS IMPRESS IN FIRST FULL-LENGTH ENTERTAINMENT FILM', the Johannesburg *Star* gave the film a full and favourable review, proclaiming 'Yes, history has been made'. The film was opened in African cinemas.

THE RAND DAILY MAIL, WEDNESDAY, 2 NOVEMBER 1949.

*Expensive American cars pull up outside the Rio Cinema at the lower end of Commissioner Street every day, and Native girls and boys jump out to book seats for **Jim Comes to Jo'burg**. The entire non-European population of Johannesburg is queuing to see the film. Natives, Coloureds and Indians line up eight deep in efforts to get in. Early last week the cinema broke its own record – set up by **Stormy Weather** – also with an all-black cast (American) – and the film is running continuously...*

*Daniel Adnewmah (Jim) and Dolly Rathebe, who played main parts in **Jim Comes to Jo'burg** are already important people. Admirers follow and ask for their autographs.*

Dolly's hair style, designed for her part in the film, is copied everywhere in the townships. It is 'cottage loaf' drawn together with a fillet of Native beadwork.

The non-Europeans are very proud of their film – made in Johannesburg by Johannesburg artists.

The Pretoria News gave the film a fair evaluation:

__Jim Comes to Jo'burg__ had its first Pretoria showing at the Empire Theatre, Boom Street, before a packed non-European audience.

> *It has no pretentions to being a great film; it has no message;*
> *it is not a bit self-conscious or proud of itself. But judged as sheer*
> *entertainment it puts most of the films shown in this country in the*
> *shade. (8 November 1949)*

Umtebeh we Bantu prophesied:

> *Future historians will look back with interest on the Johannesburg*
> *of 1949 and the record provided by the first full-length motion*
> *picture with an all-African cast shown at the Rio Theatre in*
> *Market Street ...*

Africans who lived within reach of the white-owned black cinemas of Johannesburg could see the film, but this was not the case for the majority of the population, who lived further away with no access to a cinema. The film was shot on 35mm for theatrical distribution, but Rutherford had retained 16mm distribution rights ('I was very young and naive in those days, I wouldn't have got into it if I wasn't young and naive, but another part of me was rather canny ...'), so he took a projector around the townships and showed the film in direct cinema fashion, effectively by-passing the distribution monopoly. In income, there was still very little to show, but it did reach a considerable black audience.

According to Rutherford, they had started out with an objective that went beyond making an African film: 'Perhaps we could set up an all-African company eventually, we'd train technicians, and we would really have a black film industry.' Zonk (December 1949) picked up on this: '... (the film) immediately opens up a new industry for the African people, and marks a further step in our progress' – an optimism that ignored the reality of cinema in South Africa. For Warrior Films (the Rutherford, Green, Swanson company), since the film never made enough money even to pay the producer and director, there was certainly no fund of money to draw on for another film that might spread this kind of empowerment. It was not in the interest of the cinema establishment to allow Africans to make their own films – who knew where that would lead? Innocuous as it seems as agitprop, Jim Comes to Jo'burg had resonances:

> *The film couldn't really be called a political film, in the sense that*
> *we had decided to make entertainment. We wanted to make*
> *something that was their own, but of course that inevitably was*
> *political ... it was an expression of themselves, of their own*
> *personality; it was a question of finding their voice. (Rutherford)*

THE MAGIC GARDEN (1951)

Dismayed as they were by the financial failure of *Jim Comes to Jo'burg*, Swanson and Rutherford did plan to make another film. This was to be a whimsy called *The Magic Garden*. Rutherford felt that Swanson, who had been the scriptwriter for *Jim*, had gone for entertainment, shutting out what was 'authentic black'. *The Magic Garden* would be set entirely in a township, without the phoney glamour lent by the nightclub in *Jim Comes to Jo'burg*. *The Magic Garden* did get made, but not by Rutherford, who claimed that although he initiated the project, Swanson deliberately cut him out. Since Donald Swanson has been dead for some years, we do not have his side of the story.

Although *The Magic Garden* is indeed set in a township, and shows people in their usual settings, even ostensibly dealing with the theme of poverty, the fairy-tale story prevents any confrontation with African life. This is an all-black film, more so than *Jim Comes to Jo'burg*, in which an irate white boss turned benefactor. *The Magic Garden* has more in common with *Cabin in the Sky* (1943), with its depiction of a poor black society supported by a sense of simple goodness to overcome the degradation of poverty.

Most of the action of *The Magic Garden* takes place within the convention of a chase film. Again *Hue and Cry* comes to mind, but of course the chase, the basis of so many comedies, is a theme almost as old as cinema itself. A thief steals the life savings of an old man in church, and the community gives chase. In his attempts to elude capture, the thief hides the money; it is discovered by different people, passes from hand to hand, and in its course does good to the deserving and harm to the wicked, before eventually returning to the rightful owner.

The man who wrote the original story, James Ambrose Brown, compared the film to the work of the Italian neo-realists.[17] But if we are looking for social awareness, we will not find it here. The absence of whites, with the domineering landlord, the rapacious shopowner and the tyrannical father all being black, neatly avoids any white responsibility for township poverty. As in *Jim Comes to Jo'burg*, crime is an aberration against which the whole township reacts. Another overwhelming problem, lack of housing, is turned into a joke: at one point, the thief hides inside a dustbin, where he is discovered by two constables. One remarks to the other, 'Man, this housing shortage is getting serious.' The patronising tone is confirmed by the lyrics of a song sung by Dolly Rathebe and Matome 'Tommy' Ramokgopa:

> *Thief: Every strong and husky Zulu*
> *Gets a long and dusky lulu*
> *And they go, with a hi-de, hi-de ho,*
> *To the dance at Alexandra.*
>
> *Lily: Every gay and charming Xhosa*
> *Tells her boyfriend that she knows a*

---

17   In an article in the *Cape Argus* of 27 February 1980.

Place she like and away they hike
To the dance at Alexandra.

Thief: If they can't get a bus
They don't give a cuss
For there's always a great big taxi,
With room at the back
For James and Jack
And Reg and Dick and Nancy.

Lily: Every crewboy leaves his kitchen,
And his little toes start itching,
As he slinks like a well-dressed zink
To the dance at Alexandra.

Thief: Oh, meningi skati

Lily: Oh, meningi skati

Thief: There's a band of crazy bantu
Beating rhythm that enchants you,
I'll bet you anything …
Down, at Alexandra.

Lily: There's a thing called …
… makes the floor more …
You must even …
Down at Alexandra.

Thief: Now each little coon fills a crack at noon
But at night when he does the rhumba,
They wag their tail like a lovesick male,
And tell their blues to hamba!
Oh, how they love to push and shove
At the dance at Alexandra!

(The text is taken from the soundtrack, which is not always clear.)

Unlike that in *Jim*, the music from *The Magic Garden* shows strong African roots, much of it being recognisably 'township' music. A minstrel playing a tin-whistle binds the plot together.

But at another level, assuredly not intended by Donald Swanson, the scriptwriter and director, the film can be read as a parable about the wealth of South Africa, and its distribution, or, if you like, redistribution. The stolen money is first of all hidden in a pumpkin-patch. When it is dug up by a penniless family, the whole neighbourhood starts to dig holes in the hope of finding money in some 'magic garden'. Later, after the money reverts to the thief, he hides it in a tree, from where it falls into the hands of a young man below.

And this is a precise, if accidental, metaphor for the wealth of South Africa, which grows on trees (agriculture), or is dug up out of the ground (mining). However, in the context of the film, this wealth is not in the hands of whites but of Africans, and its redistribution causes a certain amount of prosperity and even egalitarian justice, because it involves taking from the exploitative rich and giving to the poor.

It is hard to ascertain what success *The Magic Garden* had in distribution. It received limited showing in the United States ('... this little film is *Laugh, the Beloved Country*', wrote a *New York Times* critic), but was not shown in South Africa until 1961, a decade after it was made. In a review in *The Sunday Times* of 22 January 1961, the writer is obviously relieved to find that it is not yet another blow at South Africa:

> **The Magic Garden** *gives a fair idea of life in the townships, and portrays with accuracy the community life of the people, their religious outlook and the poor conditions under which they live. But there is no bitterness ... in* **The Magic Garden**. *On the contrary, a strong sense of humour and vitality pervades the film.*

But despite the non-controversial nature of his work, Swanson never succeeded in making another film. As for Rutherford, he became more and more disillusioned with life in South Africa. The growth of the apartheid state brought with it a bureaucracy that, Rutherford felt, was not concerned about the welfare of Africans, and there was increasing alienation between whites and blacks, which made co-operative work across racial boundaries much more difficult.

ZONK (1950)

According to Rutherford, African Films were so peeved at not getting the distribution rights for *Jim Comes to Jo'burg* that they decided to make their own all-black movie. They had been stung into realising that there was a potentially lucrative African market, but that if it was the right kind of film, they could attract white patrons as well. Learning a lesson from the Rutherford–Swanson production, they opted for black entertainers. They took the name of a new and popular African magazine *Zonk*, and, like *Jim*, followed a Hollywood formula.

Widening the scope, they went beyond the nightclub to a presumed stage performance. African Films did not attempt to tie the whole thing together with any kind of back-stage story, the usual Hollywood device. *Zonk* is simply a series of musical numbers, relying heavily on Hollywood stereotypes of the black as entertainer. The music ranges from 'Dixie' presentations of a darkie in straw hat and overalls, chopping wood as he sings *Deep River*, to Harlem dance-hall for *Jumpin' Jive*, to Broadway top-hat and tie. The decor is very elaborate; the direction by Hyman Kirstein has none of the rough edges of *Jim Comes to Jo'burg*. The only indigenous pieces are a gum-boot dance and a well-known song.

Zonk confirms the impression from *Jim Comes to Jo'burg* of the overwhelming influence on township life of American music disseminated through films. The last reel contains a musical number that, in the context of South Africa during the early years of apartheid, seems vertiginous. The tuxedoed compere stands in front of the stage curtains, and announces: 'Most of you good people have heard Europeans impersonate darkies. Tonight, ladies and gentlemen, we give you a darkie impersonating a very famous European who impersonates the darkie.'

To fully understand the convolutions of this speech it has to be appreciated that 'European' is used in the South African sense, to mean a white man. In fact, the 'European' in question was an American, Al Jolson (whom Africans would have known through *The Jazz Singer* and its post-war sequel). The curtains part, and with the singer's opening phrase, 'Mammy!' we are witnessing a cameo of a black man imitating a white man in blackface. It is worth trying to untangle the different cultural and racial strands that are enmeshed in this grotesque caricature.

The American 'nigger minstrel' tradition, whatever its precise origins, seems to have been a way of gaining access to, and co-opting, black culture while at the same time keeping a certain distance from it. With classic ambivalence, the minstrel show mocked Afro-Americans while tacitly paying tribute to the consummate skill of black performance, which the white entertainers copied. Even when giving straight performances of supposedly minstrel dances – and in the case of Jolson, sentimental songs – the painted facial mask (with lips enlarged and emphasised in white), effectively turned the black image into a racial cartoon. So in the performance there was a built-in ambivalence that mocked at the same time as it exploited.

That was in the American and Western European context. In the African environment, it is doubtful if any pathos for 'darkies' (outrageously exploited by Al Jolson) would have been socially permissible.

The historical background to *Zonk* was the early 1950s, the beginning of the entrenchment of apartheid with its social engineering, and its apparatus of racial classification and segregation. The devastating irony of Sylvester Phahlane singing *September in the Rain* in this film is that we have a black man imitating ('passing for') a white man (i.e. Al Jolson), something strictly against the laws of apartheid. And he does it in full view of the audience, of society, by being on stage and in a film. Now, it would have been unthinkable for a black man to do this, even in playing a part. But in this context, the performer can get away with it because he is not simply playing a white man, but *he is playing a white man playing a black man* – that is to say, it is a self-caricature. And it is this extra twist that gives it licence.

Incongruously enough, *Zonk* ends with the performers singing *Nkosi Sikelel' i Afrika*. At this point, the film makes its only concession to the medium's ability to expand beyond the unity imposed by the pretence of a stage performance, and supplies a visual foreground to the music, in the form of views of what was then called Basotholand – not even part of South Africa. What most likely happened here is simply that for this footage, the director had recourse to another film, or the out-takes from another film, probably a travelogue.

Whether Hyman Kirstein appreciated the significance of *Nkosi Sikelel'i Afrika* as the black national anthem, or whether (more likely) he simply regarded it as a nice African hymn, cannot be determined. But it is certainly curious in the context of the times.

SONG OF AFRICA (1951)

Zonk must have had some success, because it was followed by yet another all-black production from African Films. This was *Song of Africa*, directed by Emil Nofal, an Afrikaner, who had worked on *Zonk*. Like *Jim Comes to Jo'burg*, *Song of Africa* opens with a disclaimer regarding the acting:

> *This picture tells a tale of AFRICA and of its Native People. It is an attempt to show you how they live and how they play. It is acted by Africans who have had no training in the art of self expression and in this respect is spontaneous and unique.*

This film, unlike *Jim Comes to Jo'burg, The Magic Garden*, or *Zonk*, is a product of an Afrikaner's concept of the African. It contains many of the clichés and self-delusions that were to make apartheid tenable. Of course, it shows a fantasy world – most movies do that – but in this case the cosmetic world depicted is completely in harmony with Afrikaner Nationalist philosophy. Which is to say, with the mass fantasy indulged by thousands of Afrikaners.

The film begins in *Zonk* fashion with a stage presentation, this time by a Zulu jazz band, and the story swings into a prolonged flashback purporting to show how the band arrived at this high point. The plot is built around the band leader, Daniel Makiza, and there is a shift to his home. This is depicted as an idyllic vision of Zululand. There are two warriors on a hillside, bare-breasted women wash in a stream, people walk around a kraal in a leisurely way. The voice-over text of the film's hero goes as follows: 'The Zulu people still keep their old customs. A man can have many wives to look after him and to keep his home, if he has to go to the city to work. For me, this is my home ...'

The film insists on the homeland imperative, central to apartheid, that Africans belong in a particular rural area, and while they may go to the city to work, the homeland is where they really want to be. And this homeland has its enticements, like numerous wives, old men swapping war stories over pots of beer, beautiful scenery. 'When I think of Zululand, it calls strongly to me, as it calls to all Zulus who go away ...'

Daniel goes to the city in search of an education. Once more, as in *Jim Comes to Jo'burg*, the fiction is maintained that African migration did not stem from dire economic need, but was voluntary – if it was voluntary, then there was no need for Africans to remain in the city, and they would clearly return 'home' at some point. Unlike *Jim Comes to Jo'burg* and *The Magic Garden*, there is no attempt to present black life in the townships, however sanitised.

We catch up with Daniel when he is on his way back home, returning to the bosom of his family, and to his bride-to-be. While he was in the city, he encountered jazz for the first time, and he has brought back with him a gramophone and the determination to start a Zulu jazz band. But to buy the instruments, he would have to sell the cattle that constitute the *lobola*[18] for Thandi, his fiancée, which he refuses to do. However, Thandi insists that the money must go to the band. To the amusement of the village, the Zulu Jazz Band starts its practice, a cacophony that quickly transforms into a swing version of *Swanee River*.

The band is ready for the Big Time; they travel to the city and win a contest, and this brings us to the stage performance that constitutes the body of the film. The staging and decor are even more elaborate than those in *Zonk*, with numbers that range from gumboot dancing to tap dancers in top-hat and tails, culminating in a highly ambitious presentation of the drum as central to jazz. A dancer prances on giant drums, with music ranging from traditional Zulu to Latin to swing and back.

But all this success does not persuade Daniel and the band to stay on in the city. Content with their achievement, they return to Zululand, where Dan marries Thandi in a Zulu wedding ceremony that does not look authentic. The band plays joyfully, and the couple go off hand-in-hand into the sunset to their homeland Eden.

As with *The Magic Garden* and *Zonk*, *Song of Africa* takes place in a world where whites are completely absent. Even when the Zulu jazz band goes to the city, the streets are established in long-shot, so that whites simply melt into the general view. The music competition is run by blacks, the theatre is filled with an all-black audience. And this lends an illusion of freedom to the characters in the picture.

The introduction of white characters would have brought with it at least intimations of those constraints that existed in South African society whenever blacks and whites came together. *Jim Comes to Jo'burg* had its white character in

---

18   The 'lobola', or bride price, was often cited by whites in film and print as the
       reason for Africans leaving the land to seek work in the cities.

the dual form of irate boss and good-natured benefactor, and each of these roles demanded a particular obsequious response from Jim. The world of *The Magic Garden* and of *Song of Africa* is already one where the process of apartheid is complete, and separation of the races is a fact. What is completely absent is the vicious manifestation of apartheid itself.

CRY, THE BELOVED COUNTRY (1952)

At about the same time that *Song of Africa* was being made, Zoltan Korda, of the famous Hungarian film family that had established itself in Britain, journeyed to South Africa to make a film. Zoltan had experience of African subjects – in the 1930s, he had made the imperialist story, *Sanders of the River*, a justification of white rule in Africa.

Now, he had chosen *Cry, the Beloved Country*.[19] This was based on the Alan Paton novel that first brought world attention to South Africa's social problems. The book had come out in 1948, and was quickly considered a classic. In a post-war Britain where the triumph of Labourite socialism brought with it a strong anti-colonial and anti-racist groundswell, it was only fitting that *Cry, the Beloved Country* should seem a natural choice for a film.

Michael Korda describes[20] how the film highlighted a rift between the left and the right wings of the family. In its way, this was a microcosm of the split in British society as a whole:

> ... Zoli (Zoltan) was...preparing to begin **Cry, the Beloved Country**, and was determined to make an uncompromising and true-to-life film ... Alex[21]... understood better than anyone else that **Cry, the Beloved Country** was the story Zoli had always dreamed of filming. His earlier movies about Africa had been struggles between Zoli's own desire to show the reality of Africans' lives and aspirations in the bondage of colonialism and Alex's determination to make films that would present the Empire to British audiences in a positive and patriotic light. Not that Alex was unaware of the black man's burden, or even unsympathetic to

---

19 There were to be other versions of *Cry, the Beloved Country* on film: the Hollywood musical *Lost in the Stars*, and the very odd Morocco/Senegal/Guinea co-production *Amok* (1982), directed by Ben Barka Souheil, with Miriam Makeba, which does not even credit Alan Paton. (In view of the grotesque distortion of the original, it is probably just as well.) In 1996, a new South African production was released, unfortunately too late for inclusion in this review.

20 In his portrait of the Korda family, *Charmed Lives*.

21 Producer Alexander Korda.

it; he simply felt that the white man's burden was more acceptable
and commercial to Anglo-American audiences ... Now Alex was
faced with a story in which the plight of the black man in a racist
society was the basic subject. He could see no way that it could be
'toned down' or made easy for a white audience to accept, nor
was Zoli willing to compromise.

Michael Korda goes on to explain the kind of pressure that Alexander Korda had
to face from friends like Lord Beaverbrook and Viscount Bracken, who would
regard *Cry, the Beloved Country* as an attack on their revered British Empire,
and would certainly not hesitate to let Alexander Korda know how they felt – but
the film got made anyway.

Alan Paton, whose first priority was clearly to get the film made, accepted a
miserly one thousand pounds from London Films for the rights to his book. In 1949
he went to London to begin work on the film. He was to work with Zoltan Korda,
Alexander's younger brother.

Zoltan thrust upon Paton the task of writing the script, which the author
undertook very reluctantly – he had no experience whatsoever in that area. Paton
describes his first script session with Zoltan:

'"Something about nature, Alan, I want something about nature."

'Then he would say apologetically, "I know the first chapters are full of nature.
But I want something – one line maybe – about small nature."

'Something about a flower?

'His face lights up, as though I had said something extremely creative.

' "That is it," he says, "a flower." '[22]

On another occasion, Zoltan muses: 'Death, there is much death in your book,
but in a film it is good. One can always play with death.' Of such stuff the mighty
industry of cinema is made ... [23]

Since Paton was involved as co-producer as well as scriptwriter, it is not
surprising that the film is quite faithful to the book. The book has been criticised as
a white liberal's view of African life, seen from the outside, with a stylised
language that no-one ever spoke, and characters accepting of the master/servant
relationship between black and white. This can no more be denied than that Paton's
motive was to see some amelioration in the quality of the master/servant
relationship that would render more social justice to the African. The world of the
early 1950s was different from that of the years of struggle against apartheid, and
the value of *Cry, the Beloved Country* in that struggle should not be underrated.

---

22 *Journey's End*, p. 19.

23 *Ibid.*

The setting of *Cry, the Beloved Country* (1952) is a South Africa that has scarcely heard the word 'apartheid'. Conspicuously absent from the book and from the film are the key political players, the Afrikaners. Paton's white society consists of English-speakers, divided between conservatives who want to keep Africans in their place, and those anxious to help them. James Jarvis, the principal white character, crosses the line between the two as the result of a personal tragedy, and this constitutes his epiphany. What pervades the film is the Christian ethic as the path both to personal salvation and to the resolution of South Africa's social problems.

In the world of *Cry, the Beloved Country*, the organs of the state are impartial, not malevolent. The police go about their duty with no overweening joy in their power, and the justice that is dispensed – releasing the suspect against whom there is insufficient evidence, and condemning Stephen Kumalo, who has confessed – seems unexceptionable. The head of the remand home is genuinely concerned about the welfare of young Kumalo.

In a sense, there are no villains – even the murderer Kumalo is a victim. Instead of villains, we are offered social forces out of control. There is an amorphous evil abroad, whose influence, although it consumes blacks principally, spills over into the white community. The real dichotomy is not between the colours, but between town and country. And at least for the African characters, the town represents corruption, and the country salvation.

In the spirit of neo-realism that gripped European cinema at that time, Korda actually filmed in the townships and shantytowns of Johannesburg. *The Magic Garden* was also shot in a township, Alexandra, but while Donald Swanson's film admitted the poverty of township life, it has none of the degradation of *Cry, the Beloved Country*, which is devoid of the stereotypical happy African, singing and dancing even when surrounded by poverty. The Reverend Kumalo's quest for his son brings him face-to-face with madness, prostitution, robbery, murder, hypocrisy and widescale degradation. For the simple country priest, it is an education in the depths of human depravity.

His initiation comes as soon as he arrives in Johannesburg. At the railway station, he is accosted by a conman, who asks him if he needs help, and then disappears with the money the unsuspecting priest gives him to buy a bus-ticket. When he relates this to the township priests later, they are only amused – it is just part of everyday life, and not the most threatening part.

A young priest, Msimangu, is selected to guide the Reverend Kumalo through the townships in search of his son. There is a telling scene in which the two priests track down the young woman with whom the Reverend Kumalo's son has been living, and who is pregnant. The father questions her about her own parents, and she admits that she does not know where they are and she does not know how she will live. After the two priests have left her, the Reverend Kumalo halts, and says that he must return to her. Msimangu objects. Gently, Kumalo gives his reason: 'You do not understand. That child will be my grandchild.' Msimangu replies, 'Even of that you cannot be sure. And besides, how many more are there? Shall we seek them all out, one by one? Will it never end?'

It is the streetwise Msimangu, worn out by the daily battle with social decay, who loses patience. There is no way to vanquish the corruption of the town. The Reverend Kumalo's sister becomes a prostitute there. His son becomes a murderer. His son's common-law wife is on the verge of prostitution. To rescue this woman, and the child she will bear, the Reverend Kumalo takes her back with him to the country, leading her away from sin. In *Cry, the Beloved Country*, the great Manichean opposition of good and evil is very clear. Kumalo's village is humble and impoverished, but it is pure. This is where the people belong if they are not to lose their souls. The structure of this rural society is medieval, with a lord of the manor who is capable of bestowing largesse on the black villeins, as when Arthur Jarvis intervenes to repair the roof of the Reverend Kumalo's church.

Alan Paton's formula for salvation in South Africa is salvation in Christian, not political, terms. The soul of the white farmer James Jarvis, who is led to God and a re-evaluation of his racist convictions by the humility, simplicity, and translucent goodness of the African priest, may be saved. But it leaves the social fabric undisturbed – the hierarchy of colour does not need to be changed.

There is another person from Kumalo's village of Ndotsheni who went to the city and did not return. This is Kumalo's brother, who became a carpenter, but also entered politics. When the reverend goes to see him, John Kumalo talks about the new spirit that is sweeping the land, which is the stirring of black political activism, although it is not so precisely defined in the film as in the book.

During the post-war period, and especially in the early 1950s, there was in South Africa a growing political awareness among Africans. It was a time of protests and of marches, of militancy and of organisation. It was the period that brought to the fore Walter Sisulu, Oliver Tambo, and Nelson Mandela, and which had at the head of the ANC the potent moral force of Chief Luthuli. It is true that the book was written some years before the political movement gained momentum, and before these were household names, but even so, the film reveals a fear of black political action.

This fear is embodied in the character of John Kumalo, the politician. When the Reverend Kumalo and Father Msimangu visit him for the first time, the scene sows doubts about his character. It is revealed that he is living with a woman who is not his wife, and that he has not taken good care of his own son and of his nephew, the Reverend Kumalo's son, Absalom – which it was his sacred duty, under African kinship, to do. At one point, he hands Msimangu a speech he has written, and inveighs against the church:

John Kumalo: The church will speak of repentance and obedience, but of the things that most need amendment, Sophiatown, Pimville ...

Father Msimangu: It speaks of those.

John Kumalo: It has spoken like that for ten, fifty years. Have you seen any change there? The laws, the wages, the poverty.

Reverend Kumalo: My brother ...

John Kumalo: Have you seen the bishop's house? Is it like your own in Ndotsheni? And you want us all to return there, me and our sister, your son, my son, and let us all be obedient to the church and the chief.

Reverend Kumalo: My wife told me you would be changed.

John Kumalo: Of course I am changed. There is a new thing growing here, stronger than any church or chief.

John Kumalo is dissatisfied with the status quo, but there is a curious restraint in his onslaught. For he does not directly attack the obvious target, white hegemony. Instead, he attacks the church, which his brother serves. Although it is never named as such, the 'new thing' that is growing is black politics. But it is subtly tainted in the film by being embodied in the personality of John Kumalo, a man of less than admirable character. Why, he will even go to the lengths of hiring a lawyer to defend his son who is accused of murder, even though he knows that his son was involved. After the trial at which the Reverend Kumalo's son Absalom is condemned while his own son goes free, John Kumalo proclaims that justice has been done. He is confronted with Msimangu's righteous anger:

Father Msimangu: Justice? Is that what I heard you say?

John Kumalo: There was a case, and a judge. Such a thing is not for you or me or any other person.

Father Msimangu: Keep your word in your mouth. And when you open it again, in your great meetings, with your great bull voice, spare us your talk of truth and justice. (He has touched John Kumalo.) Where can I wash my hands?

When Msimangu tongue-lashes John Kumalo for his hypocrisy, he extends his condemnation to his politics. Since this is the only portrait we have of a black politician in the film, the character of John Kumalo gives the impression that black politicians are merely demagogues.

In *Cry, the Beloved Country*, there is no scene where a black man is shown being demeaned by a white man (although, white to white, racist thoughts are expressed). On the contrary, the white officials behave in an exemplary way, from the reform school head to the judge who condemns Absalom to death. Neither of the priests, neither the young priest who knows at first hand the degradation of the township slums, nor the old priest who is brutally initiated into it, takes the logical step of denouncing the system, because that would mean condemning whites. There is some questioning of the way whites behave towards blacks, but this questioning comes from whites, principally from the young Arthur Jarvis (and after his death, through his writings to his father, prompting the latter's soul-searching). There is the unsettling impression that South Africa's vast social problems can be repaired through charity, the donation of money to a boys' club here, the repair of a leaky church roof there. This reinforces a sense of *noblesse oblige* – if society is to change, it must be through white action, while blacks remain essentially passive.

The natural critic of this position would be the Msimangu of Sidney Poitier. But instead he opts for passivity: 'There is nothing you can do.' However, that is not necessarily the lesson the black audience drew from seeing Poitier. Memory itself can be politicised, and in recalling the confrontation between Msimangu and John Kumalo, black South Africans often forget that the object of the young priest's rage is a black man, and substitute a white man.

This clearly fits better with Poitier's film persona, typically that of a black man who may be subject to white prejudice (*Guess Who's Coming to Dinner, In the Heat of the Night*), who may be in chains (*The Defiant Ones*), who may even be killed by a white bigot (*Edge of the City*), but who himself never gives the appearance of being anything but a free man who cannot be intimidated.

Just as there may be a distortion of memory about exactly what Poitier did, films can carry messages that even contradict what is being said or done. Here was a black man whose body language carried lessons not intended by the film-makers, possibly not even recognised by them, and the implications of which Poitier himself may not have realised. Poitier's movements, his behaviour, his demeanour, said, 'Here is a black man who as a hero is the equal of any white man you have hitherto seen.' And that carried its own political message:

> *John Kani: I know it was a white story, I know it was written by a white person, but ... you must understand, to see our people on the screen, to see people who will become our heroes, in it, and be able to say, 'I'm not Tex Ritter, I'm not Roy Rogers, but I'm Sidney Poitier!'* [24] *(interview, 1990)*

---

24   When Africans of the star-quality of Poitier appeared on the political scene – a Mandela, a Biko – then the white authorities would have to jail them for life, or kill them.

In making *Cry, the Beloved Country*, Korda was naturally looking for a world market. So he felt that he needed world-class actors. This meant that he had to turn to America since, inadequate though Hollywood was in turning out films with black actors, such films and such actors did exist. For his two principal actors, he chose Canada Lee as the old priest the Reverend Kumalo, and Sidney Poitier as the young priest, Msimangu. With Lee, Korda was taking a risk – Lee's leftwing activities had put him on the Hollywood blacklist, and Korda was jeopardising American distribution by using him. In fact, the film received very poor distribution in the United States.[25]

But this was a period when a number of American actors and entertainers with leftwing sympathies found a haven in socialist Britain, and to his credit, Korda was not intimidated. It is true that Canada Lee's role did not require him to confront white authority, and so the part draws the accusation of Uncle Tomism. Nevertheless, Lee's performance is invested with dignity and moral weight, a fine foil to the impatience and passion of Poitier's performance. It was Canada Lee's last film.

Despite Lee's fine performance, as Paton records, Zoltan Korda's relationship with the actor was 'tinged with contempt', implying that Lee was punch-drunk from his years as a boxer.

On arriving in South Africa, Korda had announced that he would be using non-South African actors because there were no professional actors in South Africa. This was true, but it was challenged by Rutherford, who had shown Korda *Jim Comes to Jo'burg*, and had great faith in African abilities. Besides Canada Lee and Sidney Poitier in America, Korda brought with him half a dozen British actors of colour, including Edric Connor (John Kumalo) and Vivien Clinton (Mary, Absalom Kumalo's common-law wife). Africans appeared in minor parts. The result is a discordant range of black-accented English – from Hollywood through the Caribbean to Britain to Zululand.

In his autobiography, Sidney Poitier describes his first meeting with Zoltan Korda in London. The director asks him to read his part 'with an African accent'– as ludicrous as if one could talk of a 'European' accent that would hold good for the vast expanse and variety of Europe. In consequence, Poitier spends the rest of the day walking around London trying to find an African.

> *Midway in my second hour I came upon an African chap with whom I shot the breeze for the better part of an afternoon, picking up in the process the rhythmic pattern of the English language as*

---

25 American distributors infuriated Korda by changing the name of the film to the inappropriate title *African Fury*, which effectively cut off any mental association with the book, and implied a totally different character for the film, changing it to the jungle genre.

*it flowed from the lips of a Kenyan whose principal languages were Kikuyu and Swahili. By the time we took leave of each other in Trafalgar Square, **an authentic African accent** was locked in the chambers of my memory (my emphasis).*

What is missing from *Cry, the Beloved Country* is the authentic beauty of black South African English.

There is a substantial argument in favour of Korda's preference for American and British actors, and that is, that both Hollywood English and London English offer the two universally accepted forms of the language which have achieved wide currency, mainly through cinema. And of course, the more films are made with those two forms of English, the more universal they become, and the harder it is for other accents to make a breakthrough.

Nevertheless, the one significant exception to Korda's preference for non-South Africans does imply that neither acting ability nor accent were a barrier. This was the choice of Lionel Ngakane to play the Reverend Kumalo's son, Absalom.

Lionel Ngakane came to this part by accident. He had gone for an interview to become a journalist, and not succeeded, so he decided to try out for a part in *Cry, the Beloved Country*, although he had no acting experience. He was in fact not unknown to Alan Paton, because his father had worked at the Diepkloof Reformatory where Paton was for a time Principal – an experience Paton had incorporated into the film. But Paton had nothing to do with his hiring.

According to Lionel Ngakane, the part of Absalom had originally been assigned to Sidney Poitier, but clearly Poitier's embodiment of the role would have changed the character considerably. Poitier's screen persona could scarcely have been made to fit into the character of Absalom, a passive victim of social circumstances. Lionel Ngakane gives a moving performance as a young man terrified of the consequences of a murder committed in an act of panic, and made to face the consequences and his conscience.

After he had finished work on the film, Ngakane recognised that despite its success in South Africa, there was no point in his staying there to try to build a career, and he accepted an offer from Korda to work as his assistant in England. There Ngakane stayed to learn his craft as actor and film director.

If Canada Lee and Sidney Poitier were the stars, they were not accorded star status in South Africa. Both of them had experience of discrimination in the United States, where at that time it was still widespread, even outside the South. In South Africa, they could not even stay in a hotel; a farmhouse outside Johannesburg had to be rented for them. Canada Lee, who had arrived in South Africa first, told Sidney Poitier that they were in South Africa as 'indentured labourers', vouched for by Zoltan Korda.

Sidney Poitier's autobiography relates how he was completely ignorant of South Africa's racial policies before he got there. (This may seem odd now, but in those days it was entirely possible.) Poitier describes (in *This Life*, p.151) how he and Canada Lee

> *were feted by two political organisations, the South African Black Congress (sic) and the African-Indian Congress (sic). In a real cloak-and-dagger manner ... we met and spoke in private with some of their leaders, who overwhelmed us with facts and figures relating to their constant struggle against a political system that considered both Indians and blacks less than human ... they leaped at the opportunity to outline in detail every aspect of their struggle ...*

According to Poitier, they witnessed a number of racist incidents, including the beating of innocent blacks at a traffic accident. He gives a long description of an incident involving his use of a white toilet at the film studio, which was to culminate some time later in a harrowing drive to the airport to catch his flight out, when he was pursued by racist thugs intent on revenge for the toilet incident. William Hoffman, in his biography *Sidney* (p.26) quotes Poitier as saying: '*Cry, the Beloved Country* gave me the chance to say some things about apartheid that needed saying. There are few roles that I've prepared harder for. I wanted to project what it was like to be black and under the iron heel of a vicious, racist white minority. I think how I felt came across in the film.' No doubt Poitier learned his lessons while he was there.

In the end, the South African world depicted on the screen in *Cry, the Beloved Country* is not so far removed from the self-delusory world of apartheid. In the film, evil does not flow from the racist state, but from the social ills of massive and uncontrolled migration to the cities – precisely the *swart gevaar*, the fear of competition from black labour, that lay behind the creation of the apartheid state.

In the Paton–Korda film, as in National Party doctrine, blacks are happiest where they 'belong' – in their homelands. While it condemned white bigotry, the film was not perceived as a threat by South Africa's rulers. The gala opening night was attended by Alan Paton and his wife; side by side with them was the Prime Minister, Dr Malan, a principal engineer of apartheid. In the glittering throng of men in tuxedos and women in evening gowns there was not a single black person to be seen, not even an actor from the film.

In the cinema, Alan Paton was seated next to Mrs Malan, who at one point asked if Johannesburg slums depicted on the screen really looked like that.

> *I do not suppose for one moment that Mrs Malan was a heartless or indifferent woman. She just did not want to believe that any*

place in the country of which her husband was the Prime Minister could look as these places looked. She was like so many white South Africans – they are not as much shocked by such places as by the fact that people write about them, especially in books that are read all over the world. If this is done by a white South African it is the worst form of disloyalty. It shows a hatred of one's country. It is called – in the miracle of language – 'fouling one's own nest'.[26]

The film was highly praised in Britain, and in America the Museum of Modern Art awarded it the Golden Laurel Award of 1952 as 'the film that made the greatest contribution to mutual understanding and goodwill between the peoples of the free and democratic world' (whether South Africa was part of this world was not spelled out). The influential critic Bosley Crowther (*New York Times*, 27 January 1952) asked pointedly: '… why our American film-makers have not yet risen to the eloquent height of *Cry, the Beloved Country* in expounding the subject of race and why have they not exposed the problem in terms stronger than wrath or sentiment?' But *Variety* (23 January 1952) recommended the film as being suitable for 'specialised and art houses', which was the kiss of death.

COME BACK, AFRICA (1959)

I had heard about South Africa and the rise of apartheid and the National Party and it sounded very ominous to me. I was very concerned about the reawakening of fascism … we had defeated fascism in World War II, but I didn't feel that it was defeated … I thought it would re-emerge and continue in different forms. So I was alarmed at what was happening in South Africa … (Lionel Rogosin, interview, 1989)

Lionel Rogosin was brought up on the leftwing anti-fascist struggles of the 1930s and 1940s. He came from a well-to-do New York Jewish family, and had used family money to get himself started in film-making. His confessed influences were primarily the neo-realist European tradition of de Sica and the American documentary film-maker Flaherty. Both these streams aspired to the look of 'pure documentary', while Flaherty nevertheless had a strong strain of romanticism. (It is arguable whether Flaherty, with his imposition of a fictional story line on his subjects, was ever strictly a documentarian.)

Rogosin's first film was *On the Bowery*, a harrowing story about life among the dead-beat alcoholics of New York's Lower East Side. His technique, like

---

26 *Journey's End*, p. 54.

Flaherty's and de Sica's, was to use non-actors in natural settings. *On the Bowery*, made completely outside the Hollywood establishment, with a subject that the studios at that time would never have dreamed of tackling, brought Rogosin a considerable reputation. Looking for a new subject of weight, Rogosin went to South Africa, reading up on the country on the leisurely boat-trip that took him there.

In Johannesburg, Rogosin did not have a sense of being in an alien country. There was an enormous American influence on both black and white life, and Rogosin felt that he knew black South Africans in the same way that he felt a familiarity and ease with black Americans. He had been given the names of useful contacts by the great anti-apartheid crusaders, the Reverend Michael Scott and Father Trevor Huddleston in England, and by others, but

> *I had decided not to contact any of them, because I felt that South Africa being somewhat of a police state ... I'd be trailed ... For two or three weeks, I didn't know what to do, I sort of wandered around doing nothing ...*

By accident, he bumped into someone who knew him and who advised him to go to the United States Information Service, where he was given the names of African journalists on *The Golden City Post* and *Drum*, so he began his real research there. At the offices of *Drum*, a lively journal of township life, he met Bloke Modisane, Lewis Nkosi, and Can Themba. They were township writers, brash, audacious, who carried on a very active social life centred around the shebeens of Sophiatown. In the South Africa of 1959, as today, several cultures existed side by side, quite literally so in the townships, which sucked in people from all over southern Africa.

The phenomenon of Sophiatown stands out, in idealised memory at least, as a *bouillabaisse* of cultures and influences. In a perverse way, this generation of African writers was peculiarly privileged, immersed as they were in the stew of many African cultures but also having access, by dint of their work, education, and personalities, to what liberal white society had to offer. Lewis Nkosi describes a visit to Bloke Modisane:

> *One couldn't believe what kind of music one listened to when one went into Bloke Modisane's little hovel in Sophiatown. Here was a man having only one room. In the corner of this room a little record player. And suddenly you are walking into this yard and you hear Mozart and Beethoven being played. Of course, this man was obsessed with all these different cultural experiences. It seemed so unlikely, so improbable, so implausible ... (Interview, 1992)*

But of course, it was so utterly human. This generation of urbanised Africans (and this they shared with their peers throughout the world) was particularly obsessed with American demotic culture, with American clothes, as with jazz and movies:

> ... *young boys were actually writing to America. They got hold of the catalogues showing special shoes like Florsheim shoes. And when these boys were going to parties, they would pull up their socks and show you these shoes, because you couldn't get that shoe in Johannesburg, they said. 'This one comes straight from New York, man, it's a Can't Get!' And it was all the influence of the films, and watching people who were very much like you, who were black like you. (Lewis Nkosi, interview, 1992)*

But at the same time, much of this seductive popular art form of cinema was denied to them simply because they were Africans. There were many films they were not allowed to see. Therefore, much of cinema had the additional lure of the forbidden. The generation of the 1950s was more politically aware than any earlier generation, and Nkosi and others bitterly resented this racist insult. They took the unusual step of petitioning Hollywood to withhold films from South Africa while that country's censorship discriminated against Africans. That there was no response from the studios should surprise no-one.

Rogosin was a studio outsider, a fierce independent. His very presence in South Africa to make a political film proved his maverick nature. The group of black intellectuals accepted Rogosin straight away, and drew him into their circle.

> *Lionel's first plus was that he directed* **On the Bowery***. A few of us had seen* **On the Bowery***, and so we knew this guy is a serious film-maker. Two, he was an American, and an American who is in the film business, for us, who had been brought up on American films, you know, he was away and running as soon as he ... introduced himself. And also of course there was the difference between white South Africans and white foreigners, the white South Africans were the people oppressing us, and there was a belief that all white foreigners were much more liberal in their thinking and in their attitudes than our own local white oppressors. (Arthur Maimane, interview, 1989)*

This small group initiated Rogosin into township life. Because access to the townships was forbidden to most whites, Rogosin was told to pretend he was an employer driving home the 'boys' sitting in the back of the car. They were stopped once by the police, who thought Rogosin might have been a bootlegger transporting illegal liquor to the township. Although they had no liquor with them, Rogosin was nervous because he thought the police would have made a note of the car's licence number. There can be little doubt that Rogosin's fear was justified, and that he would have had problems if the police had known his true purpose.

In contrast to those foreigners who had visited South Africa before him to make films, Rogosin wanted a film that came directly out of the black South African experience. From the start, he worked directly with Africans, taking them into his confidence, asking them for their advice, valuing their judgements. This had not happened before in film-making. 'Suddenly there was a rapport. An American artist, who seemed a committed artist, coming to us and then suddenly discovering ways of presenting our lives to anybody who really wanted to know what we thought we were like' (Nkosi). Beyond a vague outline – 'I wanted a very simple story from the point of view of an African, to show simply what life was like for an African, what pressure he's under, what humiliations, what pain, what suffering Africans have under apartheid' – Rogosin had no preconceptions. He got Bloke Modisane and Lewis Nkosi to write the script for him. In one Saturday afternoon brainstorming session, they talked the story through, and that was it – 'a piece of cake' (Rogosin). In any case, in his films Rogosin always relied heavily on improvisation and spontaneous dialogue, and the natural language and speech patterns that these were expected to bring with them.

Similarly, Rogosin chose his actors off the street:

> *I found Zachariah, my main character … in the railroad station. (Bloke and I) stood in the railroad station, and probably 20 000 people in that hour passed me, very rapidly. And I saw two people, and I picked them. Like, him and him. And Bloke ran over and they looked very frightened. They probably thought we were the police …*

In his essay 'Interpreting Reality,'[27] Rogosin describes the individual he chose, Zachariah Mgabi, and how he approximated to his preconception of the leading character:

> *Zachariah's character and background fit perfectly into my image of the film's protagonist. At our first practice session, Zachariah's acting turned out to be incredibly natural. Without any preparation or training, he expressed my ideas fully. His personal history was almost identical to the script. I had not only sought someone with a tribal background but one whose essential goodness would show in his face. He was born in the heart of Zululand and grew up with almost no education. He had come to*

27   In *Film Culture* No. 21, Summer 1960.

Johannesburg a few years ago where he had met and married his Xosa (sic) wife. When I went to see his employer to get him permission for a leave of absence, I was told Zachariah was a splendid worker, completely reliable, the highest paid African in the office.

Zachariah's face had said much to me. Other experience has also confirmed my feelings conclusively about the crucial importance of the face in the portrayal of a role. At least, it was true in the making of **Come Back, Africa***. My aim was to express realism in a dramatic and poetic manner, to abstract and then humanise, or better still, synthesise. This is how the film evolved. The plot was neither purely factual nor really fictional …*

The characters, of course, were found in and came out of the place itself. But they were molded, according to their dramatic, humorous and symbolic significance, to what the system of repression was doing to them. Since they were all its victims, I let them express and bring to the surface the deep emotional effect of 'apartheid'.

For his white characters, Rogosin worked with 'mostly progressive white South Africans. But they were so aware, so familiar with the brutalising aspects of black and white life in South Africa, they were able to project this so authentically, that to me a lot of it still makes me wince …' (Lewis Nkosi). Rogosin chose to work with left-wingers because he knew that they would be sympathetic to the film, and would not betray him to the authorities.

What was fresh about Rogosin's film (no earlier film had done it, and it is still avoided in Hollywood) was his willingness to allow African languages to be spoken, even if this meant subtitling. In an early scene, Zachariah, who has just arrived in Johannesburg to work on a mine, is sitting on his bunk and exchanging experiences with an established worker. Both are speaking in Zulu. Zachariah explains – and this is quite likely no more nor less than his own personal experience – that he had to leave his village and come to find work because he could not feed his family.

With these simple words, for the first time a film takes the single great theme of African life that earlier films like *Jim Comes to Jo'burg* and *Song of Africa* had been able to deal with only in distorted form, and looks at it frankly.

This was the theme of mass migration to the cities, which has proved a well-nigh universal experience in Africa. The shock that African peasants experienced when they left the land to enter modern society has been a rite of passage for millions during this century. In South Africa it was traumatic, involving radical breaks with tradition and with everything that had held families, clans and societies together.

The economic forces compelling migration had been hidden in earlier films, which maintained the fiction that Africans left home to earn money to buy a wife, or to get an education. It was stressed that they would return, sooner rather than later, to the places they had come from.

In Rogosin's film, Zachariah is plainly in the city to make a life, and his wife and children come to join him later. The theme of the film is Zachariah's odyssey through a society that places minimal value on black labour, and where he is subject to the tyranny of the pass-book. He begins by working on the mines, and then tries to better his condition by looking for work in town. He gets work successively in a garage, in a hotel, and as a domestic servant. He is thrown out of all these jobs because of some delinquency – in one case, he joy-rides in a car he is supposed to be repairing, in another he accidentally sees a white woman in a state of undress, and in a third he amuses himself by stealing liquor and dancing to the radio when he should be working.

His lack of understanding of work discipline is certainly typical of thousands of Africans who are forced unprepared into a modern industrial society. Eventually, he is seized by the police from the bed of his wife, who is working as a domestic servant, and hauled away for not having a pass. He returns from jail to find his wife has been murdered by a tsotsi. In the final scene, Zachariah gives way to rage. The frustrations and indignities the system has heaped on him are summed up in a montage that intercuts his fist beating on the kitchen table, images of his search for work, and life on the mines, all to the accompaniment of an urgent drumbeat. It is clearly the intention to place the blame for all that has happened to him on a vicious society.

Yet the word 'apartheid' is conspicuous by its absence. This implies what is almost certainly true, that the word, even inside South Africa, was not as current as it later became. (It is recorded as being first published in an Afrikaans newspaper in 1943.) First of all, it was a 'foreign' word not only to someone like Rogosin, who may not have been much aware of its existence while he was in South Africa, but also to the non-South African audience that he envisaged for the film. Inside South Africa, while the word of course represented the ideology that was the cornerstone of Afrikaner Nationalism, for blacks it probably had less significance than its solid manifestations – the pass-system, the racist police, the superstructure of bureaucratic control that hobbled their lives.

Unlike films from the 1980s, Afrikaners are not singled out in *Come Back, Africa* as the villains. Zachariah's bosses are all English-speaking, and Zachariah does not come up against Afrikaners until he is arrested by the police. This was the first decade of apartheid, and the ideological goals of Afrikaner Nationalism, especially in the post-war period of shrinking colonialism and apparently diminishing racism best represented by the institution of the United Nations, could seem preposterous. Lewis Nkosi says that the aims of apartheid at that time seemed too far-fetched to be taken seriously.

Tragic as Zachariah's fate is, much of what happens to him in the film did happen to Africans before apartheid was institutionalised in 1948. Similarly, the social imbalance that produced the murderer Absalom Kumalo pre-dated institutionalised apartheid. Zachariah and Absalom Kumalo are both victims, demanding our pity.

While it does not show us 'bull-voiced' orators of the kind condemned by Alan Paton through the persona of Father Msimangu, *Come Back, Africa* does give an intimation of the political undercurrents of the time. The film itself has a clear and unashamed political agenda: what cause could be more worthwhile than an attack on racism and exploitation?

But *Come Back, Africa* is not only about the African as victim. There are other characters who are adjusted to the lives they live, even if not reconciled to poverty and degradation. These characters appear in the two scenes set in a shebeen, or illicit drinking den. These scenes include Rogosin's writers, Bloke Modisane and Lewis Nkosi, as well as Can Themba, all from *Drum* magazine. Modisane, Nkosi and Themba essentially play themselves. This is how Arthur Maimane, a journalist contemporary with them, describes the scene: 'That was not acting, in that that was what happened in shebeens every night. You know, long philosophical arguments about everything and nothing. It was our place of entertainment. You have a drink and you talk to people about anything from the latest crimes in the township to the state of the nation and the state of race relations and so forth.'

Because selling liquor to Africans was illegal, shebeens were the equivalent of speakeasies, liable to be raided at any time. But they were the centre of social life in the township, just like the Irish pubs they were named after.

At one point in the shebeen, Bloke Modisane attacks the figure of the Reverend Kumalo in *Cry, the Beloved Country*, as an Uncle Tom, subservient to the white masters ('this slimy, slickly Reverend Kumalo'). And even though Canada Lee's portrayal of the Reverend Kumalo has far more dignity than Modisane's condemnation would suggest, there is certainly a wide gap between the Africans who appear in *Cry, the Beloved Country* – the simple country priest and his terrified criminal son, the degraded women – and those who appear in *Come Back, Africa*. Themba, Modisane and Nkosi are not defeated by their environment; rather they are stimulated by the complex culture of Sophiatown, feeding on it and adding to it. Of the characters in *Cry, the Beloved Country*, two do give some intimation of the generation that would dominate by the end of the decade. Sidney Poitier's young priest gives no suggestion of inferiority – but then, he is never put in a situation of confrontation with white authority. The other character is John Kumalo, the black politician painted as a demagogue.

*Between the appearance of a film like **Cry, the Beloved Country**,*
*and the making of **Come Back, Africa**, a whole number of changes*

have taken place in South Africa. If we want to talk about it in symbolical terms, we could say that there has been a usurpation of the role of the reverend gentleman by John Kumalo, as far as the younger generation of Africans are concerned ... the man who becomes the signal figure by the end of the 1950s is not Reverend Kumalo, but his brother. (Lewis Nkosi, 1989)

The 1950s was the proving decade for the African National Congress Youth League that had begun to flex its muscles after the Second World War. The young men who had come out of the Youth League – Walter Sisulu, Oliver Tambo, Nelson Mandela, Mangaliso Sobukwe – were challenging white power through massive demonstrations and strikes, foremost among which was the Defiance Campaign of 1952. The Defiance Campaign was crushed by the government, but it brought widespread respect for the African National Congress, and revealed an energetic generation of Young Turks no longer content to wait for the kind of change of heart among whites that would finally allow them access to their birthright.

The Christian *caritas* that Paton yearned for in *Cry, the Beloved Country* was made even more unlikely by the ruthless laws introduced by apartheid, which were intended to control and restrict all aspects of black life. In the bleak apartheid landscape, the energy and activism of the ANC offered a ray of hope.

The very difference in film titles reveals the change in the political atmosphere of South Africa that took place between the beginning of the 1950s and its end. *Cry, the Beloved Country* is a lamentation for the condition that South Africa has fallen into. *Come Back, Africa*, on the other hand, is a translation of the rallying cry of the period, *'mayibuye i Afrika'*, the exhortation to Africans to seize again the country that rightfully belongs to them. As Bloke Modisane says in the shebeen scene, reflecting the new confidence of the era, 'They can keep the vote. We want the country – then we'll give them the vote!'

Come Back, Africa, then, while on the one hand depicting the degradation of a system that denied value to black life and labour, also reflects the optimism of the period. The kind of free speech that the government was everywhere cracking down on in public at least existed in the shebeens. Can Themba, Lewis Nkosi and Bloke Modisane engage in lively discourse that includes social and political criticism. If it had no cinematographic value at all, *Come Back, Africa* would have inestimable worth simply as an historical document. Just as *Jim Comes to Jo'burg* captured Dolly Rathebe, Dan Twala, Daniel Adnewmah, the African Inkspots and the Jazz Maniacs, and preserves them for posterity, so *Come Back, Africa* is the unique record of a handful of black intellectuals from that period of social and cultural ferment who nowhere else appeared on film. Moreover, outside the shebeen, the very streets of Sophiatown were being bulldozed to make way for whites. Together with a couple of newsreel cameramen, Rogosin was the last to film Sophiatown before it disappeared completely, and he was the only one to offer a glimpse of a rich culture that was ruthlessly expunged.

Events inside South Africa were covered at that time by newsreel cameramen, often freelance. It was only with the protest marches of the 1950s that black life began to receive serious attention outside South Africa – inside the country, there was a tacit gentleman's agreement neither to film nor project such activity. So, in a pattern that would continue up to the collapse of apartheid, the outside world often had a more accurate visual image of African activism than white South Africans, protected as they were by a newsreel blackout.

Naturally – and this has not changed much – the outside world saw this African activism through the mediation of a white cameraman and a white reporter. However, foreign newsreels in this era of liberalism were not antagonistic to the African cause. But it was interpreted to the world by mediators who put their own bias on the events. What was distinctly missing was a black point of view, and part of this can be attributed to the limitations of the technology at that time. Sound recording instruments were heavy and unwieldy – the hand-held self-blimped sound camera would not come into general use until the early 1960s. The unblimped film camera, however, was light and easy to manipulate. But it offered no sound. So reportage consisted of a series of images that were edited and narrated thousands of miles from where they had been shot. It was unthinkable that either the cameraman or the narrator could be African, and no-one was about to haul an African into a sound studio to do an interview. As a result, although there are pictures of ANC leaders making speeches, these speeches are without content. The newsreels were effectively silent movies. There was no African voice. Rogosin changed that.

> *With* **Come Back, Africa** *a whole lot of languages have become available for the film-maker. What you see is not only black intellectuals articulating their own experiences so far as black life in the cities is concerned. You even hear African languages being spoken in the film as dialogue … (Lewis Nkosi, 1989)*

This was a liberating experience similar to that offered by *Jim comes to Jo'burg* – the experience of access to something hitherto denied. But, to the glamorous world of cinema, *Come Back, Africa* added access to a *political* forum. And this experience was not only liberating to the Africans who participated in the film, but was also a revelation to those who saw it. The writer André Brink was a young student in Paris when he had the opportunity – denied in South Africa – of seeing *Come Back, Africa*:

> *It never occurred to me, by the time I went to Paris, that a black could be anything but a servant or a labourer. In all my relations*

with them, there was never any possibility of a real exchange of thoughts or ideas … So that the way blacks lived, the fact that they did all these things like eating and chatting and talking and singing, that was a closed book to me as a white. And seeing this in the film, the ordinary domestic scenes in **Come Back, Africa***, a man sitting at a table eating, people talking around a burning lamp, it came as a revelation, just this rediscovery of the most important of all things, that we are all human. That remains with me of that film more than anything else. (André Brink, interview, 1990)*

The film in the can, Rogosin left South Africa for New York. Wherever it was shown, it aroused feelings like these expressed by Anthony Carthew of the London *Daily Herald* when he saw it at the Venice Film Festival of 1959:

I have just seen a film that makes me ashamed of being white – ashamed of belonging to a race which can oppress and terrorise people of other colours … It shows how coloured men are so hedged about by restrictions and brutal laws that their lives are little better than the lives of animals in a cage … I recommend any white South Africans who read this to look up the word humanity in a dictionary. It seems the word is no longer in current use in their country … I've no doubt the film is going to cause a political storm … (4 September 1959)

The influential Bosley Crowther wrote in the *New York Times*: 'The helplessness and frustration that the average African must feel in the face of the social dilemmas that exist in South Africa today are put forth in clumsy stagy fashion but with a certain amount of raw vitality …'[28] and *Time Magazine*, which reached millions of readers, commented '… a timely and remarkable piece of cinema journalism; a matter-of-fact, horrifying study of life in the black depths of South African society …'[29]

To counter such uniformly bad press, South African government officials suggested that Rogosin was trying to introduce 'a form of sensationalism' (*Rand Daily Mail*, 8 June 1959) into the apartheid question. The director was smeared with the communist tar-brush: '… it was discovered that one of the members of his crew had communist connections and … the police found that they were making regular contacts with known and named communists in South Africa'. (One of

---

28   Interestingly, Bosley Crowther hated the shebeen scene: '(it) is not only verbose but stagy and stuffy in tone' (*New York Times*, 5 April 1960).

29   *Time Magazine*, 1959.

Rogosin's cameramen was in fact expelled from South Africa shortly after the shooting of the film.)

Rogosin had worked with people he must have known to be communists, and it was evasive of him, if understandable in the climate of the Cold War, to have given a reply that was less than candid: '... we met and worked with perhaps 500 people and one or two of them may have been communists, I don't know for sure' (*Rand Daily Mail*, 8 June 1959). Apart from the communist angle, the South African government attacked Rogosin for lying to them about his intentions. Peter Nel, director of the South African Information Office in New York, said that Rogosin had entered South Africa as 'a *bona fide* tourist' (*Rand Daily Mail*, 8 June 1959). There was no conceding on the part of either the government or even the South African newspapers that to film underground might be the only option open to someone who wanted to portray the reality of apartheid.

SOUTH AFRICA THROUGH A DISTORTED LENS
By Julian Neale, film critic

One of the greatest hoaxes in cinema history has just been unveiled in New York – and South Africans are not going to like it at all. But it is doubtful if they will ever see this film, Come Back, Africa, which has been described as 'the most appalling document of 1959'.

If curiosity ever gets the better of ruffled national feelings, South Africans will be in for an unusual experience. They will see Johannesburg through the eyes of an American who firmly believes our society to be on a par with Nazi Germany.

* They will see a white policeman making a pass at a black girl.

* They will watch the destruction of Sophiatown, without any mention of the existence of Meadowlands.

* They will see one and a half hours of what the director, Lionel Rogosin, calls 'a preview of the coming South African revolution'.

*... **Come Back, Africa** is a high-powered, emotionally-charged attack on apartheid and South African race relations. It is bitter, biased and cynical.*

It also happens to be brilliant ...

Make no mistake, this documentary is about to gain worldwide fame ...

> *(But) the result is lopsided: a selection of facts, carefully*
> *screened to present a grim, ugly picture, with all hope removed.*
> Rand Daily Mail, *12 August 1959*

The Johannesburg *Sunday Times* of 6 September 1959 ran a piece as follows:

ACE LIAR HOAXED SOUTH AFRICAN POLICE WHILE MAKING FILM, NOW USES IT TO BESMIRCH UNION ABROAD

> *... While squalid scenes of shanty-town Sophiatown are shown*
> *with its forced massed movings, there is nothing to be seen of*
> *Meadowlands, where the people were later housed.*
> *There are only stark misery, domineering policemen and*
> *debauched, pathetic shebeen scenes, with nothing of the laughter*
> *and smiles of street corner kwela players ...*

The *Sunday Times* editor was compelled to add a footnote:

> *The omission from the film of Meadowlands and other enormous*
> *Native housing schemes around Johannesburg points to Rogosin's*
> *malice in making the film. He obviously intended to give only a*
> *distorted picture – and he seems to have succeeded.*[30]

The similarity between the government's criticism of *Come Back, Africa* and that of the English-language press points not so much to collusion as to similar interests in protecting the good name of South Africa. It is standard practice for those who have something to hide to attack a film for what it *does not* do, rather than to face up to what it *does* do; but what is distinctly odd is to add a scene to the film that is not there, namely, the destruction of Sophiatown. Both the *Rand Daily Mail* and the *Sunday Times* do this. This suggests at the very least an inattentive viewing of the film.

The dispute was really about image control. Governments everywhere and at all times have tried to control certain images: it was of course the compulsion to do this that led the South African government to regulate those who came into the country with the intention of making films. Just a few years before, the wrath of the Nationalist government against the relatively innocuous film *Black and White in South Africa*, made by the National Film Board of Canada, had forced the fellow Commonwealth country to withdraw the film from showing anywhere in the world.

---

30 These reviews contrast strongly with the reception given to *Come Back, Africa* when it was finally shown in South Africa for the first time, almost thirty years later. Tony Jackman wrote in *The Star* (9 May 1988) '... for white South Africans, the film ... will inspire guilt, whether current or retrospective ... *Come Back, Africa* remains relevant'.

But Rogosin, as a private individual, as an independent, and someone not without means, was not susceptible to such pressures.[31]

Rogosin had his own public relations skills, and was helped by the quality of his product; but even more, the clumsy brutality of events in South Africa rendered the counter-attack ludicrous.

By the time *Come Back, Africa* found its way into theatres around the world, what was left of the good name of South Africa was already in tatters. The film's release coincided with the Sharpeville massacre of March 1960, an event which more than any other wiped out the optimism of the 1950s – as Lewis Nkosi, who as a young journalist reported on the massacre, says, 'We'd seen horror.'

A solitary newsreel cameraman arrived in Sharpeville soon after the police fusillades, and recorded the dead and wounded. The cameraman seems to have shot no more than one roll of 16mm film, a hundred feet, barely two-and-a-half minutes. Most obscene among the images is that of a white police officer leading four black constables who are carrying a dead body in a sheet. Amid the carnage, with people still dazed from the shock, where no-one is offering any conceivable sign of resistance, this white policeman is brandishing the symbol of white power, a sjambok.

More than any other, these Sharpeville images would define apartheid to the world for the next decade and a half, when they would be superseded by other powerful images. They sent the message that the price of white rule was African blood. In the wake of Sharpeville, the government declared a State of Emergency, and used it to ban virtually all meaningful political activity on the part of the African opposition.

In the cinema, this meant that black South Africans were once again voiceless. The promise offered by *Come Back, Africa* – the 'shift from white people trying to express a vision for blacks, and allowing blacks to express themselves, to be in control of their own discourse' (Lewis Nkosi) – was stillborn. A similar opportunity would not present itself for another thirty years.

---

31   When Rogosin could not get any major distributor interested in *Come Back, Africa* he
      took a lease on the Bleecker Street cinema in Greenwich Village in New York,
      where he showed his films and other films he approved of for many years.

Erica Rutherford

Sam Maile

Museum of Modern Art

Daniel Adnewmah
and Dolly Rathebe.

Jürgen Schadeberg

Nightclub scene
from *Jim Comes to
Jo'burg*.

...in 1951 *Song of Africa*.

Cry, the Beloved Country, the first film to highlight South Africa's racial and social problems.

The Perils of City Life

Above: Jim is mugged. *Jim Comes to Jo'burg*, 1949.
Right: The country priest is conned as soon as he arrives in Johannesburg. *Cry, the Beloved Country*, 1951.

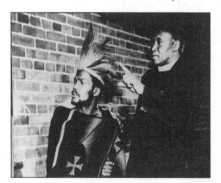

Above: Fresh from his homeland, Makwena is tricked out of his money by a phony priest. *Dingaka*, 1964.
Right: Encounter with a prostitute. *Come Back, Africa*, 1960.

Romance to Reality

Erica Rutherford

Lionel Rogosin

From homeland idyll (*Jim Comes to Jo'burg*, 1949) to the reality of a migrant who can't find work in the city (*Come Back, Africa*, 1960).

The Attempt to Launch a Black Film Industry

Production team of *Jim Comes to Jo'burg*, 1949. Eric Rutherford, Dan Twala and Gloria Green on the left; Donald Swanson at far right.

The first film to include blacks as script-writers. There was genuine white and black co-operation in making *Come Back Africa*, 1960. *Left to right*: Can Themba, Bloke Modisane, Lewis Nkosi, Lionel Rogosin.

'Buddies'

During the 1960s, the races were drawn further and further apart; Africans were uprooted from their homes on a massive scale, and laws were enacted to prevent socialisation between black and white. Education was structured to separate the races throughout life. This was the ineluctable logic of apartheid put into everyday practice. But, paradoxically, both inside and outside South Africa, a series of films was made that showed forms of partnership across the colour line. There was certainly no kind of collusion in the making of these films, and they were all set in a fictive South Africa that bore little resemblance to reality. This very fact was paradoxical: the stories showed a South Africa where black/white friendship existed, by misrepresenting the harsh facts of real South African life – but by so doing, the films held out the promise of such friendship.

DINGAKA (1964)

The first of these films is also the most problematic. *Dingaka* was made by the Afrikaans film-maker, Jamie Uys. Uys was a journeyman film-maker who had come up through an Afrikaans cinema deliberately nurtured by the Nationalist government as a counterweight to 'English' culture which, in the government's eyes, included the power of Hollywood. Uys was known for his homespun comedies, which depended for their success on a complacent belief, on the part of the Afrikaner *volk*, that they were basically a folksy, lovable people.

In the 1950s, Uys had made a short propaganda film for the government about slum clearance. *The Condemned are Happy* shows a migrant family living in a shanty town, where they are prey to rapacious black landlords, crime, disease. They are persuaded to move to a new town built for them by the authorities, where the rents are reasonable, the children can go to school and day-care, the elderly grandfather has access to an old people's home and the streets are safe.

> *What I was saying (in **The Condemned are Happy**) is that these slums developed because the black man had to adapt to the industrialised society. He couldn't make a living in the bush or the veld anymore, he had to stream to the city because of drought and so on. And there was no housing and so these terrible slums evolved. And there was a genuine effort there to alleviate the conditions by creating living areas for them, and even helping them to build their houses and so on. I believed implicitly in what I was saying at the time. (Jamie Uys, interview, 1990)*

A fervent acolyte of apartheid, the Uys of the 1950s was convinced that the policies of the Nationalist government were benevolent towards blacks. The villains in *The Condemned are Happy* are a black landlord and the evils produced by slum conditions. The whites who appear are there solely to rescue the migrant family from the conditions in which they live: their slum housing is 'condemned', but they are 'happy' because they can go to improved living conditions.

Continuing the theme of black life, Uys followed *The Condemned are Happy* with another film, *The Fox has Four Eyes*. Uys's earlier life had included a stint as a magistrate in the bush, and *The Fox has Four Eyes* concerns an African from a tribal area who lands up in prison, where he learns that 'witch doctors are liars and robbers and murderers'. He is persuaded of the superiority of white justice. In 1964 Uys turned the plot of this 20-minute black-and-white film into a much more ambitious production in panavision. This was *Dingaka*, starring Stanley Baker and Juliet Prowse, which would launch Uys into world cinema. Here is a synopsis of the plot: set in some vague native area, the film opens with a choreographed stick fight, with women watching and cheering. The winner, Temba, is lauded and stroked by adoring women. The vanquished man, Masaba, looks vengeful. Frantic, frenetic dancing, with much wagging of bottoms and joggling of breasts. Mpudi, the comic element, gets drunk and performs a funny dance. Loud, insistent drums all through – very much a staged presentation.

Masaba visits the witch doctor, Haqeba. (It is a fault of the film that its title, *Dingaka*, is never explained. It means 'witch doctor'.[32])

The witch doctor lives in a cave on top of a sheer cliff that can be scaled only by ladder. Masaba demands medicine that will make him strong. Haqeba says Masaba 'must eat the heart of a child', a small girl who must be a twin. He demands payment for this recipe.

Colourful sequence of village life. We are introduced to Ntuku, who cures leather, has a wife, a baby son, and two small daughters, twins. He and his family sing while they work. Ntuku is a happy man. Close by, women wash clothes in the stream while adolescent boys slide down rocks into a pool. Mpudi, the comic element, has a headache from drinking the previous night. Women offer him something to drink, to clear his head. One of Ntuku's young daughters, Oneka, is chosen to fetch water for Mpudi. She goes off, calabash on head, singing.

Ntuku milks a cow. The mother, preparing food, misses Oneka. She calls to Ntuku to look for her, but Oneka is not to be found. In desperation, Ntuku visits the witch doctor, who refuses to say where Oneka is. Ntuku grabs the witch doctor by the throat, and the witch doctor says that Masaba has killed her. Ntuku stalks away, and Haqeba runs after him, threatening him because he laid hands on his person.

Villagers hear the witch doctor's threat. Haqeba addresses the village from the cliff-top – Ntuku must be banished. Ntuku spies Masaba, and runs after him, but Masaba stuns him with a rock. Ntuku's wife begs for help, but no-one will help her

---

32   I use the term 'witch doctor', rather than the more acceptable 'traditional healer', because the former is used in the film.

because of Haqeba's curse. She scales the ladder to the witch doctor on top of the cliff, and begs him for help. The villagers are singing down below in chorus. Haqeba shouts 'Someone must die!' and the wife loses her balance and falls off the cliff. Since the gods have exacted revenge, someone can now help Ntuku, proclaims the witch doctor.

The terrified Masaba goes to the witch doctor and asks him for help. Haqeba says he must go to the white man's city, where Ntuku won't find him.

The injured Ntuku is borne away in a litter, the whole tribe following in a set-piece march. Ntuku buries his wife. He says the gods have punished him, but that he will find Masaba and exact revenge. A chastened Ntuku goes to the witch doctor and apologises. Haqeba accepts his apology. Ntuku asks him where Masaba is, and Haqeba tells him. Haqeba gives Ntuku potions to help him find Masaba, and asks for payment in cattle.

Ntuku ritualistically burns down his family hut and, with Mpudi as his companion, sets out to look for Masaba. They walk past herds of elephant and giraffe, and imposing baobab trees.

Johannesburg – never named as such – the big, alien city. Streets busy with people and traffic. Ntuku runs after a scooter which he believes, mistakenly, is driven by Masaba, and gets separated from Mpudi. A priest stops him, asks if he is from the Makungwe people, and offers to help him. The priest takes him to a church to protect him from *tsotsis*.

The African church is quite luxurious, and people are singing music that is more like American gospel than South African church music. The priest, who has taken Ntuku's money to look after it, says he'll go for food. The service ends, the congregation leaves. Ntuku is left alone. The lights go out. A cleaner comes. He and the real priest disillusion Ntuku about 'the man of God' who has conned him. The cleaner finds Ntuku a job on a mine.

There is a scene of minework, choreographed. There is a shebeen scene, also choreographed. Ntuku is watching mine dancing when someone tells him that the Makungwe do not dance, but do stick-fighting on the 'white mountain' (the mine dump). The climb up the mine dump, with other mineworkers heading in the same direction, is also choreographed. Ntuku sees Masaba stick-fighting, and decides to kill him, but later. He confronts Masaba at night, when Masaba is wearing a tuxedo and is with a woman, boasting about his prowess at stick-fighting. Ntuku attacks Masaba, and believes he has killed him. Ntuku is arrested. In jail, he rediscovers Mpudi, who is there for being drunk. In jail, says Mpudi, 'I get plenty food, but no drinks!'

Ntuku is advised by another prisoner not to talk to lawyers. Enter lawyer Davis, who has been forced to take Ntuku's case. Ntuku says he doesn't want a lawyer, and has no money. But Davis is a legal aid lawyer, so doesn't have to be paid. He tells Ntuku that Masaba is not dead, but in hospital. Ntuku refuses a lawyer, saying he will speak for himself. He is returned to jail. Back at the office, Davis complains of being given a legal case he doesn't want.

In court, Davis says his client is not co-operating with him. The first witness is Masaba, and Ntuku attacks him physically in open court. Davis is then visited in his office by his wife Marion, who says they can adopt a child – they have not succeeded in having their own. Davis is grumpy, and says he wants his own.

Back in court, Ntuku gives evidence. He says that Masaba killed his little daughter; a surprised Davis says he didn't know the facts of the case. The judge calls for an adjournment, saying that Masaba will be brought to trial. Marion Davis quarrels with her husband about his lack of commiseration with Ntuku. Davis visits Ntuku in prison, and tries to gain his confidence. Ntuku insists that the law of his tribe gives him the right to kill Masaba in revenge. Davis says he wants to be his friend; Ntuku says that to prove this, he must find work for Mpudi. Then he tells Davis about Masaba.

In court, Ntuku tells his story. He says that Masaba told him that he had killed his daughter. When he is asked how Masaba told him this, Ntuku says Masaba's eyes told him. He says that Haqeba, the witch doctor, accused Masaba. When asked how this came about, he says he squeezed Haqeba's throat. Ntuku accuses Davis of betraying him, because they won't hang Masaba.

Davis argues that Ntuku believed Masaba killed his child. He contrasts tribal with 'civilised' justice, to the detriment of the latter. Davis maintains that Ntuku was obeying the laws of his tribe, and that he had a 'simple and abiding belief in justice'.

> *Davis: In complying with the laws of his tribe, he became a criminal in the eyes of the state.*
>
> *Judge (to Ntuku): The state, not you, will punish offenders if they are guilty.*

Ntuku is sentenced to two years' imprisonment. Back home, Davis talks to Mpudi, whom he has taken on as his gardener, about Haqeba, the witch doctor. Does Haqeba do good or bad things? Later, at a cocktail party given by the Tribal Commissioner, the Commissioner says that they suspect Haqeba, but do not have any proof against him.

> *Commissioner: … the whole tribe lives in fear of him.*
>
> *Davis: What kind of hold does he have over them?*
>
> *Commissioner: The usual – superstition. He puts the fear of the gods in them. They hate his guts, they're terrified of him – so they worship him.*

Davis's obvious concern about Ntuku effects a reconciliation between Davis and Marion. To cap it all, her doctor tells her at the party that she is pregnant.

In another choreographed scene, convicts are breaking rocks in a quarry, singing as they do so. They wear eye-protectors against rock splinters. They are overseen by black warders, who are armed with spears. Seizing an opportunity, Ntuku makes a dash for freedom. He is struck by a spear, but he runs through burning brush and leaps over a cliff into a river to effect his escape.

Davis is told of Ntuku's escape. He, Marion, and Mpudi go to the Makongwe tribal area to find him. Davis and Marion behave as if they are on safari:

> Marion: It's like a little paradise.
>
> Davis: Here? I still can't find a point for my electric razor.

Davis goes to visit Haqeba, who has two bare-breasted women in attendance. Haqeba's familiar, a snake, crawls over Davis's foot in an attempt to intimidate him. Davis questions Haqeba about Ntuku's child. Haqeba says Davis should look after his pregnant wife. Davis threatens Haqeba that if any harm comes to Marion, 'I'll kill you myself.'

Back in camp, Davis says to his wife, 'That heathen up there certainly can weave a spell … a bloody shyster.' Ntuku reveals himself to Mpudi who tells him that everyone now knows that it was Haqeba who murdered Ntuku's daughter, not Masaba, and that Temba saw him do it. But Temba is now dead. Ntuku returns to what is left of his family, who confirm that Haqeba is the murderer.

On his cliff-top, Haqeba summons the tribe with his ox-horn. He calls for a feast that night. The feast begins, heavily choreographed with an undulating snake-dance, and sexy dancing by the women.

Ntuku grapples with a problem: 'If a man kills my child, I must kill him. But if I kill Haqeba, the gods will kill me. What must I do?' Ntuku's soul-searching is intercut with bacchanalian scenes from the revels. At his wife's graveside, Ntuku determines to kill Haqeba, come what may. The dancing increases in intensity. The drums become more and more insistent.

Davis, now sporting a pistol in his holster, finds Ntuku in his hut with his children. Davis wants the people of the tribe to testify against Haqeba.

> Davis (to Ntuku): Haqeba has committed many crimes – I want you to talk to the tribe, to give evidence against him, and he will be hanged.
>
> Ntuku: You cannot hang Haqeba. He is the son of the gods. The gods will destroy all of us … a plague will descend on the country, and everyone shall die.

Davis: He's a man, that's all. He's a liar, he's a thief, he's a murderer, but he's only a man. He sucks the blood of your people, he grows fat on them. We must see that he's punished ... he's a fake, that's all, just a fake. (Ntuku) get rid of this man, then your tribe can be happy, can be free.

Marion gazes tenderly at Ntuku's sleeping children. Sounds of festivity and thunder outside intermingle.

Back at the dance, Haqeba is borne in on a litter. Female dancers gyrate seductively around him. Ntuku ponders about what he should do. The drum tempo increases. A female dancer is tossed by male dancers. Ntuku walks in on the scene, and announces he has come to kill Haqeba. Thunder and lightning. Haqeba exhorts the tribe to help him, but the crowd is intimidated by the thunder and lightning. Haqeba retreats, screaming in fear. Ntuku attacks and strangles him, while the tribe cowers in superstitious dread at the elements. Haqeba is dead. The skies clear. Ntuku pronounces, somewhat surprised, 'He was just a man.' The tribe, now free of a tyrant, breaks into a dance of triumph. As Ntuku walks away, he meets Davis and Marion.

Ntuku: Now they can hang me for killing Haqeba.

Davis: They won't hang you. You've got a lawyer now, chief.

Jamie Uys's film, as much musical as drama, with the fantastic in all its elements, nevertheless deserves serious analysis. For it is awash with the social and historical currents of its time. It was made by a confirmed Afrikaner Nationalist, a believer in apartheid, a man who, both in his career as a magistrate in the bush, on which experience *Dingaka* is supposedly based, and in his film-making, had constant contact with Africans. It is a distillation of Uys's experience, and it is more: it is a syncretising of apartheid's delusions.

Despite Uys's presumed extensive acquaintance with Africans and African customs, there is scarcely a single element in the entire film that can claim to be authentic. The picture-book village where the Makongwe tribe lives comes not out of the decrepit tribal homelands of South Africa, but out of cinemythology.[33] It is related to the Zululand of *Song of Africa* made ten years before, yet even further removed from the South African reality. Its topography rises out of the fantasy

---

33 A letter to *The Star* from an African who had seen the film complains: '*Dingaka* has certain mistakes that we feel ought to be corrected before it is sent overseas for distribution. We would ... like to know on which tribal customs this film is based, because Ntuku's wife and children wear Xhosa costumes, but Ntuku himself is in a Basotho blanket. The warriors and the girls are in Zulu costumes. The same with the vernacular in the film – they seem to be from all different dialects. Perhaps Mr Uys can explain it to us.' (18 June 1965)

world of apartheid, an Afrikaner Disneyland. The insistence on the Edenic nature of the place appears in the carefree life led by the people, filled with song and dance, and pleasant water-slides. Marion even draws attention to this, with her 'It's like a little paradise.' But this Eden has its serpent – literally so in Haqeba's familiar, which threatens Davis. And it is precisely this threat, a challenge to white authority, that reveals the dimensions of the evil.

The concept of 'the tribe' was a European invention. In the literature of exploration and empire, and in the film canon that built upon it, the tribe was a faceless mass, almost invariably subject to a tyrannical single ruler. The tribe performed the will of its chief, and where this will threatened the colonisers, their only recourse was to the Mauser and the Lee-Enfield, the Maxim and the Gatling and further refinements of the 'civilised' technology of death, not excluding aerial bombing. The tyrant would not listen to reason (i.e. the white point of view, usually that he should give up his land with grace), and therefore he and his tribe must listen to the gun.

Dingaka exists on screen as an entertainment, but it has its roots in a particular time – the early 1960s – and a very particular place – South Africa, so any claim to innocence it might have, is tainted. Jamie Uys said (interview, 1990), 'I had made a movie called *Dingaka* in the early 1960s, and I thought that I was going to put no propaganda and no message into it.' Uys could avoid the reality of apartheid only by creating a dream world.

The problem with dream worlds is that they can draw attention to precisely what they are designed to hide – the real world of the dreamer. If we place *Dingaka* in its time and place, a very different interpretation can be made of Uys's supposedly apolitical entertainment. What exactly was happening in this South Africa of the early 1960s was a government scheme called Bantu Authorities. Bantu Authorities was a plot cooked up by apartheid's ideologues to substitute traditional leaders in the homelands with puppets who would dance on the government's strings.

The quisling leaders were often fiercely resented, most noticeably in Pondoland, where some of them were killed. This rebellion was suppressed by force in 1960. It did not get much attention in the outside world, which was more affected by that year's bloodier Sharpeville massacre. (The Pondoland troubles were not captured on film.)

The traditional leaders who were displaced, if they were activist at all, were active only in their local area. During the preceding decade, other leaders had come into prominence of the stamp of the John Kumalo of *Cry, the Beloved Country*, discredited by his own creator, Alan Paton, as a rabble-rouser, but embraced by the new generation. In the repression after Sharpeville, when the African National Congress was banned, these new leaders were arrested, or fled into exile, or went underground.

The government tried to taint these leaders with the accusation of communism. Some of them of course were, but the accusation was levelled most notoriously at Nelson Mandela, who was never a communist. But in the view of the government, a communist was anyone who furthered the aims of communism, one of which was asserted to be the overthrow of the government of South Africa – *ergo*, whether Mandela was a *de facto* member of the Communist Party was immaterial.

For conservative Afrikaners (which at this period, the early 1960s, meant the majority), communism was only partly a political threat, the latest manifestation of the *swart gevaar*; it also struck at their rigid Calvinist roots. Communism in the form of the ANC was no less than the anti-Christ, 'Satan incarnate', as André Brink described it in an interview in 1990. Which brings us back to Haqeba. Haqeba, the witch doctor on the cliff-top, whose evil will misguides the tribal mass, springs full-blown from a Satan-obsessed psyche.

In the film, the Tribal Commissioner says that the tribe are in superstitious fear of Haqeba, and *sangomas*, or traditional healers, are customarily depicted in white fiction as arousing such superstition. But this depiction is itself suffused with a superstitious incomprehension and fear of the unknown – not to mention the bigoted rejection of an alien religion.

When Haqeba threatens Davis, the lawyer, he is challenging white authority. A white South African audience – not exclusively Afrikaner – would recognise this without the need for articulation. So what is being played out in Uys's melodrama of African life and mores is very much an unconscious metaphor for what was happening over the broader landscape of South Africa – the overthrow of not only the traditional but the popular leadership of the African people.

Haqeba, with his bee-hive hairdo (prescient forerunner of the 'Afro') is the personification of evil, just as the ANC leadership, *qua* 'communist', was the anti-Christ. What the fictional lawyer Davis says of Haqeba – 'That heathen … certainly can weave a spell … a bloody shyster' – could equally be applied, from an Afrikaner Nationalist point of view, to the 'atheistic communistic' leadership of the African National Congress.

The overthrow of Haqeba is an allegory for what was happening in fact all over South Africa. Davis, the representative of white law, urges Ntuku to take the law into his own hands and challenge the traditional leader of the tribe, Haqeba. In the climax, Ntuku does so, by killing Haqeba. The due process of white law is thereby scoffed at, but Davis promises that Ntuku – whom he now addresses as 'chief' – will not be punished. Again, this does not seem different in kind from the manipulation of the law that forced Bantu Authorities onto an unwilling populace.

And *Dingaka* came out in 1964, the year in which Nelson Mandela was being tried for sabotage in the Rivonia Trial. Stripped of his fancy lawyer's suit, was not Mandela the ultimate witch doctor, able to bend an ignorant and superstitious ·

people to his will? And was it not right, therefore, to dethrone him and sentence him to prison for life? (Mandela and his co-accused narrowly escaped hanging.)

The courtroom scenes in *Dingaka* present white justice as impartial and correct, which Uys, himself a former functionary of the legal system, believed to be no more than accurate. This echoes the courtroom scenes of *Cry, the Beloved Country*. The Rivonia Trial had the same veneer of justice; the Catch-22 was, of course, that the ANC had no part in the Parliament that enacted the laws governing black people.

The lawyer Davis sympathises with Ntuku's point of view: 'In complying with the laws of *his* tribe, he became a criminal in the eyes of the state' – which is not far from Mandela's defence that he was not bound by the laws of a state that did not recognise him as a full citizen. It is this empathy on the part of Davis that leads him to strike up a friendship with Ntuku.

But in the end, Davis assumes a manipulative role parallel to that of the white advisors who pulled the strings of the puppet leaders in the homelands, when he incites Ntuku to overthrow the traditional head of his tribe, and in so doing, condones murder.

In the context of the film, just as in the context of the larger society of South Africa, this was justified as being for the good of the tribe. So if this is the first of the 'Buddy' films, the relationship places the white half in the elevated position of Big Brother who uses the black man as a tool.

The part of Ntuku was played by Ken Gampu, who was to become, as a result of the chance accorded by this film, the first internationally recognised black South African actor. Gampu, who is not a bitter man, describes how, despite having the leading role in *Dingaka*, he was still subject to apartheid rules on location:

> When I became an actor, it was '63, '64. But those days, as you know, we were not allowed to sleep in a hotel. They used to have 'boys' room' at back. Now, we were filming up in the Northern Transvaal, in a place called Louis Trichardt. We were filming the whole day. I was running up and down the whole day. At night, the crew went of course to their rooms in the hotel, and I was supposed to go at the back and sleep in the 'boys' room'. On principle, I said to myself, 'I'm not going there, I'd rather sleep in the car'. I slept in Jamie Uys's car, on principle. (Ken Gampu, interview, 1990)

Uys was enough of an orthodox Afrikaner not to fight for Gampu's right to sleep in a hotel bed. Yet at the same time, in the film's imaginary world, the African character created by Uys and embodied by Gampu is a long way from the concept of 'kaffir'. Ntuku is not intimidated by white law or white prisons, and Davis has to woo him for his friendship.

Like Sidney Poitier's priest in *Cry, the Beloved Country*, Ken Gampu has a screen presence that says more than the story requires him to say. The dignity of Gampu remains inviolable. Of course, this held advantages for a film aimed at a world market more and more conscious of the meaning of apartheid.

It is as well to point out that Uys's South Africa (in the film, the country is never identified by name) does no disservice to the apartheid cause in his depiction of a country where blacks have freedom of movement and job-seeking, and where the whites are enlightened liberals.

It is noticeable that Uys skirts all the landmines of South African life by turning them into musical interludes – instead of the misery of the tribal 'homelands', life in 'Makungwe' is made up of singing and dancing, and the rigours of the mines and prison become ritualised, and therefore acceptable, through choreography.

GOLD! (1974)

This Michael Klinger production, set on a gold-mine in South Africa, suppresses the realities of mine life, as *Dingaka* does, although it does not resort to choreography to do so. For our purposes, the main characters are Slater, the mine trouble-shooter (played by Roger Moore), Kowalski, an aggressively racist white miner, and John Nkulu ('King'), a black miner (Simon Sabela). (There is a love-interest for Slater in the form of Terri Steiner, the mine-owner's daughter, and there are numerous white villains.)

Although much of the action takes place on the mine, black/white relations are for the most part glossed over, with the exception of one confrontation integral to the plot. Underground, the team-leaders are white, the team black. 'King' Nkulu is the only African to have a name. Nkulu is assaulted by Kowalski, the gang-boss, and championed by Slater, since '(African miners) can't hit back' – a statement which is never explained, though we can read into it that to challenge a white overseer carries prohibitive consequences, probably dismissal.

Apart from Nkulu, who is not intimidated by Kowalski, all the black miners are background figures. As usual, the depiction of South Africa confirms whites as owners and doers: the opulent lifestyle, the Rolls-Royces and swimming pools, bowls club, the country hideaway replete with game, the discreet servants – all these constitute a domain for whites only.

At one point, Slater and his lover Terri escape from it all by flying to her father's country estate. The flight in the small plane pre-dates but is reminiscent of a scene in *Out of Africa*, and performs precisely the same function: the elevation above the landscape and animals implies lordship over them – those in the heavens are the elite to whom Africa belongs, not the people down below in the muck.

This sense of domination is compounded when Slater and Terri land. They are greeted by an aged retainer who, Terri explains, is a former mineworker deafened in a mine blast. Since he was no good for mine work any more, her father the mine-owner had given him this job. This is clearly to be read as an act of charity, rather than an indictment of mine conditions.

In an unusual twist, *Gold!* is a story of capitalist villainy. A group of international investors plots to flood the mine to force up the price of gold. The climax comes when the mine is flooded, and Slater and Nkulu join forces to go down below in a rubber dinghy to stop the flood. Nkulu uses his great strength to hold shut a door against the force of the tide long enough for Slater to join a wire that will enable him to activate the safety switch. The wire joined, Slater tells Nkulu to blast. This will save the mine and the trapped miners, but kill them both. Nkulu cuts the rope holding the dinghy with Slater in it, and Slater is swept away to safety while Nkulu activates the blast, thus sacrificing his own life.

It is a classic Faithful Servant situation. The two men have acted like buddies to save the mine, Slater supplying the brain, Nkulu the brawn. But tradition demands the sacrifice of the Faithful Servant, for this enhances the stature of the white hero. The Faithful Servant thinks highly enough of the hero to save his life at the cost of his own. And not only does the white hero not have to share glory with a black man, but the black man's deeds accrue to him, as the sole survivor – it is reported over the mine loudspeaker that 'Slater has saved the mine'. As a bonus, Slater gets the girl, an option never open to the Faithful Servant.

The subject of apartheid was suppressed completely in *Dingaka*, a South African film with international pretensions. In *Gold!* racial discrimination is muted almost to the point of non-existence, appearing only as a psychotic racism. If it could be maintained that until Sharpeville, more than a decade after the introduction of institutionalised apartheid, the world did not fully comprehend the inexorable nature of the Nationalist government, South Africa's domestic policies were revealed during the 1960s to be fundamentally racist.

This period saw a number of documentaries shown on television outside South Africa that clearly laid out the actions and intentions of white South Africa towards its black population. There was a great deal of press coverage, and organisations like International Defence and Aid were part of a worldwide network disseminating accurate information about the country. Yet it was not deemed to be a fit subject for fiction films. This avoidance of a dramatic, urgent and profoundly human subject was paralleled by Hollywood's avoidance of America's own civil rights problems, which came to a head during the 1960s.The only logical explanation for this seems to be a fear of dealing with a subject that might antagonise a section of the potential audience, primarily white America.

While Hollywood's ignoring of the subject could, with strained charity, be said to be motivated by financial considerations, in South Africa, the financial was inextricably tangled with the ideology of race. The South African film industry woverwhelmingly white: only at the very lowest echelons, movie-making's equivalent of 'hewers of wood and drawers of water', could blacks participate.

During the 1960s and 1970s, the industry was heavily subsidised by the government. To have attempted to make films challenging government policy would have been to risk censorship, loss of audience, and forfeiture of the subsidy.

It was bread-and-butter politics, and there were few who were tempted to outface it. Those who tried, like Ross Devenish, came up against a no-win situation, and felt that they had no option but to leave. But South African feature films of these two decades in some ways went beyond what had already been achieved by the exertions of the South African government.

In a country of 30 million people, 25 million of whom were black, the South African movie industry, often supported by foreign investment, made film after film without showing a black face. It thus succeeded in doing what the government signally failed to do in real life – it wiped blacks off the map of the country. The director Antony Thomas describes his experience as an actor in South African films:

> *All the white characters lived in homes where there were no black servants present … one felt that one was contributing to a myth, one was contributing to a dangerous myth … I'm afraid most propaganda and most censorship is self-censorship. Directives do not come down to directors … in South Africa that they've got to follow this certain line. But they do follow it because they think it will be acceptable to the powers that be. (Interview, 1989)*

And not only to the powers that be, but to the international film scene, for those films had to compete in a cut-throat market overseas dominated by Hollywood's own brand of exclusion.

The civil rights movement in the United States of the early 1960s could not be completely ignored by Hollywood. Its profound and disturbing effects did eventually filter through to that olfactory zone of Hollywood sensitised to sniffing dollar returns on moral tales. The film industry, itself far from free from racist practices, laboured and brought forth a few well-meaning movies intended to prove that African-Americans could be human also. These were films such as *The Blackboard Jungle, Edge of the City, The Defiant Ones, Guess Who's Coming to Dinner?* and *Raisin in the Sun.*

What these films had in common besides their theme was the actor Sidney Poitier, virtually the only black actor since Paul Robeson to have achieved proven box-office appeal. So when Hollywood finally came to deal with a South African subject, it was inevitable that Poitier would be cast in the lead.

THE WILBY CONSPIRACY (1975)

The film that would be Poitier's vehicle was *The Wilby Conspiracy*. It is a mixture of ill-digested information about apartheid South Africa subordinated to a story-line that depends heavily on action. Which is to say, it was typical Hollywood. The hero, Shack Twala (Sidney Poitier), a character loosely based on Nelson Mandela, has been on Robben Island for ten years. When the film opens, although still a prisoner, he is once more on trial. He is defended by a woman advocate, Rina van Niekerk. The following unbelievable representation of South African justice takes place:

> *Advocate van Niekerk: The State accuses my client of violation of the Terrorism Act. Shack Twala … was in his fifth year of imprisonment when this Act was passed by Parliament. I put it to Your Worship that he cannot be guilty retroactively.*
>
> *Judge: Under what statute do you contend that he cannot be guilty?*
>
> *Advocate van Niekerk: Section 9, Article 11, Paragraph 2 of the Universal Declaration of Human Rights of the United Nations, of which the Republic of South Africa is a founding member.*
>
> *Judge: The reality is that the laws of South Africa are made in Cape Town, and not at the United Nations in New York. What is your position?*
>
> *Advocate van Niekerk: The Defence requests a dismissal.*
>
> *Judge: Any objection, Dr Schroeder?*
>
> *Dr Schroeder (State Prosecutor): To the contrary. The Defence Counsel's point is well taken. The State is withdrawing its case. The Republic of South Africa is not insensitive to the criticism levelled against us by the world community, however misinformed it may be. We have therefore decided to withdraw the charge, trusting that a greater justice will have been served.*

And Shack Twala is duly released. Also present at the trial is a rather bored British engineer, Jim Keogh (Michael Caine), lawyer Rina van Niekerk's lover, who is visiting South Africa. After the trial, the newly-freed Twala, Rina van Niekerk and Jim Keogh are driving through the streets of Cape Town when the car is stopped by the police. Twala is brutally arrested and handcuffed when he cannot produce a pass. Keogh intervenes when his girlfriend is assaulted by a policeman, and he and Twala escape together.

Twala and Keogh are now fugitives. Keogh is totally uninterested in politics ('I'm neutral') and resents the enforced relationship (which copies the plot situation of the highly successful *The Defiant Ones*).

Twala's agenda is to find some diamonds belonging to his liberation group, which he will take to the head of his organisation, Wilby Xaba, who operates from across the border, and who will use the diamonds to buy weapons. But Twala's release in the first place turns out to have been a ruse on the part of the Machiavellian Major Horn, of the Bureau for State Security, who is tracking the fugitives' every movement. Horn wants Twala to lead him to Wilby Xaba, which Twala eventually does, after a series of less and less plausible adventures. In a denouement situated just across the border in Botswana, Horn and his men seize Wilby, who has come to meet Twala. Before they can fly him out to South Africa, however, Twala and other Africans hang on to the floats of the helicopter, forcing it back to the ground, where an angry crowd attacks Horn and rescues Wilby. A defeated but still arrogant Major Horn claims that he will return, whereupon Keogh, who has been reluctantly converted to the cause of the revolution, summarily executes him.

The two veteran scriptwriters, Rod Amateau and Hal Nebenzal, who co-authored *The Wilby Conspiracy*, based on the book of the same name by Peter Driscoll, approached the task not in the spirit of an anti-apartheid campaign, but as a standard Hollywood adventure film, genre Wild West. This is how Amateau described their task as they saw it:

> *Think Shane, think Shane a minute. The guy (i.e. Keogh) comes through town, wants to mind his own business … cannot mind his own business, is forced into the life of the town, and eventually leaves the town, leaving it better than when he found it … (Interview, 1991)*

When The Man Riding out of the West was applied to revolutionary situations, the locale for the Saving the Revolution genre was usually Mexico. The impression left with films set outside the United States was that while the cause of the little folk was just, they needed the help of a heroic Anglo-Saxon to solve their problems, for they could not do it alone.

While Mexico was right next door, and there was already an established *padrón* mythology about it, Hollywood knew nothing whatsoever about revolutionary stirrings in Africa. Africa was not part of the Saving the Revolution genre, it was part of the Jungle genre.

There had been films about the Mau-Mau in Kenya, but these were treated as 'restless natives' stories, with all the sympathy going to the besieged colonials. Nebenzal and Amateau claim not to have been so naive as not to have known something about the political situation in South Africa at the time they came to do the script – around 1974 – but they were anxious to disclaim any political motivation behind their writing. (The interview took place during the neo-conservative ascendancy of 1991. Even without a blacklist, it was impolitic to be considered a liberal.) When asked about parallels in the script with South Africa of that time, they eschewed any taint of political correctness:

> *Nebenzal: I think the question is overloaded with portent –*
> *Amateau: – and hindsight.*
> *Nebenzal: – we approached it professionally. Here was a truly interesting story, worth telling. And we told it, and we honed it, and we refined it, and changed it minutely, we found certain raisins to put into the pudding, and that is really what we did, we didn't sit down like two guys who came from the New School of Social Research ...*
> *Amateau: ... We went to it from a filmic rather than a, you know, geopolitical experience ...*

In contrast, Michael Caine claimed at least a kind of commitment:

> *My abhorrence of this system (i.e. apartheid) lay dormant for many years as it did for most of the world – until a chance came for me to do something concrete about it. The film was called **The Wilby Conspiracy** ... the theme of the film was anti-apartheid... This film was my first foray into that very risky realm of 'message pictures', and as such proved a bit ahead of its time, but I am still proud that I made it anyway.[34]*

But Michael Caine's conflict, expressed here, turns out to be much the same distaste expressed by Amateau and Nbenzal for anything overtly 'political' – where of course 'political' means anything what could be construed as leftwing. The scar tissue from the Hollywood blacklist era had by no means healed over. One wonders in what sense – a quarter of a century after the introduction of institutionalised apartheid, fifteen years after *Come Back, Africa* – was *The Wilby Conspiracy* ahead of its time. It was only ahead of Hollywood box-office time.

In his turn anxious not to offend anyone, Martin Baum, the producer, would say: '... we recognise that there are many South Africans who reject apartheid completely, but the film *is* against any system which creates second-class citizenship in whatever form or for whatever cause' (quoted in the biography *My Name is Michael Caine*).

---

34 *What's it All About?*, Ballantyne Books, New York, 1992, p. 324.

Pace Amateau and Nebenzal, the film's sympathies *are* with the fictional black organisation, the Black Congress, which stands in for the African National Congress. Jim Keogh represents a sceptical white audience that looks upon the black liberationists as Marxists in disguise. Amateau and Nebenzal wrote a witty little scene between Shack Twala and Keogh which takes place when they are on the run in a car:

> *Keogh: Talking back to that policeman – you are what is known as a cheeky kaffir.*
>
> *Twala: That is exactly what I am, Keogh. For which please thank the GMS.*
>
> *Keogh: The what?*
>
> *Twala: The Gospel Missionary Society. They sent me to their schools, and instead of Mark and Luke, I discovered Marx and Lenin, and from there I had absolutely no difficulty getting into jail.*
>
> *Keogh: Are you a communist?*
>
> *Twala: Because I read Marx and Lenin? I also read **Mein Kampf** and Magna Carta and **Winnie the Pooh**.*
>
> *Keogh: Well, what the bloody hell are you then?*
>
> *Twala: The most feared species in all of Africa – a kaffir who cannot be broken.*

After twenty-six years, it is understandable that Hal Nebenzal would not remember the precise details of the story of *The Wilby Conspiracy*, and just as understandable that he would not be familiar with important details of the life of Nelson Mandela. At one point in the interview, in describing the character of Shack Twala, Nebenzal said: 'Sidney Poitier, the role he played was that of a non-violent, of a thinking opponent to apartheid. In the same manner, you cannot see Nelson Mandela reaching for a gun, it would be atypical.'

In point of fact, Mandela *had* 'reached for the gun', first of all in planning sabotage, then in leaving the country in 1961 in order to undergo military training and to obtain weapons for the African National Congress. Nebenzal, perhaps again influenced by the rightward swing of politics in the 1980s and 1990s, forgot that his own Shack Twala wants to recover the hidden diamonds in order to purchase weapons for his rebel organisation, the Black Congress.

The use of Poitier, when compared with the role he had played in *Cry, the Beloved Country*, also reflects a change in the way the world, as reflected through the viewfinder of cinema, had come to perceive South Africa. The priest in Korda's film is so inured to degradation that he is reduced to passive anger; the part that Poitier plays twenty years later is of a leader actively working to overthrow the government.

The main achievement of *The Wilby Conspiracy* is in its villain, Major Horn. (Horn is supposed to be an Afrikaner, but Nicol Williamson plays him with a straight middle-class English accent. Just as well, because there were certainly many English-speakers among apartheid's heavies.)

This is the first film for cinema (there were depictions, certainly, in British television) to show BOSS, the infamous South African Bureau for State Security, at work. The first time we see Major Horn it is in a typically arrogant confrontation with a man ostensibly his superior, a police brigadier:

> *Brigadier: You fanatics shout 'national security' whenever you do anything immoral or illegal.*
>
> *Major Horn: And damned lucky for you we do! Three million whites surrounded by eighteen million blacks? Listen: we built this country, every town, every factory, every farm, mine and Christian church, and I protect it. And that's the way it's gonna stay. Because no Zulu twenty years out of a tree is ever gonna shove fifty cents in my hand and tell me there's a freighter waiting to ship me out of the land I built. All righty?*

Although cast in only a semi-realistic fictive form, the film does convey the message that BOSS is a diabolical agency, deep into manipulation, murder and torture, all in the name of protecting the state. According to Amateau and Nebenzal, this zeal even extended to surveillance of the picture while it was being made.

> *… things that happened during the pre-production period, when we were in London. As an example, we had a lovely English woman who was in charge of the wardrobe, and she needed information on South African police uniforms. So we asked her to go down to the South African Consulate in London, and talk to the people, and we cautioned her, we said, For God's sake, don't talk about **The Wilby Conspiracy**. Very smart, very lovely woman. She went down there, and she said, We're going to shoot a television segment that plays in South Africa, and can you help us with South African police uniforms? And they were very nice, and said, Of course, they gave her stills, pictures, etc, she said, Thank you very much, and as she walked out, they said, And good luck with **The Wilby Conspiracy** (laugh). (Harold Nebenzal, interview, 1991)*

Both Amateau and Nebenzal also believe that there was a spy on location with them in Kenya, where the film was shot. 'The strange thing is, we didn't feel that we were propagandising at all, we deliberately tried not to propagandise, and we didn't want to show, you know, the inhuman conditions and all of that, you know – we leave that to the professionals.' (Amateau)

Perhaps the most astonishing part of the Amateau/Nebenzal approach to the subject was that they felt that they could treat a subject like South Africa apolitically. According to Nebenzal, they were making 'an anti-apartheid point without politicising it' – which requires the kind of double-think that Hollywood, after all, is well versed in.

In the person of Major Horn, Amateau and Nebenzal had created a personification of evil, and the conventions of Hollywood – this was still the 1970s – demanded that evil not go unpunished: 'You know, in the final analysis, you could not rationalise with total evil. At one point, you've got to pull out the gun, and pull the trigger. You have to kill the snake.' As the scriptwriting duo explained it, this posed a dilemma, because in the script, Major Horn had just been captured, and had handed over his gun. It thus involved the execution of an unarmed man, which the natural candidate, Twala/Poitier, could not do, since he was established as Mr Clean. There was only one other candidate, Keogh/Caine.

The scene is set up with Horn, his scheme to capture the rebel leader Wilby frustrated, in the hands of Twala and Keogh. His arrogance undiminished, Horn says that he will be made part of a prisoner exchange, and promises 'I'll be back'. At this threat Keogh, who has been unloading the gun taken from Horn, stops to consider: 'You know, I really believe you will.' Whereupon he raises the gun and shoots Horn through the head. 'To the dismay of United Artists, imagine, your leading man turns and shoots an unarmed villain point blank! I mean, this is not American movies ...' (Amateau).

When I put it to Amateau and Nebenzal that since it is a white man who does the shooting, this could be interpreted as a plea for whites to get involved in the anti-apartheid struggle, to bear arms, even, on the side of blacks, the two writers rejected this interpretation vehemently.

> *Nebenzal: We didn't see it in cosmic political –*
> *Amateau: – grandiose –*
> *Nebenzal: – grandiose proportions at all.*
> *Amateau: No, we saw – it's a knighthood quest, in other words, the knight comes to the town, the villagers ask him, Hey, do me a favour slay the dragon, and the guy says, Jesus, it's not my dragon, what am I going to slay him for? I mean, it's your dragon ...*
> *Nebenzal: It's the Kurasawa picture –*

Amateau: Right.
Nebenzal: The guy comes into town, does his job, and moves on.
Amateau: Right, right. He's not permitted to move on without doing this.

But precisely the invocation of the ancient mythology of dragons, and of the modern mythology of Kurasawa's *The Seven Samurai* places *The Wilby Conspiracy* in a cosmic context. There can be little doubt that the film signally failed to rouse hordes of whites – or even one white person – to take up arms against apartheid. Nevertheless, Keogh, in Nebenzal's own words, 'grew politically'. From a bored bystander – at Twala's trial he is absorbed by the racing results in a newspaper – he becomes more and more deeply involved, until finally his execution of Horn is a serious commitment to the cause of the liberation struggle.

The act has other resonances. Because it is a white man who kills the BOSS agent, this has the effect of disempowering the black man Twala, whose race has been most affected by Horn's machinations. The act of retribution would most fittingly have been carried out by an African. (That was to happen, a few features down the line, with *Dry White Season*.)

The Wilby Conspiracy is clearly in the line of buddy movies, following *Dingaka* and *Gold!* But there is a fresh development. Whereas in the two preceding films the white man is the senior partner, the big brother who in some way guides his African buddy, in *The Wilby Conspiracy* the terms of the relationship are far more egalitarian.

The extent to which the convention is being dramatically altered appears in a scene where Twala and Keogh are on the run. Twala asks Keogh to stop the car, so that he can relieve himself. But that is not all: since Twala is handcuffed, he cannot unzip his fly, which Keogh therefore has to help him with. But even that is not the limit of his incapacity, and an extremely reluctant Keogh has to help him still further ...

Of course, the scene is played for laughs. But it involves some interesting role reversals. In the script, the character of Shack Twala is continually under pressure to play the role of the subservient native – the first confrontation with the police comes about because Twala will not address the white policeman deferentially as 'constable', and later, when they meet up with police once again, despite the need to placate them, Twala behaves with ill grace when they address him as 'boy'.

Keogh is continually trying to impress on Twala the need to behave like his servant so that they do not excite suspicion. Instead, it is the white man, who, in a very basic way (by helping him with his natural functions) becomes the body servant of the black man. Beyond that, always protesting, Keogh is drawn into serving the cause of the revolutionaries, which is Twala's cause. Until in the end he becomes their voluntary hit-man. That he has gone through a process of education is made clear, when Keogh shoots Horn, by Twala's remark that 'Now you understand'.

Twala is never subservient to the will of Keogh, he simply goes his own way, dragging the white man along with him. In the process, we are convinced of the rightness of the Black Congress cause. This is elicited by the contempt and sadism of Major Horn and his sidekick, and by the incidents of repression that we see. Shack Twala is no Faithful Servant, nor is he passive: he is dedicated to his cause, and in the end is instrumental in defeating Horn, by himself grabbing the runners of the helicopter as it rises, bearing away Horn and his captive Wilby. Twala's act inspires the cowed peasantry literally to rise up to help him drag the helicopter down, and in a memorable scene they tear the helicopter to pieces with their primitive implements. It is a victory of the masses over the men and the technology repressing them.

That this scene was shot a year or so before the Soweto uprising must be catalogued as coincidence. It was never shown in South Africa, so it had no influence there. As has been indicated, the government was aware of the film and its content and, according to Nebenzal, put pressure on the local South African exhibitors, who advised the studio, United Artists', that not only that film but other United Artists' films could be affected. This threat was viewed indulgently by Amateau:

> *That wasn't a threat, that was economic leverage … they said openly, Look, you can't expect us to show this picture and then show the other pictures with the enthusiasm we have in the past …*

As a result, United Artists made only a lacklustre effort to distribute anywhere, and the film has largely been seen on television, where it appeared long after its release.

Although the popular rising depicted in the helicopter scene had of course nothing whatsoever to do with the Soweto uprising, it is indicative of a current of popular, uninformed sentiment outside South Africa, the kind of sentiment shaped precisely by the genre of Peasant Revolt films that constituted history for Hollywood and in consequence for much of the world. Hollywood's imperative to solve all the problems of the world in one-and-a-half hours combined with the mythologised history of America's own revolution to create a belief that once oppressed peoples were moved to rise, no force could keep them down.

In 1976, with no help from Hollywood, disaffected students did rebel, without arms, in a defiance that awed the world. But whatever victory was ultimately achieved came about as the result of an intricate chain of circumstances that began with the televised image of the Students' Revolt, was then processed by an international network of anti-apartheid activists, and finally led to punitive action against the South African government by a number of states. But this took fourteen years of repression, of torture, and of bloodshed.

During the almost thirty years of apartheid that preceded the Students' Revolt, it had been South African government policy to create barriers between white and black. By the 1970s, a whole generation of Africans had been schooled to know whites only as masters, and of whites to know blacks only as servants. In the face of this, it seems perverse that another Buddy film should be made; it seems doubly perverse that this film should be the creation of an Afrikaner; and beyond perversity that it should prove to be one of the most successful films of all time. This film was *The Gods Must Be Crazy.*

THE GODS MUST BE CRAZY (1980)

Jamie Uys had made the first of the Buddy films, *Dingaka.* Even as early as 1964, when *Dingaka* appeared, the film revealed many of the tensions within Afrikanerdom that were summed up in the great debate between the *verlig* and the *verkramp* – the 'enlightened' and the 'restricted', or 'conservative' – that preceded the undermining of Afrikaner power (*kragdadigheid*) in the late 1980s.

Whether it was due to his experience as a magistrate in a tribal area or not, Uys does seem to have developed a kind of respect for Africans that was not common at that time. The hero of *Dingaka*, Ntuku, draws our sympathy by his independent search for justice, and his manipulation by the white lawyer Davis could escape a casual observer.

The subtext of *The Gods Must be Crazy*, which came out at a critical time in South Africa's history, also needs to be clarified for the majority of people who saw in it no more than a slapstick comedy that could laugh at serious issues. *Gods* is as disarming as it is entertaining. And it is as treacherous as it is both.

The appeal of *Gods* lies in a yearning for idyllic simplicity in the face of an increasingly complex and stressful world. Uys's hero is the Noble Savage in the person of Xi (played by N!Xau) the Bushman, and much of the plot revolves around his confrontation with a society that does not understand his ways, and of which he has no need. Observe that the African chosen by Uys is more exotic than his own black countrymen, who in that time and place – South Africa after the Soweto uprising – would not have been easy to romanticise. It is a typical trait of Uys, in *Gods*, to transform the South African reality to make even its worst features palatable – just as in *Dingaka* he had used choreography. *Gods* is a psychogenic parable about white South Africa, an exploitation of its myths in an attempt to exorcise the Black Devil by means of laughter.

The story of *Gods* is made up of a number of intertwining plots of more or less equal value. First, there is the story of Xi, the Bushman of Botswana. As depicted by Uys, the life of the Bushman people is idyllic. They are completely in harmony with their environment, living communally, until a careless aviator throws a Coke bottle into their midst. Possession of this unfamiliar but desirable object becomes such a cause of friction within the little tribe that Xi determines to get rid of it by returning it to the 'gods' whence it came, even if it means going to the end of the world. Second, in a neighbouring black-governed country, the revolutionary Sam Boga attempts a coup. He is unsuccessful, and together with his followers flees into Botswana. Third, a white woman suddenly tires of her meaningless job in a city office and on a whim takes a job as a teacher in a black school in Botswana. There, she meets up with the male lead, a shy, awkward zoologist who will eventually win her favours. These three plots converge at the denouement, when the black revolutionaries seize the white teacher and her black pupils as hostages, and they are rescued by the zoologist and the Bushman working as a team.

The Gods Must be Crazy is set in Botswana. This was expedient for a number of reasons, paramount being that Botswana is not South Africa. Some of the filming was done in Namibia, but in the late 1970s, when *Gods* was shot, Namibia was still ruled by South Africa, and there was a guerrilla war going on there, so this would not have been a felicitous setting for the film either. Botswana, a non-controversial African country, was the *locus* of choice.

Uys even had the audacity to list the film as a Botswana production, thus avoiding the odium that a South African film might attract. Uys's Botswana is a bogus topography that only accidentally resembles the real country of the same name. Like the homeland depicted in *Dingaka*, it is above all an imaginary landscape limned by the self-deluding imagination of apartheid. In its details it resembles the massive con-job the South African government sold as the Bantustans. These were supposedly independent, self-sufficient countries where Africans could develop in their own way according to their own customs, and find a place in the sun. In fact, the Bantustans were built out of dust, dumping-grounds for the so-called 'surplus appendages' (the Nationalist euphemism for non-productive blacks) that the apartheid economy found so tiresome. The Bantustans were intended to hem people in, to prevent their migration; the free movement of people across a landscape, with which *Gods* is filled, was simply not possible in pass-bound South Africa.

The form adopted and adapted by Uys for *The Gods Must be Crazy* is that of the travelogue. By means of the travelogue, in the comfort of cinema seats, we are shown exotic landscapes, strange peoples and dangerous animals. Our guide is the omniscient narrator, who owns the images and whose task it is to make them accessible to even the most boorish of intellects. If these exotic landscapes, strange peoples and dangerous animals do indeed exist, it is for our entertainment.

The screen onto which threatening yet harmless images are projected is a symbol of that other screen, the one between the Third World and the privileged of this earth. Whatever we see on the screen – be it starvation, desecration or carnage

– repels, intrigues, titillates, but does not touch us. The newsreel itself, which dominates our sense of the world, has become simply another form of travelogue. In its different manifestations, the travelogue has been virtually the only form by which most people in the First World have experienced Africa.

During the latter part of the nineteenth century – the years marking the Scramble for Africa – perhaps to salve a Christian conscience that had earlier that century abolished slavery yet still needed to exploit the labour of Africans, the phrase 'the white man's burden' was invented. This was intended to imply that the white man was in Africa not for his own profit, but out of a sense of duty – to Christianise and civilise the native. Why else would a white man choose to go to such a God-forsaken hole? Uys had a more honest assessment of the phrase: 'When I was young, the whole world was racist. The white man looked down on the black man. We called the black man "the white man's burden". ' (Interview, 1990)

The true nature of the burden is epitomised in a scene from a South African film from the silent era, *The Copper Mask*. Having to ford a river, an irascible white man beckons a native over, and, climbing piggy-back, orders him to wade in. The cunning shifting of the burden from the back of the African to that of the white man was typical of the hypocrisy that often characterised the white presence in Africa. So many of the films about Africa are about the shifting of burdens, about the transfer of guilt and of responsibility from the strong onto the weak, from the oppressor onto the oppressed.

The travelogue, a film form, was itself descended from the great literature of exploration of the nineteenth century, the period when Africa was being 'discovered' and opened to exploitation. But the relating of exploits, of journeys, of encounters, did not constitute all that the literature, as well as the fact, of exploration was about. For it was also about the process of self-discovery, of testing oneself to the limit. For Europeans, Africa was never so much a place as a state of mind, a perdurable 'heart of darkness'.

The title of Conrad's novel of course echoes Henry Morton Stanley's *In Darkest Africa*. For its narrative, *Gods* draws on the great tradition of the trek through Africa. Not the safari trek, where you hunt for animals, but the missionary trek, where you hunt for the souls of human beings.

This was essential to the white man's view of Africa – you did not go to such a benighted place unless you had a *mission*. To Africa, Europe sent its fanatics. Made fifty years after the events it depicts, the Twentieth Century Fox film *Stanley & Livingstone* (an earlier work by the 'Africa expert' Henry King – see *Untamed*) totally without irony echoes the religious mania that drove the missionaries through the words of the New York publisher James Gordon Bennett:

> *Christians who believe in spreading the Word of God among the heathen ... heroic figures in the dark places of the earth ... The*

> *Dark Continent – mystery, fever, heat, cannibals, a vast jungle in*
> *which you could lose half of America ... unchanged, untouched*
> *since the dawn of history.*

And when Stanley is depicted taking up the mantle of Livingstone, his explorations take place to the march of the battle hymn *Onward Christian Soldiers*.

The Afrikaner early on decided that *his* mission was to bring the Word of God to the wilderness. Unlike Livingstone, he had no desire to share that Word with the kaffir, the unbeliever, for Afrikaners were God's chosen people, and the chosen do not share with the unchosen, for then how would you tell the difference? And above all, Afrikaners wanted to preserve that difference. By the middle of this century, the Afrikaner's mission had come to mean the protection of white Christian civilisation against the unholy alliance of the *swart gevaar*, or 'black terror', and communism.

In apartheid South Africa, communism and the black terror became synonymous. The communists were out to overthrow the government, which would lead to black rule – also the goal of the African nationalists. In Uys's film, the two are fused in the persona of Sam Boga, leader of the terrorists.

The name Sam Boga is not an innocent coinage. In part it recalls Sam Nujoma, head of Swapo, which was fighting for the liberation of Namibia; in part it is close to the plural sound of the Afrikaans word *sambok*, which is written in English as 'sjambok'. Now, a sjambok is a long bull-hide whip; if you hear 'sjam' as the swish of the whip, and 'bok' as the impact, the word is nicely onomatopoeic. In its country of origin, it has customarily been used by the South African police, and as such is a fearful symbol of white authority. It has never been associated with blacks – except on the receiving end. But in one of the frequent inversions of Uys's distorting mirror imagery, it becomes the personification of Black Power. The mission of Sam Boga, the Whip, is a destructive one: the overthrow of established order.

The white heroine's mission is escape from the rat-race of modern society through good works, specifically teaching African children. The inversion here is that in reality missionaries customarily went *to* South Africa, and were so effective in their education that they came under attack from the South African government. (See Shack Twala's reference in *The Wilby Conspiracy*.) That same government had been grossly neglectful of the education of its own black population, and this had been a source of great discontent inside South Africa.

The mission of Andrew Steyn, the Afrikaner zoologist, is scientific discovery, in the innocuous form of examining elephant droppings. His presence in Botswana is clearly non-exploitative, even ecologically correct.

Xi's mission in travelling to the end of the world with his Coca-Cola bottle is the protection of the Bushmen; both Steyn and Xi are curators of a way of life.

Perhaps the deepest, unconscious, irony in the film is a small part played by Uys himself – that of a Christian missionary.

All these plots entwining, all these people scurrying across the landscape of southern Africa, colliding with comic pratfalls, constitute a distorted microcosm of the clash of peoples, customs, and ideologies that is in reality deeply tragic. What Uys does in *The Gods Must be Crazy* is to create the never-never land that the architects of apartheid would have had us believe in, where their intentions are for the good of everyone. In this land of make-believe, an entire village drops its work to turn out to sing a hymn of welcome to the white teacher – the relationship of black towards white is gratitude for help being given, and that of white towards black is protective paternalism. This peaceful, symbiotic, unequal relationship would continue forever were it not for the eruption of the terrorists onto the scene.

Uys's terrorists are caricatures of the white nightmare, the black guerrilla. Sam Boga's men are bumbling incompetents, who hardly know how to use their weapons. Uys insists that this is no more than an accurate depiction: 'Your terrorist, or your black soldiers, or freedom-fighters, were still very amateurish and inefficient, which was true at that time.' Uys's terrorists bungle everything, from an attempted coup to a kidnapping – Uys even has the audacity to have one slip on a banana skin.

Such a representation of the black guerrilla was a common image among whites, encouraged by government propaganda and the Afrikaans press of the time – he was an ignorant native whose innate inferiority prevented him from ever being a threat. The African's limited intellectual capacity means that he is not capable of effective leadership: thus, in *Gods*, long-haired Sam Boga is not even black, he is of 'coloured' or 'mixed blood'.

With the same kind of disinformation, the government regularly reported that the master-mind behind Umkhonto we Sizwe, the ANC's armed wing, was the white communist Joe Slovo. The intention of government propaganda was to tranquillise white fears. Uys builds on this groundwork to create his own exorcism of the 'black terror' through ridicule. White South Africans laughed in relief; those in other countries who laughed were unconsciously ingesting this propaganda of contempt.

When the terrorists kidnap the schoolchildren, the white scientist comes to the children's aid. There is a white platitude about Africans, often expressed, that they are 'like children'. In *Gods*, they literally *are* children, who need the help of a white man.

Reading *The Gods Must be Crazy* demands that it be constantly put in its context, since it did not spring from a vacuum. That context was the Students' Revolt of just a few years earlier, 1976. This had begun with the repeated protests of thousands of Soweto children against the use of Afrikaans, the language of the oppressor, as an instruction medium and came to a head when the police fired on a crowd of protesters.

The Students' Revolt is commonly regarded as the beginning of the end for apartheid. At the time, it was blamed on the usual vague suspects, Black Power, alias the Communist Party, alias 'outside agitators', or, as a South African newsreel of the time put it, 'filthy elements'. Trapped in their own mesh of propaganda, it was virtually impossible for the authorities to concede that the students were driven to revolt by government policies. No, they had to have been 'led astray' by sinister forces.

This is what we see in metaphorical form in *Gods*, when the terrorists kidnap the children for their own political ends, and lead them 'astray' over the countryside. The threat to the children in the film is from the terrorists; in the real world of South Africa of 1976-77, fears that the *minds* of black youth were being subverted by Marxists did not prevent the authorities from sacrificing some 800 of their *bodies*. The truly lethal threat to the children came not from guerrillas, but from the police.

The kidnapped children in *Gods* are rescued by the scientist, but the scientist *in conjunction with Xi the Bushman*. The white scientist sends Xi on a mission to rescue the kidnapped children. In itself, this constitutes a perversion of reality, for during the Namibian war of liberation, the San, or Bushmen, were routinely enlisted by the South African army to track down and fight Swapo, the Namibian freedom-fighters. This was a classic example of the use of one indigenous people to defeat another, and equally classically, the San (Bushmen) themselves were destroyed in the process. (The Americans did the same with the hill-people of Vietnam.[35])

Incompetent as they may be, Uys's guerrillas are well armed. In *The Gods Must be Crazy*, it is they who have the weapons, while the white hero goes unarmed – a reversal of the gross imbalance, in reality, between the weaponry of the South African army and the very modest fire-power of the African freedom-fighters. Unarmed as he is, in order to overcome the abductors, Steyn turns to white man's magic – science.

In the cinema, it is a cliché that ignorant savages can be defeated by tricks of science known only to the white men – in *King Solomon's Mines*, for example, the knowledge that there will be an eclipse of the sun saves the white adventurers from execution.

The superior totem owned by Steyn is a sleep-inducing drug used to stun animals, but he will not administer it himself – this task falls to the Bushman, who, a child in size, can mingle easily with the captured black children. Xi is made a

---

35 Documentary Educational Resources of Boston claims that during the guerrilla war in Namibia, the Bushmen had the highest rate of military service of any ethnic group in the world. This was because the San were indigent, and the army offered employment. Out of this came the ever more rapid erosion of their way of life, with destruction of clan and family ties following hard upon alcoholism and prostitution.

miniature bow-and-arrow for that purpose. We had early on seen the Bushman hunting with bow-and-arrow tipped with a soporific drug, and it is fair to ask why the Bushman is not allowed to use his own drug – would this not have been tidier? Tidy, perhaps – but that would have made it Bushman magic, and not White Man's magic.

To make a figurative interpretation of the plot: blacks are like children who are easily led astray by anarchic forces (black liberationists). When this happens, the threat is not only to blacks, but to the white race, personified by the heroine, the schoolteacher, who is also abducted. To save black and white alike, white organisational skills must mobilise all indigenous peoples and even nature itself (a poisonous bush). Andrew Steyn, the pacific, unworldly scientist – the personification of a technologically advanced but entirely non-aggressive South Africa – beats all the odds.

Of course, the South African state of the turbulent 1970s was neither unarmed nor non-aggressive. It had by far the best-equipped and most efficient fighting forces on the sub-continent, and these were used constantly as a tool of policy: South Africa invaded its weak neighbours purposefully and often, killing hundreds of black civilians. It paid and equipped insurgents to destabilise countries of the region, reducing Angola and Mozambique to levels of starvation and poverty from which they may never recover. All this terror was carried out in an attempt to contain its own 'black terror' – South African English for those who sought democratic rights. This was the reality behind Uys's parable.

Who are these 'gods' who are crazy? They are the technologically advanced whites, whose very garbage is a source of wonder to the Third World. In his simple wisdom, the Bushman rejects what white society has to offer, symbolised by the discarded Coca-Cola bottle.

This rejection is an anodyne to white angst, because it means that the Bushmen do not covet the white standard of living, and so can never be rivals for it. This might have been a desirable state of affairs for white South Africans, but it was far from the reality of the masses demanding their rightful share of the South African pie.

The Gods Must be Crazy is a Buddy film close to the ethos of Uys's earlier film, *Dingaka*. Once again, we have a sympathetic and independent black character who works in conjunction with a white man to achieve a goal. In *Dingaka* it was a common goal, in *Gods* Xi essentially does the will of Steyn. He is the familiar Faithful Servant in the guise of a free agent.[36] In both cases, the enemy is black.

. There is no sense in either film of black/white friction. Whether we want to call this propaganda or not, it served superlatively well the goal of the government,

---

36   Note that Xi is released from prison through the intercession of Steyn. Xi thus owes Steyn a debt, like the Kaffir in *A Kaffir's Gratitude* and the Zulu in *A Zulu's Devotion*. He does in fact become Steyn's employee.

which was clear from the disinformation films that the Information Service was producing to counteract the impact on world opinion of the Students' Revolt. These films aimed to prove that the intentions of South Africa's homelands policy were essentially benign, and that the country was on the way to becoming a just society.

Proficient as these films were in public relations, nevertheless, their appeal was largely to the ignorant and to apartheid's supporters overseas. For the most part, these propaganda films did not make it onto the television screens, whence people around the world get most of their information. There, viewers were more likely to see Antony Thomas's poignant trilogy, *The Search for Sandra Laing, Six Days of Soweto* and *Working for Britain*. This was where the popular image of South Africa was formed.

For most people, South Africa was a country of discrimination, racism, brutality. And then along came this unassuming low-budget film about 'Botswana', which offered an altogether new and appealing topography to the political landscape of southern Africa. Folly, foibles, pratfalls; winsome maiden and shy wooer; blundering villains; machines that have a will of their own; the world speeded up, like the old silent films – it is not Buster Keaton, but that is the mould. How could you discern apartheid amid all the slapstick?

The final ingredient, the one that made the film an unprecedented success, was the Bushman. In Uys's lens, he becomes a modern version of the Noble Savage, the focus for jaded modern appetites seeking to escape from the complications of Western society. Uys readily confesses to his own nostalgia:

> *(O)ne of the themes in my movies is that I seem to be sad about the Africa I knew as a child disappearing. The Africa that was untrammelled and didn't have white civilisation sprouted all over it. Where the wild is still the wild, and the animals still roam free. And the people who live there lived as Africans without our trappings and our hangups and our problems. (Interview, 1990)*

According to Uys, he had been intrigued by the Bushmen when he came across them while making his film *Beautiful People*, and they lingered in the back of his mind as a possible subject for some years. When Uys did eventually take up this subject, his path literally crossed that of the American ethnographic film-maker John Marshall, who actually filmed Uys on location for *The Gods Must be Crazy*.

John Marshall has been the great chronicler of San, or Bushman, life over the last forty years, a period of catastrophic change for a people who have been persecuted for centuries. Marshall first went to the Kalahari in 1950, and since then he has devoted most of his energies to recording a way of life that has now completely disappeared, the hunter-gatherer existence that was caricatured by Uys.

In showing their spartan existence, this is how the narration in *The Gods Must be Crazy* describes the Bushmen:

> *But the slender and graceful little Bushmen of the deep Kalahari live here quite contentedly, and in complete harmony with their environment. They must be the most contented people in the world. They have no crime, no punishment, no violence, no laws, police, judges, rulers or bosses.*

In the 1950s, Marshall's cameras captured San people still living by hunting and gathering, but these were the last images of a way of life lost forever. Marshall reacts strongly to the very term 'Bushman': '"Bushman" is a racial classification … in South Africa, (its) use has been to exterminate and dispossess people who are classified as "Bushmen".' (Interview, 1991)

Marshall describes a systematic erosion of San territory until by 1970 'there was no more hunting-and-gathering. Everybody in fact was rounded up and lived in a slum, in a rural slum around the shining houses of the white officials in Tsumkwe, which was the administrative capital of Bushmanland.'

Although Uys may have gone to the Kalahari in the late 1970s to look for the classical hunting-and-gathering Bushman (if he did, his research was sadly deficient), what he put on screen was not the reality, but a construct based on found images from books like Laurens van der Post's *Bushmen of the Kalahari*, and indeed Marshall's own films – although Uys sanitised these sources.[37] Out of them, he fabricated his own romance of Bushman life, which turned out to be one that had massive appeal throughout the world.

Uys's Kalahari, far from being a semi-desert, is turned into a Garden of Eden, where even the lack of water is no problem, because the Bushmen know how to collect and drink the morning dew, and where the hunter apologises to his game before he kills it.

John Marshall concedes Uys's right to let his imagination run free: 'Uys made a fiction film, anybody can make any fiction film they want. The problem comes up when he says to … reporters who are presenting ostensibly facts, that N!Xau actually lives that way, that there is such a place out there …'[38] And that is precisely what Uys does do:

---

37 For example, contrast Marshall's stark images of hunters killing a giraffe (in *The San*, shot in the 1950s) with Uys's Bushman killing a springbok.

38 The devastation of the San people is depicted in the films of Documentary Educational Resources, especially the damning portrayal in *N!ai, The Story of a !Kung Woman*, by John Marshall, Adrienne Miesmer, and Sue Marshall-Cabezas (1980).

> *When I was casting for* **The Gods Must be Crazy**, *I decided that I had to see every Bushman in the whole world before I chose my leading man. I'd heard there were about 30 000 Bushmen still existent in the whole world ... we found (N!Xau, who plays Xi, the lead) in Botswana, because his hunting-ground straddles across two countries, Botswana and Namibia. And they move freely across the border, because where they are there's no Customs ... (Interview, 1990)*

John Marshall has known N!Xau for some time, and points out that he never lived by hunting-and-gathering, was not nomadic, and, most prosaically, earned his living by cooking for the children at the school in Tsumkwe. In Daniel Riesenfeld's interview with him in 1990, N!Xau himself said that he had never worn skins or used a bow-and-arrow.

The line between fact and fiction becomes non-existent when film critics repeat unquestioningly the Uys hyperbole:

> *(Uys needs to find his star) Bushman and sometime actor N!Xau ... Trouble is, N!Xau is somewhere out there in the Kalahari Desert. All last week, Uys circled the area in a light plane ... waiting for N!Xau to light a fire to show where he is, down below. As of Sunday, Uys was still circling, still looking for smoke. (Jerry Tallmer,* **New York Post**, *29 November 1984)*

Such willing suspension of disbelief perpetuates the fantasy of *Gods* well beyond its 90-minute running time in the cinema. John Marshall sees this sentimentalising of the Bushman reality as actually life-threatening, since it obscures their critical plight.

There is a telling scene near the end of *Gods* when Xi takes leave of Andrew Steyn. Steyn offers him money for his assistance, but the interpreter tells him that Bushmen have no concept of money, and don't know how to use it. This is a very clear enactment of the self-serving cliché common to all forms of exploitation based on race or class: that the lower order does not need more money, or if it had it, would not know what to do with it.

This quaint notion was played out in real life when Uys engaged N!Xau to act in the film. At that time, N!Xau was earning about 300 rands a month from his duties at the school, and in local terms this was a respectable income. Marshall states that Uys paid N!Xau 1 200 rands for his appearance in *Gods*, and if he is correct, N!Xau might even have lost money by working for Uys.

> *(Uys) said he paid the Bushman $300 for his first 10 days work, then realised it was a mistake, because he has no use for money. 'I found out later that the money had blown away,' Mr Uys said.*

*Next, the Bushman was paid with twelve head of cattle, 'because he liked the idea that cattle don't run away when you hunt'. Lions killed eight of them, and the Bushmen ate the others hurriedly, Mr Uys said. (Judy Klemesrud, interview with Jamie Uys, **New York Times**, 28 April 1985)*

Uys's flippancy regarding the Bushman contempt for money was rebutted in a scathing letter from Toby Alice Volkman, staff anthropologist of John Marshall's Documentary Educational Resources, of Watertown, Massachusetts:

*If N!Xau's $300 film-star salary had, as Mr Uys puts it, 'blown away', this is not because he had no use for money. Money was a pressing concern in Bushmanland when Gods was filmed in 1978; subsistence hunting and gathering had almost ceased, and people depended on government handouts and purchased foods ... people quarrelled intensely over money and other possessions ... (**New York Times**, letter dated 30 April 1985)*

Even though *The Gods Must Be Crazy* earned considerably more for its distributors than for its producer, *Gods* certainly made Uys the richer by several million dollars. With the help of a lawyer, N!Xau eventually did win more money from Uys (in the interview with Judy Klemesrud above, Uys states that he had sent N!Xau $100 a month for the last few years, and that he had set up a $20 000 trust account in his name) but it could not compare with the money that Uys earned in his use of N!Xau.

So the Buddy relationship between Steyn and Xi in the film, where Xi, to no advantage to himself, obligingly helps the white man, seems a replica of the apparently exploitative relationship between Uys and N!Xau. This is Jamie Uys's own description of his first meeting with N!Xau, which supposedly took place in the bush:

And then I asked my interpreter (another Bushman) to ask him, Would he come and work for us, we would pay him. He said, That is not interpretable, because for one thing, we don't have a word for working for someone. Payment we don't understand either. (Interview, 1990)

Confusion between what is script and what is reality is complete. But it is still possible to distinguish what is expedient. Marshall's judgement, '... for Uys to say that this is a simple child of nature who doesn't understand money is just another way to rob somebody, you don't have to pay them' (interview, 1991) seems by no means too harsh.

Uys's film never utters the word 'apartheid'. Different races seem to interact without friction, but a closer look reveals that the film faithfully observes South Africa's racial gradations. The 'Bushmen' – men, women and children – appear to have been selected for their lightness of colour.

Almost all the blacks behave in a clownish fashion, from the terrorists who try to topple the black government, to that government's army, to border guards. There is the distinct impression that blacks are funny, and usually incompetent. People are killed violently in the film – during the coup attempt, and when the helicopter is blown up during the banana plantation shoot-out – but there is no sense of seriousness about these deaths, because they all happen to blacks.

> *For South Africans to make films about apartheid, it doesn't work*
> *for me because we are in the scrum, we can't see clearly ... I have*
> *never felt like making a film about apartheid because I just know*
> *that when I talk about apartheid, I even contradict myself ... (Uys,*
> *1990)*

Nevertheless, behind the comic veneer, *The Gods Must be Crazy* is saturated with the mindset of apartheid, and in some places it ran up against protests. The New York Southern Africa Solidarity Coalition paraded in front of cinemas where it was playing, and handed out fliers:

> *... it is not the 'Gods (Who) must be crazy', but the mad dog*
> *racists and their friends who constructively engage in promoting*
> *slanderous propaganda who are crazy. The movie-going public of*
> *New York should not be crazy enough to go for South Africa's*
> *slimy games!*

But the protests had little effect. In Stockholm, Paris, New York, *The Gods Must be Crazy* ran for years.[39] Although it had no government backing, the film was a huge propaganda success for the South African government. N!Xau's face appeared often in government publications and the South African press, which upheld the Bushman myth:

---

39 Although *The Gods Must Be Crazy* was an overwhelming box-office success inside South Africa, it was not an unqualified critical success. '*Gods* is good for a few laughs but the humour is slapstick and palls long before the end...' (*The Pretoria News*, 10 September 1980), '...a confusion of conflicting styles as if Uys is not sure of what he's trying to say or achieve...' (*The Star*, 20 September 1980). The *Pretoria News* writer, Diana Frylinck, also repeated the earlier complaint levelled at Uys for *Dingaka*, that he had been cavalier of ethnic accuracy: 'The tribespeople, supposedly Tswanas, are dressed in Tsonga clothes and sing the odd Zulu chant and Venda hymns...'

*(T)he Bushman who starred in Jamie Uys's film, **The Gods Must be Crazy**, says that Western civilisation does not fascinate him as much as most people would expect. 'I enjoy visiting you, because you are also fond of me, but I will always go back to my wife and seven children, where I belong,' he said recently in an interview before setting off on a promotional tour to France. The diminutive Bushman will return to his family in the Kalahari immediately after the tour, to help his family look for food and survive the coming winter ... (Die Vaderland)*

Vincent Canby, the influential reviewer of the *New York Times*, was effusive in his praise of the film, and came to the quaintly comfortable conclusion that

*I think it's safe to guess that Mr Uys is certainly neither a racist nor an apologist. Nobody with the sense of humor that he displays in **The Gods Must be Crazy** could be. Nobody who would take the time to choreograph the kind of elaborate sight gags that are the reason to see this film could support the sort of self-interest officially sanctioned by the South African government. Such narrowness of vision is antithetical to the creation of laughter. (**New York Times**, 28 October 1984)*

N!Xau, whether you believe Uys's version of his discovery or not, was certainly plucked out of the wilderness, and became an international star, even though none of the millions – perhaps hundreds of millions – of people who saw him could pronounce or remember his name. Uys lamented

*I'm afraid lately he's starting to realise that he is regarded as something special ... **The Gods Must be Crazy** ran very well in Japan. One of the networks there bought the movie for broadcasting and they wrote to me and said, Could I bring the Bushman out there for promotion? and I said, No, I don't want to do that because you'll want to kind of display him as a freak. They said, He's a big hero here, he's a sex-symbol and a big hero in this country. I said, If you put on Western clothes, you're going to spoil the image of this Noble Savage, and this strong person. So they had the best designer in Japan design a kind of cloak for him. Which worked very well. It didn't take any of his dignity away ... and from the moment we landed in Japan, and from the moment that we were there, he had these millions of people worshipping him ... Now, you would think it would make his head swell, or something. He just smiled and enjoyed it ... completely unselfconscious. He just loved these people and they loved him* *back. Afterwards, we took him to France, because the French wanted him there too. Then I noticed he was getting a bit self-conscious ... he is picking up our hang-ups, our social diseases ... (Interview, 1992)*

After receiving the adulation of the world, N!Xau returned to Tsumkwe, in Namibia.[40] At the time of our interview in 1990, he seemed to have aged considerably since making the follow-up, *Gods II*. He shuffled rather than strode, and, in his well-worn European clothes, had little of the dignity he had had when naked except for the skin that Uys asked him to wear. He did not seem different from all the other people, flotsam left after the carving up of Bushmanland into game preserves and farms.

If N!Xau came out of the experience with any profit, it was not easily visible. He complained that the government was not handing out the food it promised. In winter, when the people cannot grow food, and when the cattle run dry, life was particularly hard. 'Sometimes you can gather mangetti nuts from here, but this year the rains have been bad, and the mangetti crop is down. Elephants eat the nuts.' For a while, during the Bushman craze, tours would come out to visit the community, and the local people would dress up like Uys's Bushmen, and do a theme-park act for the tourists. People will always pay for fairy-tales.

Meanwhile, John Marshall continues with his fight to secure land for the San people, so that they can farm it, and gain some kind of security and dignity.[41] He is convinced that it is their only chance for survival.

The Gods Must be Crazy came out in the period after the Soweto uprising had apparently been controlled. The black anarchy depicted in Uys's film seemed to have exhausted itself. It is true that there was a low-level guerrilla war going on, but it was hardly more than a pin-prick to the elephant that was the South African military state. *The Gods Must be Crazy* was one of the best antidotes to the poisonous name that apartheid had gained throughout the world, laughing it into non-existence. Jamie Uys died in January 1996. I am sorry he did not have the opportunity of turning his comic talents to the post-apartheid era.

STATE OF EMERGENCY

The willingness of Afrikaner leaders, sincere and candid people, fully able to deceive others as well as themselves, to admit that they had made mistakes, made it

---

40   '"But never forget that his soul is in Tsumkwe with his wife and seven children,'"
      said Miss Gerda van den Broek, who is looking after N!xau...' (*Citizen*, 2 March
      1984).

41   Eloquently revealed in *Pull Ourselves Up or Die*.

tempting to believe them when they said they wanted to change the face of apartheid.

Their preoccupation with the image of South Africa meant that they had missed the principal lesson of the spasm of 1976, which was that they could no longer discount the black majority. Despite the killings, the beatings, the enforced exiles, the deaths in prison, the black population was not subdued. The South African government had failed to come up with a satisfactory policy of damage control by the time it was hit by the next cycle of violence. This started with a rent-strike in 1984, and spread to townships throughout the country in a way that was both more spontaneous and better organised than in 1976. Media coverage had also improved: the correspondents were in place, with vital contacts among the dissident community already established; the crews now included something that had been missing in 1976, black videographers – when the confrontations took place, often these were the only ones who could gain access to the townships; and satellite transmission gave immediacy. In the media battle, white South Africa was decisively outgunned.

The police could harass the crews, whom they hated. Many were arrested, Brian Tilley was shot in the leg, and the police stood by while George De'Ath, a cameraman for Independent Television News, was hacked to death by township pro-government vigilantes. But newsfilm was haemorrhaging out of South Africa, and the impact on the American public – the critical mass – was enormous.

During this period it became quite clear that there was a chain reaction that began with the pictures of unrest and repression in South Africa, and passed through living-room television sets into people's awareness, which led them to put pressure on American business with interests in South Africa to pull out, and to force Congress to impose sanctions.

The township unrest could be contained, but the economic threat implicit in sanctions was a deadly blow to South African security. White South Africa could live with American indifference, but not with American hostility. In the urgent words of a police officer at the time, 'We have to stop bad news about South Africa from getting out.' The government had lost control of the image.

To wrest it back from the anti-apartheid forces, in 1985 a State of Emergency was declared, permitting the authorities to restrict severely what reporters could do, and in the following year censorship openly directed against the 'media terrorists' (in the phrase coined by Stoffel Botha, Minister of Information[42]) was imposed. There is no doubt that this action was aimed primarily at foreign television. Looming in the minds of National Party leaders was the spectre of Vietnam, which had been 'lost' to America through the machinations of the 'liberal press', wittingly or unwittingly playing the communist game. The liberal press had

---

42   In Parliament, 20 May 1988.

'lost Vietnam', and it could 'lose South Africa'. This was a view shared by American conservatives.

That they took so long over such an obvious measure against the foreign media suggests an agonising debate inside ruling circles. Their own propaganda aimed at the West had always stressed that they were part of 'the Free World', which implied freedom of the press. By imposing censorship on the Western news media, they took the calculated risk of alienating Western public opinion. They rationalised the decision by claiming that they were in a situation akin to war, and in wartime, censorship is normal. They went so far as to accuse the foreign news media of provoking unrest, but no concrete charges to this effect were ever brought against foreign news agents.

The authorities must have been as astonished as they were delighted by the results of their prohibition. The American networks bleated some token protests, and then silently capitulated. It is not known if they ever considered going underground, but the star system of on-the-spot news reporters made this virtually impossible. So closely tied to the news that they reported were the network personalities that anything that did not emanate from the mouths of these demiurges was suspect, indeed, could even be deemed not to have happened. How could they use local people to report the news? – even though behind every American who did a stand-up before the camera lay a number of South Africans who had been gathering the news, often at great personal risk, which was then fed to the reporter, and regurgitated as his own.

There remained only one arena over which the government could exert no control outside the country, although it would be censored inside. This was feature films. With an audience well-primed about the situation in South Africa from watching television news, by the early 1980s the film industry was poised to cash in on this general awareness.

Recalling the period of the 1980s, Mfundi Vundla, who was an expatriate writer living in Los Angeles at that time, estimates there were probably twenty to thirty projects with a South African theme in development.

> ... they wanted a commercial story ... Hollywood is a commercial venture, it's a business, so they are not really into the charity business, or into the business of making people conscious about things. So it all rides on whether they can make money ... (Interview, 1991)

Hollywood's record on South Africa was dismal. None rushed to follow the lead of Woody Allen, who in the mid-1980s had a clause written into his distribution contract with Orion Pictures forbidding his films to be shown in South Africa. Paul Newman and Tony Randall marched in Washington to protest the Reagan administration's policy towards South Africa, and Harry Belafonte joined the continuing picket outside the South African Embassy there. Headed by Ed Asner, then president, the Screen Actors Guild passed a very weak resolution encouraging members to engage in 'peaceful, lawful demonstrations against the apartheid system'. But American actors too numerous to mention by name flocked to South Africa to work, in defiance of the United Nations ban.

The reason for this collaboration was simple: actors need to work. The reason why the studios and distributors never challenged apartheid was also financial: South Africa was a major market for American films.[43]

When Hollywood finally challenged apartheid, its motive was not sympathy for the resistance movement but, again, financial. Hollywood perceived that television had created an awareness which it could transform into a market. And yet, for all its predatory instincts, Hollywood can – rather like the scene in *Frankenstein* where the monster is charmed by a little girl – offer a glimpse of something that looks suspiciously like a heart.

Hollywood's own record of racism, which includes sins of omission as damning as any of commission, dating from long before even *Birth of a Nation*, was undoubtedly a major factor in the persistence of racism in the United States. But when some producers became convinced of the humanity of black people, then, belatedly but not ineffectually, they began to offer films – *The Defiant Ones, Edge of the City, Guess Who's Coming to Dinner?, Raisin in the Sun, In the Heat of the Night* – whose message was anti-racist.

But it took Hollywood a depressingly long time to take up the question of apartheid. First of all, this was *Africa* – and Hollywood had a very definite image of a jungle as big as a continent, bursting with wild animals and savages, into which there was no way of fitting the complexities of South African society and its discontents, where the whites were little better than Nazis, but where the blacks, even if they were the victims, showed disconcerting leanings towards Marxism. This was clearly dangerous territory. But through television's saturation coverage, it eventually became impossible to ignore. In the end, it was clear even to Hollywood that here was an issue of Manichean simplicity.

Mfundi Vundla describes how he used to go around the United States talking to interested groups about South Africa, and inevitably the question of how many whites in South Africa supported the anti-apartheid movement would come up. Vundla had truthfully to say, 'Not many'. And Vundla sensed their keen disappointment:

> ... *you could see the pain amongst progressive whites in America who are concerned about South Africa, you know. And I guess, it seems to me the powers that be, the people who get movies made, that pain was in them too. (Interview, 1991)*

---

43   See 'Hollywood Acts?', in *American Film*, Vol.11, No. 2, 1985.

And so, in a not unfamiliar twist, the films that eventually got made compensated for that pain, not simply by contributing to awareness, but by showing whites playing a significant anti-apartheid role.

The box-office was a major, perhaps the decisive, factor in the way South Africa was presented. Mbulelo Mzamane, then Professor of Literature at the University of Vermont, observed:

> *The one thing about Hollywood is, Who gets the lead? And one presumes that a lot of the crowd pull is going to be dependent upon that … Nine out of ten times these are white actors. And so therefore the conventions of Hollywood, but also a long tradition of racism demands almost that you look through the eyes of a white star, a white hero. (Interview, 1991)*

Mfundi Vundla supports this analysis:

> *Hollywood is of the opinion that black leads in a motion picture do not make money. So that if you are going to make a black film, you've got to have a black with a white guy, you know. Have Danny Glover with Mel Gibson, have Kevin Kline with Denzel Washington, have Danny Glover with Martin Short, have Danny Glover with Willem Dafoe, have Sidney Poitier with Tony Curtis, you know, there's a tradition with that kind of movie in Hollywood. (Interview, 1991)*

All the 'Hollywood' films made about South Africa during the 1980s fitted this formula of legitimisation of a black story through a white hero. It was true of *Cry Freedom*, *A World Apart*, and *Dry White Season*. The most blatant was the first, the blockbuster *Cry Freedom* (1987). Almost everything about *Cry Freedom* causes one to look askance at the process by which films come into being. There is certainly cause for concern when one reflects that for future generations, *Cry Freedom* may well constitute the only 'history' of the liberation struggle in South Africa for millions of people.

CRY FREEDOM (1987)

Steve Biko, a leader of the black consciousness movement, had died as the result of injuries inflicted by the police in his prison cell. He was not the first to die in this way, but the contempt with which his death was treated by the authorities inspired his friend, the newspaper editor Donald Woods, to question the official version of the affair, and this turned it into a *cause célèbre*.

Biko died in 1977. There were books and television programmes in the wake of his death, and the subject caught the attention of Richard Attenborough, who was responsive to something that promised to be of a stature approaching his enormously successful *Gandhi*.[44] Attenborough needed no special spur to be interested in South Africa. The director is a product of leftwing liberalism, which has a long lineage in British cinema, and for which no apology is needed. Even as British society turned towards the right, anti-apartheid principles remained firm throughout the media.

In the film and theatre unions, there were real penalties against those who broke ranks and went to work in South Africa, which was never the case in the United States. Attenborough has said of his work: 'I'm interested in cinema's ability in narrative form to make a statement, set up a circumstance, question a view, challenge a position. I'm a political animal.' With regard to *Cry Freedom*, he was open about his 'passionate abhorrence and opposition to the repressive regime which presently operates in South Africa'.[45] In his introduction to the publication 'Richard Attenborough's *Cry Freedom*', Attenborough wrote:

> ... *I didn't wish to make a film of despair. In one way Steve Biko's life, ending as and when it did, followed by a sham inquest only held due to pressure ... was a tragedy. Nothing could alter the appalling fact that one of the brightest, most charismatic, intelligent and fascinating men ever born in South Africa was murdered whilst in police custody. But what had developed, due to the publication of Donald's book, was that Steve's life became an inspirational rallying point for black people, not only in his country but throughout the whole of the African continent ...*

I think that it is seriously to be doubted that Donald Woods's *Biko* had that much of an influence on Africans. Inside South Africa, Steve Biko would have been known wherever the black consciousness movement was active, and he became more widely known as a result of his death and the controversy surrounding it, of which Donald Woods's confrontation with the authorities was certainly a part. The book that Woods wrote afterwards probably counted for less inside South Africa, where it was banned. Outside South Africa, it would have had a much wider appeal, although more to European and American readers than to Africans.

Attenborough had already made one film that touched on aspects of racism in South Africa, *Gandhi*. This film includes the formative impact on the young Indian lawyer of his experience in South Africa. The film led to a confrontation with the

---

44   Andrew L. Yarrow (*New York Times*, 27 November 1987) called Attenborough 'a sort of Cecil B De Mille of social change films'. With self-deprecatory humour, Attenborough described himself as '... a sort of aging male Mary Poppins ...' (*Newsweek*, 9 November 1987).

45   *Horizon*, November 1987.

South African authorities, with Attenborough attempting to have it shown only to desegregated audiences in South Africa.

He was not successful. When it came to his new project, Attenborough felt it incumbent on him to visit South Africa to speak with Biko's widow, Ntsiki.

While there, trying unsuccessfully to remain incognito, he also visited Winnie Mandela, which led to an attempt by the South African propaganda machine to inculpate him in 'terrorist activities'. This was done largely through an SABC reporter, Freek Swart, who followed Sir Richard to Winnie Mandela's house of exile in Brandfort, and claimed to have overheard from outside the house the conversation between Sir Richard and Winnie Mandela.

Sir Richard's visit took place in 1984, and I visited the same house a year or so later, and interviewed Mrs Mandela there. It was a small house, and it would be theoretically possible to overhear conversation from the inside if one was standing at an open door. But this presupposes that speakers inside did not go out of their way to disguise what they were saying, even by the simple precaution of lowering their voices.

Freek Swart reported on SABC that

> *(Richard Attenborough) asked Mrs Mandela several times during their conversation for secret addresses where documents could be sent to her from London and also repeatedly referred to Bishop Trevor Huddleston.*[46]

This quotation is taken from a report in the *Rand Daily Mail* of 13 February 1984, which also said that:

> *According to the SABC report, Sir Richard allegedly told Mrs Mandela that he planned to make a film to improve the image of the ANC overseas. The film, he reportedly told her, would be finished by Christmas. Its release would be timed to coincide with protests and strikes in South Africa ...*

In its report on the SABC item, *The Daily News* stated: 'Mr Swart alleges that Sir Richard said he "approved of Russian aid to the ANC"...' That Swart had heard something, and had not fabricated the whole story, is apparent from *The Daily News* interview with the director in England:

> *Angrily pacing his study yesterday, Sir Richard said: 'The reference to the Russians and the ANC is an utter distortion. It was put to me that the ANC had to be kept alive, and if that meant taking money from the Russians, that was the way it would be. I*

---

46   Trevor Huddleston was among the most indefatigable of the anti-apartheid campaigners.

said in the circumstances I could understand that point of view. It is true I asked Mrs Mandela for an address or addresses where I could send mail.

As for the allegation about finishing the film by Christmas to coincide with demonstrations, this is a downright lie. If I do decide to make a film about South Africa, it would simply not be possible to begin filming until some time next year and it would not be ready for release until probably some time in 1986.

Sir Richard said he bitterly resented the smear that he associated himself with violence in South Africa ...

The artless nature of Sir Richard's response, and the fact that he and Winnie Mandela apparently made no attempt to hide their conversation, strongly suggests that they were far from the conspiracy that Swart's report tries to implicate them in. And Swart's contention is clearly compromised by the fact that although the reporter carried out an interview with Sir Richard after he finished his conversation with Mrs Mandela inside the house, he never thought fit to question Sir Richard on camera about the conversation he had just 'overheard'. Perhaps he was too embarrassed to admit he had been eavesdropping.

Sylvia Vollenhoven, in *The Sunday Times* of 5 February 1984, underlines the great fear for the South African political establishment: 'Observers have pointed out that a Biko film on the scale of *Gandhi*, which won eight Oscars, could be a severe blow to South Africa.' *The Star*, a few days later, carried a weird article by Martin Spring, a former editor of *The Citizen*, in which he managed at the same time to dismiss Biko as a 'nonentity' ('Only after his death did the media, the left and the enemies of South Africa, following the pattern of the Nazis with Horst Wessel and the communists with Patrice Lumumba, raise him from obscurity and make him into a martyr ...') and at the same time make him the black leader chosen by the CIA to take over South Africa: '... the South African Minister of Police told me that Biko was "almost certainly the paid agent of a foreign power" and "had more money at his disposal than anyone else in South Africa".'

Martin Spring went on to quote unspecified 'intelligence sources' who suspected that the CIA had 'put so much money and effort behind Biko that, when he died, they were outraged and resolved to unleash a whirlwind of publicity against South Africa in a spirit of revenge'. Although he did not go so far as to suggest that Richard Attenborough's film would also be secretly funded by the CIA, Spring confidently expected it to be financed by 'the Anti-Apartheid Movement, the Defence and Aid Fund, the UN Committee Against Apartheid, or some other similarly disinterested party'.

For all his years as a journalist, including editing the *Financial Gazette*, Spring had clearly never learned that the 20 to 30 million dollar costs of making blockbuster movies like *Gandhi* or *Cry Freedom* were far beyond the coffers of any of the diabolical agencies he mentions.

The Cape Times (14 February 1984) complained that:

> *The vendetta being waged by the SABC against Sir Richard Attenborough is quite disgraceful. One of the world's most respected film directors has been portrayed to the nation as subversive and potentially criminal.*

The tactics used were substantially the same as those used against Lionel Rogosin almost a quarter of a century earlier. In comparing the two cases, what is perhaps most instructive is to see how the communist demons circling the laager had swelled their legions by the addition of the CIA and the anti-apartheid forces of the West.

But while Sir Richard was certainly innocent of plotting the violent overthrow of the white government with Winnie Mandela in her house of exile in the Orange Free State (a house which itself would become victim of an act of terrorist arson about two years later), he was to be accused of insensitivity by some of the very people he truly believed he was helping. Despite the best of intentions, in his interpretation of *Cry Freedom* Attenborough was working against tendencies in the British media towards empowerment for minorities, most notably in Channel Four, of which, ironically enough, Attenborough was Deputy Chairman.[47]

Whatever his inclinations, the director was trapped by the system, and perhaps by a certain ingenuousness. Biko died in 1977; it took some years for his life to become hagiography, and even more years for Attenborough to raise the money to make the film. It took almost a decade after the Soweto uprising for 'Hollywood' to decide that South Africa could be good box-office, and to select among the myriad stories that were being offered. And then, to compound everything, far from being the Steve Biko story, what was settled on was the Donald Woods story.

> *What Hollywood was basically looking for about South Africa, was ... a story that had a major white character, who was a major civil rights or human rights person, and somehow this person's life intertwined with African life, to a great degree, and was an exciting, action-packed story, poignant, moving ... **Cry Freedom** was like that. (Mfundi Vundla, 1991)*

Donald Woods, who had indeed had to make the choice to leave South Africa, was open to the accusation of having cashed in on his relationship with Biko, and of inflating and sensationalising his own role in the anti-apartheid struggle.

---

47   Channel Four embarked on many programmes by and for minorities.

Attenborough was of course free to construct his own script around Biko's life and death, but he elected to go with the Donald Woods version. To tell 'the South African story' predominantly through a white character.

However, the projected film was always known as 'the Biko story', and Attenborough had to insist, defensively, that it had always been the intention for Woods to be the central character. But in that very decision lay an affront. As Mfundi Vundla points out, 'There were whites who were active in the struggle, there's no question about it, you know, but infinitely more blacks were ...'

It was a question of trying to correct a stubborn imbalance, of recognising faces out of the black masses, of doing homage to men and women who had suffered incomparably more than all but a handful of white South Africans. It was a political question because at the time *Cry Freedom* was made, the struggle was ongoing, and there was no end in sight. Most devastating for those who knew what the black consciousness movement had meant was the distortion of its ideology.

Cry Freedom continues the tradition of the Buddy film. Defying racial barriers, Biko and Woods become friends. In one scene, Biko guides Woods through a township, which Woods has never before visited, describing the ills of township life. Biko becomes the white man's mentor, the one who will instruct him in the meaning of the apartheid system. His conscience stirred, Woods becomes the voice of righteousness within the white community. When his buddy dies, Woods carries on the fight alone ...

At surface level, it seems that Woods becomes the willing agent of the fighter against apartheid, transmitting Biko's message to white South Africa while Biko is alive, carrying it to the world when Biko is dead. But it is not so simple. There are multiple mediators: there is the real Biko, whose teachings were absorbed by the real Woods; these in turn were transformed into the screen Biko's teachings, as mediated by the screen Woods, *as interpreted by the scriptwriters and director*. What is left of Biko's message is what the director wanted left, and that could well be not only inadequate, but a distortion.

The effect of *Cry Freedom* is to disarm Biko, to make him non-threatening to whites – but a prophet of black South Africa in the 1970s would have made no impact on his fellows with a simple 'love thy white neighbour' message. That was not how Biko was perceived by his generation, and that was not his message. For Attenborough, the friendship between Biko and Woods becomes a paradigm for a new South Africa. But the paradigm is one which yokes Biko once more with a white man, when the entire thrust of Biko's philosophy was to free blacks from dependence upon whites: 'Black man, you're on your own!'

It was widely recognised by black and white intellectuals alike that Attenborough had betrayed the black consciousness movement in abusing the message of one of its leading spokespersons in this way. Attenborough's defence was to claim that he was not making a film for them: 'I'm not interested in preaching to the converted at all. I want to go to the non-converted, I want to go to people who are indifferent, I want to go to the people who are ignorant, not because they would so wish to be in that state of mind, but because information has simply not been placed in front of them.'

Realistically, after a decade of saturation television coverage of civil unrest in South Africa, there could not have been that many ignorant people left. Information in abundance had been placed in front of millions, nightly. But the information had never been presented in this form before, that is to say, as a Hollywood epic, with wide screen, star actors, a dramatic story. Twenty-one million dollars worth.

Attenborough's zeal was that of the missionary, carrying the anti-apartheid message to the benighted. Because it was presented as a story, 'with human interest', it was accessible to those people bewildered by the intricacies of South Africa's problems. It could touch people emotionally in a way that documentary or news footage usually does not. Recognising the appeal of a Hollywood treatment, the African National Congress gave full backing to Attenborough and to the film. They accepted the film's ambiguities, settling for the public relations advantages. (In this acceptance, there lay an irony: in its beginnings, the black consciousness movement did not always see eye-to-eye with the African National Congress; yet this film could not have been made without their fiat.)

There can be no doubting the passion of Attenborough's commitment. In an interview with John Burns (*New York Times*, 1 November 1987), Attenborough said:

> *Through Biko, I wanted to show what life in South Africa means to blacks, and in certain circumstances what it means to whites. My objective was straightforward – to insure that having seen the movie, nobody will be able to remain indifferent to the situation in South Africa, and to encourage them to stand up and say, 'This is intolerable!'*

The opening scene, of an attack on a squatter camp, succeeds in conveying some of the terror of lives that are subject to random brutality. But then immediately the interest switches to the photographs that have been taken of the raid and the white photographer who took them, and thence to Donald Woods as the newspaper editor selecting the pictures that will be published. And we only arbitrarily return to the black experience.

What is played out on the screen is a kind of rugby match, as segregated as any such match in South Africa at that time, where the ball is the African people. The police can raid the squatter camp, thereby exhibiting their control over black bodies. But when the bodies are turned into photographs – images – the control passes to the white journalist. Control will pass back and forth between the opposing teams, the government and police on one side, the white journalists on the other.

Two-thirds of the way through the film, Biko disappears from the story, and the persecution of Woods takes over. In terms of the film's narrative, it is not far-fetched to say that Biko dies for the glory of Woods, for Woods inherits Biko's 'message', and carries it to the outside world, outwitting the forces of evil to do so. And with the concentration on Woods's exploits, the plight of Africans – 'what life in South Africa means to blacks', to quote Attenborough – disappears from the screen. A white hero displaces a black one, and triumphs where the black one, by dying, signally failed. It perpetuates the image of the African as victim, someone whose fate is in the hands of others.

Other aspects of Biko's life are pre-empted and insidiously incorporated into the martyrisation of Woods. That Woods will in a real sense take over Biko's experience comes when Woods takes the decision to defy the government, and hears Biko's voice: 'In a war, people take great risks ...' In the film's presentation, the threat to Woods overshadows what was the far greater lethal threat to Biko and other blacks. The (standard Hollywood) family of Donald and Wendy Woods and the attack on it blot out the sketches we have of Biko and his wife and child.

The flight of Donald Woods is described in minute detail, and wildly overdramatised, so that it outbalances Biko's death. In recognition of this, Attenborough tries to compensate by means of a flashback. As Woods and his family are flying to freedom, Woods dwells on the culmination of his friendship with Biko, at the time of the Soweto uprising.

This event – which the black consciousness movement certainly influenced – is offered us as the outcome of Biko's teaching. In a telescoping of events that took a year to unfold, we are shown with cinematic licence the shooting down of students by the police. But in an unintended fashion, the true relationship between Woods and the people and the bloodletting is revealed: up in the sky, Woods is above it all, and can fly free (see *Gold!*, *Out of Africa*). There was no such option for blacks in the streets of Soweto below ...

The clumsy attempt by the South African government's propaganda machinery to implicate Sir Richard Attenborough in 'terrorist activities' during his research visit to South Africa had negligible impact overseas. In South Africa itself, it would have invoked the chimeras of an international communist conspiracy directed against the Afrikaner nation, in which a hard core astonishingly still believed. But when the completed film was submitted to the censors in South Africa in 1987, the judgements of a Publications Committee were surprisingly acute and sophisticated, and could even be termed 'liberal'. Here are some of its comments:

> * *The scenes of police violence, bulldozing of a squatter camp at*
> *Crossroads and the shooting at Soweto are horrifying – but of*

limited duration. They do have emotive force but nevertheless would not directly lead or call for violence – there is never a call to violence or revolution – only confrontation.

* *The black people live with intimidation and violence on a daily basis – the scenes of violence shown are everyday facts of life to them – in fact, they would criticise the fact that so much exposure is given to Woods despite his sympathy for their cause.*

* *The present policy of peaceful reform and negotiation, plus power sharing needs to be emphasised as being sincere and ongoing. Despite currently having a state of emergency, the unconditional approval of this film despite its one-sided point of view publicly demonstrates that South Africa is politically mature, unbiased and fair by allowing all points of view for public screening.*

This decision did not satisfy the Minister of Home Affairs, Stoffel Botha, who thereupon directed the Publications Appeal Board, the highest bastion of official censorship, to review the decision of the Publications Committee. In itself, this process was tactical, since it delayed the film's opening; and of course, Minister Botha, simply by turning to the Appeal Board, was signalling to that Board that he expected it to reject the film. The appeal process took a further six months, and as Botha had hoped, the Publications Appeal Board took issue with the lower level Publications Committee:

Although the Board is in agreement with much that the Committee says, it must be pointed out that the Committee seems to have mistaken their (sic) function in so far as the following aspects are concerned: its concern in 'demonstrating that South Africa is politically mature, unbiased and fair by allowing all points of view for public screening' is, of course, commendable, but smacks of policy-making ... such considerations fall outside the ambit of the Committee's task, which is to determine whether the film is 'harmful' to race relations ...

The Appeal Board, headed by Cobus van Rooyen, stuck closer to the letter of its brief, but not unsympathetically so:

Within the context of this film this Board finds that nothing said by the character, Donald Woods, is of such a nature that it might be regarded as an incitement to racial hatred, violence, civil disobedience, and the like. In fact, as the hero of the film, he is portrayed as an advocate of non-violent political change. He initially regards Steve Biko's views as a deplorable exposition of Black racial prejudice, and then, gradually, through discussion with Biko, Woods comes to realise what Biko stands for: confrontation without violence, Black pride and nationalism, justice, equality ... In so far as the security violations of Woods are concerned, they lose prominence since the film shifts into something of an adventure-story. In fact, it would be quite understandable if a substantial number of viewers were to find the film's heavy accent on the actions of Woods, who becomes the hero of the film, questionable or even deplorable in the light of his real role in relation to that of Biko, who, in the eyes of many, is something of a martyr-figure.

Such a reaction against the film and its producer and script-writer is, of course, not undesirable in terms of the Publications Act. In fact, it is likely to neutralise emotions which might otherwise have arisen as a result of the screening of the film.

The paragraphs I have highlighted above seem to reflect a knowledge of the debate that had already arisen outside South Africa regarding the focus of the film, and clearly it hopes for a backlash against Attenborough if the film were to be shown inside South Africa. However, while the Publications Committee plainly accepted that police brutality was a fact, the Appeal Board had a different perspective:

A further aspect – and probably this is one of the more problematic aspects of the film – is the depiction of members of the Security Police and the ordinary police as rather stupid, brutal, and generally despicable. This Board is of the view, however, that ... (t)heir portrayal is so obviously negatively biased that, in our opinion, even a foreigner would realise ... the extent of this ... 'overkill' ...

With some members of the Appeal Board voting against the film, it was passed for viewing by people over 18 years old.

The reason for this relatively benign response from the censorship apparatus to a film that only a little earlier would have been condemned out of hand, came about as the result of a new policy on the part of the authorities. At a time when the government had taken unprecedented steps to control the image of South Africa by muzzling and manipulating the foreign electronic media it was also trying to give the impression of being more tolerant towards expressions of dissent in the arts at home.

The head of the Publications Appeal Board, Professor Cobus van Rooyen, was credited by the *Weekly Mail* with having 'wrought tremendous changes, particularly in greatly broadening what is considered "acceptable" in the arts'.[48] The Board listened sympathetically to both aesthetic and political judgements about *Cry Freedom* from a range of experts. One of these, Professor Pieter Fourie, head of the Department of Communication Sciences at Unisa, rejected the idea that *Cry Freedom* was propaganda, and insisted that it was entertainment. Asked whether it contained factual errors, Fourie acutely invoked the Afrikaner nation's own epics:

> *It is dramatised historical documentary. There can be factual errors in this genre – in the films **The Voortrekkers** and **Ons Bou 'n Nasie**[49] there were factual errors. You must allow space for the director's dramatisation.*

However, this was not the last word. The film opened on 29 July 1988, in thirty theatres throughout the Republic of South Africa. That same day, the film was seized by the police. Police Commissioner General Hendrik de Witt, who had the authority to override the censors, issued a statement saying the film 'endangers the safety of the public, the maintenance of public order, and will delay the end of the State of Emergency imposed in June 1986'.

Minister of Information Stoffel van der Merwe said that the censors were not in a position to judge 'the situation on the streets'. He also stated: 'The security forces are portrayed in such a negative light that their public image would be seriously undermined. Whites are typified as privileged and surrounded by wealth, as opposed to blacks living in great poverty and subjected to exploitation and repression,' which the Minister claimed was not accurate.

Coincidentally or not, there were bomb blasts at two of the theatres where the film opened that day, and threats to others. Such occurrences could have been the act of rightwing terrorists or of government *agents provocateurs* but they did appear to strengthen the wisdom of the Minister's decision to ban the film. *Cry Freedom* was not opened up to debate inside South Africa.

On hearing the news, Attenborough made a threat: '(The American distributors) are furious with the way *Cry Freedom* has been treated ... There is a very real possibility the Motion Picture Association of America will impose a total ban on South Africa.' But there were no serious indications from Hollywood to back up this threat, any more than there had been any response to the petition of Lewis Nkosi's generation thirty years earlier. Cinema was a business, and put economics before politics. South Africa had always been a lucrative market. But I have no

---

48   *Weekly Mail*, 5 August 1988.

49   (sic) The actual title is *Die Bou van 'n Nasie*.

doubt that a ban on the exportation of films to South Africa would have had at least as great an impact on white society in South Africa as did the sports boycott.

Cry Freedom did well in Europe, and indifferently in the United States. Whatever the equivocal nature of its content, it can be claimed to have strengthened the anti-apartheid movement in much the way that Attenborough had intended.[50]

DRY WHITE SEASON (1989)

As a black film-maker, my first responsibility was to make a film about the situation in South Africa. But I wanted to make it from the black point of view. It was impossible, because the people who have got the money here to make films, they are not interested in films with black leads. So I had to look for a solution to circumvent this problem. So I started to look, you know, to read books about South Africa, written by South African writers, and I found that one from André Brink which actually gave me the opportunity to deal with black characters and white characters. So I started in my mind to develop the film, and said, OK, I know exactly what to do with that. (Euzhan Palcy, interview, South Africa Now, 1989)

Euzhan Palcy, a film-maker from the French Antilles, who had made her name with a film called *Sugarcane Alley*, was impelled by similar motives as those of Attenborough, although an additional spur was her blackness. Up to this point, all fiction films about apartheid had been made by whites (with the exception of Gibson Kente's *How Long?*, which was never released). But despite her good intentions, Palcy was under the same Hollywood constraints as Attenborough. There are of course many stories written by black South Africans about black life. Whatever film she would make, it still had to have a white person as the central character, so Palcy had to look among white authors. She chose the novel *A Dry White Season*, by André Brink.

Like Donald Woods's book on Biko, Brink's novel was an exposé. It was fiction, but it was based on Brink's outrage at the reports of deaths in detention in the mid-1970s. The search for the truth undertaken by a simple Afrikaner schoolteacher follows Brink's personal odyssey, the progress of a conscience-

---

50   Some days before the South African censors came through with their surprise
      decision in favour of the film, Thomas Pollack, chairman of Universal Picture
      Group, in an ecstasy of philanthropy not common in Hollywood, offered to donate
      all profits from the film's distribution in South Africa to the United Nations
      Children's Fund for southern Africa relief, if the film was allowed. By the time the
      film was permitted several years later, this offer appeared to have been forgotten.

stricken Afrikaner through the society that formed him. Brink's refusal to accept the sanctimonious lies of apartheid placed him outside the laager:

> *When an English(-language) writer, Nadine Gordimer or whoever, attacked apartheid, it was mainly greeted with a shrug 'What else can you expect from the English?' And even more so when it came from a black author. But when an Afrikaner, who through his language culture belonged to the power establishment in the country, attacked the whole system by which the country lived, that was regarded as the most treacherous act of all. Real back-stabbing .... (André Brink, interview, 1990)*

His writing made him a renegade, subject to threats and police searches, censorship and confiscation of his writing. The experience was undeniably harrowing. And since Brink chose to stay on in his own country, the harassment was longer-lasting than that of Woods.

Both *Cry Freedom* and *Dry White Season* revolve around the writing and hiding of a manuscript. This manuscript contains unpleasant truths about the regime which, it is assumed, will affect public opinion abroad and in some way undermine that regime. What is unsettling about this formula is that it places this power in the hands of righteous white men – Donald Woods, Ben du Toit (the hero of *Dry White Season*) – to the exclusion of blacks. Why cannot blacks gather and pass on these facts? There is, unfortunately, a vexing truth in this presentation.

Indeed there were blacks who had all kinds of information damning to apartheid to pass on, just as there were dozens of African journalists who, like Woods, were forced into exile. But the majority of these Africans had to make out as best they could in African countries – they were not whisked away to fame in the West. Those who controlled the media in the West trusted and dealt with those they perceived to share their values.

This meant not only that black pain was mediated through middle class whites, but that there was a certain appropriation of that pain: in fiction form, with the murder of Ben du Toit and in the account of Donald Woods (in *Cry Freedom*), where at certain points in the film a parallel is drawn between Woods's current experience and what Biko had to endure. (For example, when Woods first undergoes house arrest, he hears the voice of Biko, now dead, reminiscing about his own experience of 'police just across the road'.)

Interestingly enough, there is a scene in *Dry White Season* where the well-meaning Ben du Toit (Donald Sutherland) tries to draw parallels between his own life and that of an African, and Stanley, the taxi-driver (Zakes Mokae), demarcates a well-defined line between them:

> *Du Toit: Then you're Zulu ...*

Stanley: Zulu, Xhosa, Sotho. I'm African, that's all.

Du Toit: Me too. My father had a farm. I grew up like any African boy, in the bush. Ate African porridge, no shoes except –

*Stanley: Bad food … no vote … carry pass-book … Careful, lani.*51

The novel *A Dry White Season* is filled with victims, mostly black, but including the Afrikaans schoolteacher, Ben du Toit. When she came to adapt the novel to the screen, Palcy rejected the black-as-victim image, and built up one of the African characters, the taxi-driver Stanley, into the embodiment of the resistance.

In scenes reminiscent of *Cry Freedom*, Stanley becomes Ben du Toit's mentor, the one who introduces the Afrikaner to the township and to African life. But unlike Biko in Attenborough's film, Stanley does not go under. In a major alteration to Brink's novel, Palcy makes Stanley the agent of revenge, when he shoots the sinister officer from state security. Palcy's Stanley does not need anyone else to act for him. Brink had no hand in the filmscript, and knew nothing about the changed ending:

> *By the time the film was made, there had been quite a number of books, articles and films and so on, in which every single time the protagonist who fights against apartheid gets killed or becomes a victim of the struggle. And she felt, perhaps rightly, that this might gradually convey the message, 'Don't rock the boat, because you can only end up a victim.' So she wanted to show that in at least some respects it was possible to beat the system. I don't altogether agree with the specific choice she made, it was a bit too glib. (Interview, 1990)*

Researching her film, Palcy had visited South Africa. 'What I discovered, what I saw with my eyes, what I heard, I think that made me just enraged' (*South Africa Now*, 1989). Out of this rage, the rage of a black person, came her solution: primitive justice out of the barrel of a gun. It is the familiar Hollywood ending, even if it does seem to empower blacks.

While it is possible to count ticket sales with a degree of accuracy, and even to chart television viewing (all the major anti-apartheid films reached television eventually), it is impossible to gauge the *political* impact of these works on the general public, and upon their governments. I have no reservations about believing that newsreel coverage of South Africa was a vital threat to apartheid, a belief demonstrably shared by the South African government. Writing at the time of the release of *Cry Freedom* in the United States at the end of 1987, the *New York Times*

---

51   Translatable as 'whitey'.

correspondent John Burns, who had reported from South Africa for a number of years, opined:

> *For those who believe that economic sanctions and divestment can hasten the end of apartheid, the film comes at an important juncture. Censorship has drastically reduced the flow of information about what Mr. Vorster ... described (to me) as 'the derogatory aspects of South African society.' It is one of the few successes that the Pretoria Government has been able to claim in recent years, and opponents of the racial system outside South Africa are worried that the world's attention may falter.* (**New York Times**, *1 November 1987)*[52]

Apartheid did indeed fall. It fell after *Cry Freedom, A World Apart, Dry White Season*, and *Mapantsula.* But to claim that apartheid fell *because* of them would be outrageous. They certainly performed a function, on one level that of 'propaganda', as Sir Richard Attenborough unabashedly confessed with regard to *Cry Freedom*. (This does not mean that they could not also be regarded as works of art.)

Cinema also has certain advantages over reportage, notably of being packaged in story form, and having characters embodied by stars; it could also do what newsreel and documentary cameras signally could not do: show us the interrogation rooms and torture chambers of the Special Branch and of the police.

But by the time Hollywood got around to making these films, the battle had already been won. The day that financiers decided that a state that insisted on apartheid was not a good investment was the day that apartheid was doomed, and no sleight of image by the government would change that.

That decision was made by the mid-1980s, and Hollywood's contribution came too late to do much more than throw some more soil on the coffin. Just as well: on the whole, the public's response to the anti-apartheid films was disappointing, deflating Hollywood's interest.

The coming of democracy to South Africa does not necessarily mean the end of the Buddy genre – in fact, there might be an even greater need for it – but certainly it will change.[53]

---

52 It is worth noting that in this same article ('Film is the Weapon, Apartheid the Target') John Burns described the African National Congress as 'an organisation long committed to violence' – which paralleled the South African government's claim that the ANC was a terrorist organisation, and revealed his position on South Africa.

53 How drastically can be seen in the post-apartheid comedy of cartoon-level sadism, *There's a Zulu on my Stoep*, which pits a black and white duo against neo-Nazis, and even has them swapping race.

THE POWER OF ONE (1992)

Perversely, the last of the apartheid era Buddy films proved to be a curious and offensive throwback to paternalist ideology – although it poses as a plea for inter-racial co-operation. This was John Avildsen's *The Power of One*. Avildsen had directed the enormously successful *Rocky* and *The Karate Kid*, formula films about beating the odds. While *Rocky* only takes on the world heavyweight champion, *The Power of One*'s hero, PK, takes on apartheid.

It must be admitted that *The Power of One* is an extremely well-made film; but its plot and characterisation are fatuous and simplistic. Based on a novel by Bryce Courtenay, it is the story of an English-speaking South African who is orphaned and sent to an Afrikaans boarding-school. There, he comes across a bigoted Afrikaner dominee who preaches virulent race hatred against Africans and English, urging the school to 'rise up and push out the English, and put down the black'. Encouraged by this, the school bully, Jaapie Botha, begins a persecution of PK, which starts with a group of boys urinating on the defenceless child, and then dubbing him '*pisskop*'. On a visit home when his mother dies, PK tells his Zulu nanny about the persecution at school, and she summons the medicine man, who endows PK with absolute courage. Later on, with the declaration of war against Germany, the Afrikaans youth, in an orgy of Nazi fervour, string little PK up by his heels for bully Botha to use as a target for his sling-shot. But this is too much even for the English-hating school authorities, and Botha is dismissed from the school.

PK is taken in by his grandfather who, having no rapport with children, passes the task of taking care of PK to a pacifist German refugee, Doc, a succulent-loving musician. (If the cactus is a significant symbol, it escapes me.)

However, as an alien during World War II, Doc is interned in a prison for Africans. (The plot is filled with unlikelihoods like this.) PK is still allowed to visit him for piano lessons, and there he strikes up a friendship with a black prisoner, Geel Piet. Piet teaches PK to box, but cannot defend himself against the attentions of a sadistic guard. Because PK speaks African languages, and treats everyone equally, Geel Piet dubs PK an *inyanga*, here translated as 'Rainmaker'. When PK questions Piet about the respect that is rendered to him by the other prisoners, Piet tells him that they perceive him as the one who 'stops the conflict, brings the rain, brings the peace'. Piet tells him that this 'myth is as old as Africa'.

Doc, as musician, is asked by the prison commandant to organise a concert for a visiting dignitary, and PK, Geel Piet and Doc use this as an opportunity to get back at the guards. PK moulds the various quarrelling ethnic groups of the prison into a unified choir, and writes a subversive Zulu lyric for them:

> *They (guards) run this way,*
> *They run that way,*

> *They are confused,*
> *They are cowards.*

On the evening of the concert, this is sung to the uncomprehending guards and guests. However, the sadistic warder waylays Geel Piet on his way to the concert, and beats him so savagely that Piet reveals the meaning of the lyrics before he collapses. Piet dies in the arms of 'little *baas*', telling him of his accomplishment in bringing 'all tribes together first time, because of you – Rainmaker ...'

PK goes on to an English-speaking school, where in contrast to the Afrikaans school, it is taught by the headmaster that 'inclusion, not exclusion, gentlemen, is the clue to survival'. PK has success with boxing, and meets a girl who happens to be the daughter of an Afrikaner academic (played by Marius Weyers), an apartheid theorist. In defiance of the law, PK fights an African in Alexandra township, where upon his victory, he is hailed by his defeated opponent as 'the Rainmaker'. This African, Gideon Duma, sets out to exploit the myth, and persuades PK to run classes to train African teachers.

The bully Jaapie Botha, PK's old nemesis from boarding school, turns up again. He is now a police sergeant with ample opportunity to indulge his sadistic bent. The Man You Love To Hate beats up Gideon Duma, blinding him in one eye; burns the mixed-race gym where PK trains; breaks up the teacher-training class, during which raid a policeman kills PK's girlfriend with a blow to the head; and finally, Botha, looking for PK, takes part in a police assault on Alexandra township, where there is indiscriminate killing and brutality.

After a final man-to-man showdown between Jaapie and PK, which PK wins, Jaapie, when he reaches for his gun, is despatched by Gideon. This accumulation of horrors convinces PK to give up his scholarship to Oxford in order to stay on and fight apartheid in his own country; silhouetted against a massive setting sun, PK leaves with Gideon to bring education to the masses ...

It is the kind of plot that makes you feel sorry even for the Afrikaner prison-guards and policemen, so crudely are they drawn. The demonisation of Afrikaners becomes caricature – there is a passing reference to the fact that racial separation was introduced by the English, but in the film, English South Africans are overwhelmingly liberal. But it is the depiction of Africans and of Africa that is most disturbing. To a far greater extent even than *Cry Freedom*, *The Power of One* disempowers Africans. The film ends with a moralistic, even political, homily:

> *In South Africa and around the world the struggle to gain human rights for all people continues.*
>
> *Changes can come from the power of many, but only when the many come together to form that which is invincible – the power of one.*

Applied to South Africa, this can only be read as a plea for unity of all the disparate African peoples, together with whites (although maybe the beastly Afrikaners are excluded). There is nothing wrong with this; indeed, the search for such unity among African peoples has been the great challenge of this century. But it is profoundly insulting to make the great unifier a white man with mystical powers of healing – 'the Rainmaker'.

To see how this comes about in the film we have to look at the way in which the central character, PK, is Africanised. His father is already dead when he is born, and he comes into a family that consists of his natural white mother, and a nanny. There seems to be no racial barrier between mother and nanny, scarcely a mistress/servant relationship. In an astonishing scene, the baby PK is shown being suckled by his nanny, who then picks up her own baby and suckles it.

The scene is astonishing not because this was something uncommon, but precisely the opposite – it was so common as to be mundane – and yet I had never seen it on film before. It was the custom in thousands of white families to have a black wetnurse, and yet this most intimate of all relationships has been suppressed in cinema, just as it was repressed in real life, with consequences that can only be conjectured. Unfortunately, what is audacious in *The Power of One* is undermined by the motive for depicting it, which is to identify PK with a mystical Africa.

First he has access to Africa through the body of his nanny. She also teaches him Zulu; later, when he suffers at school, this same nanny ('like any good African mother', since his own mother is now dead) heals him by having him treated by Dabola Manzi, an *inyanga*, or medicine man, who endows him with extraordinary courage. Through the naturalist refugee Doc, he is instructed in African nature; Geel Piet, the black prisoner, recognises the power that the *inyanga* has placed in 'little *baas*', and adores him as a messiah for Africa, which conviction is readily accepted by the other prisoners, and later by PK's boxing opponent Gideon Duma and the people of Alexandra.

The reiterated theme of the film is that it is PK's mission, the mission of a *white youth*, to lead the tribes to 'freedom through unity'. (At the prison concert, he appeals to the assembled prisoners 'Tonight let us be one under the African sky'.)

Only Hollywood would not be able to recognise the demeaning nature of this theme to a people that had been fighting for human rights throughout this century; but the naivety of Hollywood knows no bounds. No doubt the makers of the film had the best of intentions, but in the end, the people of Alexandra look suspiciously like the superstitious tribe of Jamie Uys's *Dingaka*, lost and looking for a leader. The plea for unity at the end of the film becomes a mockery when what we have been offered is the story of a white hero who, Rocky-like, triumphs over adversity as an individual, and not as part of a group.

To the viewer, the 'One' of the title is clearly PK, and not some vague incipient African nation. PK's African friends – his nanny, the prisoner Geel Piet, and finally

Gideon Duma, with whom he sets out to overcome apartheid – appear more as throwbacks to the Faithful Servant persona whose function is to inflate the central white hero rather than as characters with an independent existence.

The Buddy films – *Dingaka, Gold, The Wilby Conspiracy, The Gods Must be Crazy, Cry Freedom, Dry White Season, The Power of One* – all depict some kind of co-operation between black and white, directed towards a common goal. In the anti-apartheid films, the goal is the destruction of apartheid. This is not the case in Uys's films, which on the one hand pretend that apartheid does not exist, and on the other, that there is a greater evil, which is black political power. The anti-apartheid films also require that the black hero becomes the mentor and teacher of the white hero – and through him, the audience viewing the film.

These elements reflect the concerns of the film-makers (scriptwriters, directors, producers). They also reflect the current of the times. They also, even while the struggle against apartheid was going on, projected a time beyond that struggle when black/white co-operation, as opposed to confrontation, would be essential. But that was still a white point of view; supposing blacks did not see it as essential?

BEYOND BUDDYHOOD: MAPANTSULA (1987)

The most interesting of the South African films to come out of the 1980s was one that should not have been made at all. *Mapantsula* was shot inside South Africa, and it involved deceiving the censoring authorities. It was low-budget, shot during the State of Emergency. It was not a Buddy genre film, and yet it did involve close trans-racial co-operation. It was made under enormous difficulties, but compared to the Hollywood productions, it was completed relatively quickly.

Oliver Schmitz was a young film editor who was working in alternative film-making in Johannesburg in the mid-1980s when he decided to leave South Africa for a while to work for German television. Abroad, he saw newsreels that would have been censored in his own country, so he had access to images of protest he would not have seen at home.

> *When I was in Germany, the only thing I saw from South Africa were those kind of scenes on television. So one of the prime motivations in my mind in starting the project was looking at that footage on television and thinking, Well, what is it like to be one of those people, what if one takes the life story of one of those people out of the crowd and looks at it in detail ... (Oliver Schmitz, interview, 1989)*

This concept fused with an idea that Schmitz had had earlier about a township gangster, on which he had shot a Super-8 featurette with an actor, Thomas Mogotlane. Mogotlane credits the black films that had been made – *Jim Comes to Jo'burg, Magic Garden* – and actors who had appeared in them, like Thomas Ramokgopa, who was his acting teacher, as his inspiration:

> *... they broke the way, because now we could take much interest from seeing them acting and seeing them on stage, and we said to ourselves, We can do this too ... (Interview, 1990)*

Mogotlane worked with Gibson Kente on his play *How Long?* which was banned for its anti-apartheid content. When Kente decided to turn the play into a film, he asked Mogotlane to help him write it. They wanted to shoot the black-financed film in Soweto, but this was 1976, the time of the uprising, and because of the police presence they had to move to a township hundreds of miles away. Gibson Kente was detained before the film was completed, and it was finished by his assistant, Ben Moyi. However, the police seized the film. Besides Kente, Mogotlane and others who had worked on it were detained for three months without charge.

After that, Mogotlane worked for Heyns Films in Johannesburg, on educational films which he translated into African languages. Through Robyn Hofmeyr, a woman who worked there and encouraged him to try writing his own scripts, he met Oliver Schmitz in 1983.

> *We talked lengthily about film-making, and I told him, Look, I've never written a film before, and I don't know how they are written, but I have an idea of how to write and to act and all that. And he said, OK. I'll give you books. You read books, and as long as you have the story in your head, put it right. Then you've got a script. And we can shoot it and make a film.*
> *(Thomas Mogotlane, interview, 1990)*

He wrote the script for the half-hour film that Schmitz regarded as the pilot for *Mapantsula*. When Schmitz was in Europe, he succeeded in raising money for a more ambitious production, again encouraging Mogotlane to write the script.

They developed the story around the character of a township gangster. In a culture of repressive laws, the outlaw has a special eminence. 'The gangster ... was this debonair figure, you know, had all the girls, maybe had money, but what struck you was that he didn't have to work for the white man ...' (Mfundi Vundla, interview, 1991)

There is a parallel in the ghettos of American cities, where, because of chronic unemployment and barriers to advancement, the drug-lord is one of the few entrepreneurial success stories. As a result, he is surrounded with glamour, and becomes a role-model for black youth.

As Oliver Schmitz points out, black society in South Africa had been criminalised by the laws that governed it – in order to survive, an African had to break them, whether by moving to a place where he or she should not be, or by looking for work illegally.

Because the laws were myriad, the breaking of them was inevitable. So there was no special stigma attached to those who broke the laws professionally. There was even a kind of toleration on the part of the police, because gangsters could often be used to spy on apartheid's enemies, the political activists. Gangsters could be persuaded to do this for money, or to avoid a prison sentence. Few of the gangsters had any political convictions.

Mapantsula is about a gangster who finds himself in just such a situation. Caught up in a demonstration, he is captured along with the protesters, and jailed with them. In jail, he is offered his freedom if he will identify some of the protesters.

The strength of the film lies in its presentation of township life and in the life of the *mapantsula*, or petty gangster, played by Mogotlane. Mogotlane directed the actors, as well as co-writing the script, and his own acting is a *tour de force*. The character he created, the gangster Panic, is an existential anti-hero, who preys on the white community:

> *... though you may not know politics much, but you know where the money comes from. Like most of the people tell you that, 'Hey, look. If you want to get money, go to the white man – he has money. Go to town and steal in town.' (Mogotlane)*

Panic picks the pocket of a white businessman on the open street, and instead of running away, leans up against a shop-front and coolly counts the money he has stolen in front of his victim, who is too terrified by the knife gripped in Panic's teeth to do anything. The scenes of Panic's picaresque life, whether visiting a nightclub, stealing or being bawled out by his landlady (Dolly Rathebe making a comeback to films after almost forty years) impress as being quite authentic. The anti-apartheid activists, on the other hand, seem somewhat wooden, over-idealised. And the denouement, where Panic refuses to give in to police pressure and betray his friends, does not seem convincingly motivated.

At the time of our interview with Oliver Schmitz in 1989, apartheid was under siege, but showed no signs of crumbling. Schmitz had considered the role of the gangsters in the struggle: '... there are a lot of gangsters, and what is interesting is their defiance, their open defiance to the society, it's just that it's a defiance that is non-political, and many people have asked themselves this question, What would happen if those gangsters actually became politicised?' This never happened to any significant degree; on the contrary, what did happen was the descent into thuggery of political youth groups of different persuasions, who terrorised many of the townships, to police indifference, or even acquiescence.

Oliver Schmitz acknowledges a comparison between Panic's experience and his own:

> *In one sense the story is about a gangster, but I see it as a story about myself as well, really, in terms of the deviance of the character. And in his politicisation, I see partly the process that I have gone through or am going through as well. And especially if you don't initially know what's wrong with your society, but you know something's wrong, and you want to do something about it, you start behaving in deviant ways ... (Interview, 1989)*

What Schmitz is describing is the position of the artist as social critic and hence as outsider. The comparison between outlaw and artist is one that is often made, not least by artists themselves. In South Africa, this comparison was facilitated by the nature of apartheid ideology itself, which saw criticism as anti-social, and determined to punish it, either openly, through censorship, or covertly by intimidation.

Both kinds of onslaught fell most heavily upon the black population, of course, but it was usually the attacks on white writers that drew international attention. It was well understood by both pro- and anti-apartheid forces that in a society like South Africa, art was subversive.

Boundaries between art and propaganda, never very clear, began to dissolve. And, typical of our times, where all forms of communication merge and interact, news reportage became fodder for cinema. *Cry Freedom* had drawn on newsreels as the inspiration for some of its scenes. In *Mapantsula*, Oliver Schmitz, as an editor of documentary, deliberately set out to imitate clips from newsreels when he recreated confrontations between protesters and police: '... before we shot the stuff, I put together a whole lot of news footage, and we watched it, and we talked about it, and it influenced to quite a large degree how we finally resolved those scenes ...'

Schmitz also wanted to bring out how the police were actually using newsreel footage – whether shot by their own Betacam crews or confiscated – to incriminate the protesters. Panic's moment of temptation comes when he is asked to identify protesters on a police television monitor.

The importance of *Mapantsula* lies in its breaking free of the Buddy genre. In *Cry Freedom, Dry White Season, A World Apart* and *The Power of One*, the black characters exist to a large degree to boost the central white character. They are adjuncts who are befriended by the white hero or heroine, and whose chief function is to reflect the humanity of the white protagonist. This is the case even when the latter seems to be acting on behalf of blacks by becoming in some way their champion.

So in the end, the black characters are variations of the Faithful Servant, however well-rounded they appear to be, and there has been no progress since the beginning of the century – indeed, however much of a caricature D W Griffith's Zulu Chief from 1908 appears to be, there is no doubt that he is the central figure, and the threatened white mother and child are recipients of his magnanimity.

Panic stands alone. Where whites appear, they are either his prey, or the police, who threaten him. Unlike black characters in the other films, Panic is conceived from the inside, not the outside. He is not so much observed as experienced, in a way that only a very few white writers are capable of.

All the other films had been written by whites. Thomas Mogotlane was offered a rare opportunity:

> *So I felt that now, it will be wonderful writing something about myself, writing something about my situation, about my people, which would be authentic and true. Down to the point. Not to let somebody write something about me, meantime, meanwhile, he doesn't know me, anything about me.*

By 'me', Mogotlane means 'blacks', and the common African experience.

Mapantsula came into being as the result of a number of deceptions perpetrated on the authorities. The phoney script that was offered to the censors was about a gangster, but with the political aspects omitted. The bait for the authorities was that it appeared to fit into a genre of black gangster films encouraged by the powers-that-be for their own political purposes.

The system of film-making by caste – whereby there was Afrikaans cinema, English cinema, and African cinema – had come about because of the Nationalist desire to nurture an Afrikaans film industry. Since an Afrikaans film industry could exist in no other way, they had to subsidise it heavily. But by the tortured logic of apartheid, which claimed to be separate but equal, they had also to pay for English- and African-language films. (The African-language films were in fact a hidden bonus to Afrikaner film-makers since – to a large degree – they supplied the producers, directors and technicians, with Africans restricted largely to acting roles.)

White, often neophyte, film-makers churned out films for Africans in much the same way as the pioneers of the film industry had done in New York and Los Angeles, working very low-budget, with a film ratio as close to one-to-one as they could get. Like the D W Griffith of Biograph days, they could shoot and edit a film in a week. Subjects that proved to be enduringly popular with their African audience were sports and gangsters. The black heroes they offered were able at times to overcome the awfulness of the craft exhibited and reach an audience otherwise saturated with white stories. The authorities were convinced that these pulp films, totally devoid of political content or social awareness, were pabulum for the masses. Oliver Schmitz and producer Max Montocchio were able to exploit this for their own ends when they offered the dummy script for *Mapantsula*.

But while it was possible to hoodwink the authorities at the script stage, and even after shooting present a version that was not the final edit, there was no way of circumventing the censors when seeking distribution inside South Africa. The final version, in all its political nakedness, was what had to be submitted. *Mapantsula*, which proved quite successful outside South Africa both on television and in art theatres, met with the following objections from the South African censors (certain words are emphasised in the original):

> * Although **one-sidedness** is not sufficient to find a film
>   undesirable, the blatancy with which this line is followed in
>   **Mapantsula**, is an aggravating factor...

> * The **propagandistic tendency** of the film is not suitable to
>   viewers in a country where emergency regulations have to be
>   enforced.

> * The film has the power to **incite** probable viewers to act
>   violently.

> * **Friction** between **blacks** and **whites** (employer and employee)
>   can result if this film is approved for general release.

> * The provocation which the **police** had to bear, is conveniently
>   set aside. But their action against riotous mobs is portrayed in a
>   manner which will generate further hatred against the security
>   forces ...Confrontation with the police is encouraged.

> * The effective closing scene communicates a clear message to the
>   viewer: refuse co-operation with the authorities and side with the
>   rebellious elements in black society. Thereby the state becomes
>   powerless to act against subversive organisations.

The preceding judgements were followed by comments that concisely outline the dilemma facing the guardians of the totalitarian system that constituted apartheid South Africa when they wished to appear enlightened:

> ... The mere fact that many people might find the confrontation
> between the police and the rioting blacks in poor taste is not
> sufficient reason for declaring the film undesirable. It is important
> to decide whether the screening of this film is likely to provide or
> contribute to sedition. Should the scenes portraying riots, together
> with the singing of freedom songs and the shouting of slogans be
> regarded as contributing towards a sense of hate for the police or
> should the scenes simply be regarded as informative as, for
> example, a news item would be? Another question which must also

be posed in the present matter is whether the confrontation portrayed between the police-force (which in the riot scenes is mainly white) and the blacks would not be harmful to the relations between black and white.

The main issue in the present matter is therefore whether the bounds of the merely informative are transgressed and that the material is presented in an inciting or provocative fashion ...

We believe that hate for the white man, as represented by the white police and 'Pretoria' is likely to increase within the minds of a substantial number of likely viewers of this film as a result of ... viewing the action portrayed during the rioting. We do not, however, believe that this means that all the scenes of rioting ... should be cut, but that certain careful excisions would neutralise any provocative effect which the scenes could otherwise have. The same difficulty comes to the fore during the interrogation of Panic by the Security Police. Although aspects of the interrogation as well as the obvious third-degree are not undesirable, we believe that the relations between black and white would be affected detrimentally when the bounds are overstepped by the Police and Panic is held at the window. The same can be said to apply when the detective says that Panic's death could be arranged straight away.

The censors were writing this in 1988; it appears that the methods of the police were by that time so indisputably notorious that even the censors saw no point in claiming that this was not the way the police behaved:

The Board in no manner denies that these scenes could take place in real life but that is not our task. What we are required to establish is whether the scenes as portrayed would be provocative or inciting.

Subject to cuts being made, the film was passed for audiences over 18 years old, and in theatres of not more than 200 seats. Oddly enough, the film was passed for *video* distribution: the censors believed that 'The large screen amplifies the dangerous political effects the film could have on probable viewers in this country.' The censors retained the same age restriction on the video – how they imagined this could ever be enforced is a mystery. *Mapantsula* was finally passed for general distribution in uncut form in 1992. When it was opened by Ster-Kinekor in December of that year, it did not do well. Part of the reason for this may have been South African distributors' lack of experience in catering to an African audience.

Buddies against the law

Right: A black convict and a white lawyer overthrow a tribal tyrant. Ken Gampu in *Dingaka*, 1964.
Below: The noble African who sacrifices his life for his white buddy – and the mine. Simon Sabela in *Gold*, 1974.

Above right: The black freedom fighter who teams up with a white man to escape the Bureau of State Security. Sidney Poitier and Michael Caine in *The Wilby Conspiracy*, 1975.
Right: The surviving white buddy takes over the heroism of the black. Kevin Kline and Denzil Washington in *Cry Freedom*, 1987.

Jamie Uys

Villon Collection

Marnie Arch Productio
Photograph: Frank Conn

The bushman as Noble Savage. *The Gods Must be Crazy*, 1983.

 *Evolution of the Black Hero*

Above: Domestication of the savage; the Zulu warrior becomes a nanny. *De Voortrekkers*, 1916.

Below: Africans with human emotions; the Zulu lovers in *Symbol of Sacrifice*, 1918.

Erica Rutherford

A fable entirely about
Africans. Daniel
Adnewmah in *Jim Comes
to Jo'burg*, 1949.

Museum of Modern Art

Africans trapped in
tragic circumstances
beyond their control.
Sidney Poitier and
Canada Lee in *Cry,
the Beloved Country*,
1951.

Lionel Rogosin

The first politically
aware Africans on
film. Can Themba
and Bloke Modisane
in *Come Back,
Africa*, 1960.

As predator (left) or as victim (below), 'Panic' stands alone. Thomas Mogotlane in *Mapantsula*, 1988.

'Zooluology'

> *Zooluology: the white myth of the Zulu; the equation of the Zulus with
> the wild animals of Africa; the domestication of these creatures; the
> Zulus as the prototypical 'African tribe'; the political uses of the Zulu
> image.*[54]

THE ZULU'S HEART (1908)

The importance of this film by D W Griffith in laying down the negative/positive
image of the African as either the Savage Other or the Faithful Servant has
already been described. Why Griffith chose Zulus for his subject is not known –
it might have been something as artless as the fact that since they were believed
to go around half-naked, Biograph, which operated on a shoestring, did not have
to pay for costumes to be made. It is likely that Griffith had never seen a Zulu in
his life, unless he had seen some travelling circus or music-hall act.

But Zulus were already well-established as part of the mythology of Africa,
through the literature of empire writers such as H Rider Haggard, among others, as
well as copious newspaper accounts of British and Boer battles with the Zulu
nation during the second half of the nineteenth century, and as recently as the
Bambata Rebellion of 1906. So Griffith could have been well acquainted with the
Zulu legend, which principally made of them a ferocious warrior people.

The Boer family in its covered wagon in The Zulu's Heart, with its resonances of
America's own highly mythologised pioneer history, automatically appealed to an
audience raised on Manifest Destiny. The white nuclear family, struggling against
savages in an alien landscape, is a dominant image of the westward expansion. (The
threatened family unit – whether threatened by Indians, psychopaths, communists,
thugs or aliens – is a perennial theme in American cinema.)

The very frailty of the little white group implies that any attack upon it must be
dastardly. But when you multiply that covered wagon by thousands, with perhaps a
cavalry or an army to back it up, but certainly with superior weaponry, it is placed
rather more accurately in the historical panorama.

As presented in the cinema, the image of the lumbering covered wagon and its
apparently vulnerable white family masks the invasion and seizure of land belonging to
others, justifying that invasion by presenting the rightful inhabitants as savages. (This
was standard practice in the literature of colonisation. Caliban, of Shakespeare's The
Tempest, is a notorious example of the indigenous inhabitant who is deprived of his
land – the island – and enslaved, and yet for whom we have no sympathy.)

Griffith was suffused with this ethnocentric sensibility, a trait so pervasive in
European and American civilisation that *The Zulu's Heart* was but the first
example of a racist mindset that has dominated films about Africa ever since.

---

54 My own definition.

RASTUS IN ZULULAND (1910)

In a bizarre, almost grotesque, fashion, a short film made some two years after *The Zulu's Heart* fused American prejudices concerning African-Americans with those concerning Africans. The producer Siegmund Lubin, under the aegis of Pathe Freres of Jersey City, had made a Sambo series of all-black comedies. This proved so successful that between 1909 and 1911 he created a second series built around the character Rastus. Films like *How Rastus got his Turkey, How Rastus got his Pork-chop* and *Chicken Thief*, portray a shiftless, feckless n'er-do-well who is always getting himself into a scrape. The series includes *Rastus In Zululand*.

Unlike the Zulu chief in *The Zulu's Heart*, the lead is not played by a white man in blackface, but by an African-American – this may be partly because Rastus is a comic character, a buffoon. In this demeaning role an African-American could make it onto the screen. The Rastus series is essentially a vehicle for mocking 'darkies' as a way of asserting racial superiority.

The publicity for *Rastus In Zululand* describes Rastus as 'an odd-jobs man, that is, he does odd jobs when he has to, but when there are a few small coins in his pocket, prefers to sleep'. Rastus takes a nap on a bench, and is shanghaied by three white men, who force him on board a ship, to become part of the crew. They are shipwrecked off the coast of Africa, and Rastus manages to swim ashore. He is spotted by spear-toting natives, and carried off to a Zulu village, where, still wearing his navy ducks, he is prepared for the cooking-pot. But his appearance charms the daughter of the chief, a fat and ugly damsel, who wants to marry him. The Zulu chief then offers Rastus the choice of the cooking-pot, or his daughter. Rastus chooses the cooking-pot. Before he comes to the boil, however, he is awakened by a policeman – it has all been a dream …

The plot emphasises the status of the African-American as victim, but this is a matter for derision rather than sympathy. In the dream, he is prey for the seamen, then for the Zulus, then for the Zulu woman, and finally, he is prey to the authority figure of the policeman, who wants him to move on.

The uniqueness of this particular Rastus episode lies in the unconscious irony that permeates the film. When Rastus is shanghaied, he is forced back into slavery, to undergo a Middle Passage in reverse, in an involuntary back-to-Africa experience – but far from this being a joyful return, it is a painful one. He receives no mercy from his brethren there, who are cannibals. He is even more victimised in Africa than in America – at least in America they only want to enslave him, not eat him. The comic punch is that he considers marriage to an ugly woman a fate worse than death. The film invites us to rejoice at his helplessness, at the sight of his knees quaking in fear, even though he does come out unscathed in the end.

But why was it necessary for the American film-maker, fifty years after emancipation, to scapegoat the black minority through the figure of Rastus – for the invitation to mock Rastus is an invitation to mock all of his race? What were the fears inspired by a segment of the population that was still virtually powerless in a country that harboured it only grudgingly? Was it the nagging anxiety that those you have harmed may one day seek revenge? It may be relevant that the period from 1890 to 1920, the time during which *Rastus in Zululand* and *Birth of a Nation* were made, was the peak period of lynchings recorded in America.

White South Africa's fears of a black uprising were more justified. Even in defeat, Africans would not cease to be rivals for the land of South Africa, and this was an ever-present chimera. (In contrast, in the United States, a policy of what amounted virtually to genocide was carried out against indigenous peoples, and when this was all too successful, it became possible to regard them sentimentally as the Vanishing Race.)

In South Africa, the very real presence of the native population demanded that the ritual of exorcism be constantly repeated. Saturated with a common racism, the films that came out of South Africa's own indigenous film industry were to prove close in spirit to those produced outside the country, but purporting to portray South Africa. The celebration of white supremacy, especially the conquest of inferior breeds, infused the art of the west during the age of empire, and endures beyond that era. (Many films about Vietnam want to deny the fact of American defeat.) Cinema's South Africa was a fictional territory filled with dangerous savages that had to be quelled – in a word: Zulus!

If asked to name one African tribe, almost anyone would come up with the reply, as did Griffith and Lubin, of Zulus. The image of the spear-wielding warrior that is part of everyone's taxonomy of Africa has been created by the cinema. When Teddy Roosevelt returned from his bloody safari across eastern Africa, he brought back with him copious film coverage. Among the pictures recorded is one trophy of a band of local Africans, who are identified as 'Zulus'. Since this is Kenya, they cannot possibly be Zulus but, by the early years of this century, the word had already come to be virtually synonymous with 'African savage'; and the attributes imposed on the Zulu people by the Western media of the time were being applied indiscriminately to peoples throughout sub-Saharan Africa.

Savage Zulus feature in *Zululand* (1911); *Queen for a Day* (1911); *A Wild Ride* (1913) which features the heroine's mad dash for freedom on the back of a pet ostrich; *The Zulu King* (1913). In the latter, Lubin, who had made *Rastus in Zululand*, continued with comedy. This is how the *Moving Picture World* of 28 June 1913 describes the film:

> *It is almost a shame to take the terrible theme of Cannibal Savage*
> *history and reduce it to comedy, but there is a humor in the*

condition, which may induce a laugh so long as the white man comes out on top. The picture is not intended to horrify the audience, but more to induce a scream of laughter, at the beautiful stupidity of the aborigines and how easily they were conquered by modern tact and wit. The picture is wonderfully true to the atmosphere of the pictorial savage ...

From the beginning, the word 'Zulu' was politically charged. The Boers, trekking away from British rule in the first half of the nineteenth century, saw their defeat of the Zulu army at the Battle of Blood River as a sign of God's grace upon the Afrikaner people, nothing short of a miracle.

For the British, who suffered the most humiliating defeat of their colonial wars up to that time at the hands of a Zulu army at Isandhlwana in 1879, Zulu military prowess had to be inflated in order to explain that defeat; this paid a bonus when the British struck back with overwhelming force – the greater the enemy, the more glory when he was defeated. These battles early on found their way onto the silver screen, and their repetition in later works had political ramifications.

Although newsreels and travelogues had been made in South Africa from the earliest years of the motion picture industry, there had been little incentive, due to the profusion of foreign imports, for an indigenous film industry. Film distribution came to be dominated by one man, Isadore William Schlesinger, who had come to South Africa in 1894 from the United States, become very successful in insurance and real estate, and branched out into show business. (His background and life have parallels among his Jewish peers who created Hollywood.) Conditions stemming from the First World War spurred Schlesinger to undertake production. All the leading film-producing countries, with one outstanding exception, were adversely affected by the war.

The exception was of course the United States, which to begin with was outside the war, and able to profit from it. Hollywood would almost certainly have gained international supremacy anyway, but the Great War quickened and consolidated it. In South Africa, Schlesinger was faced with rising prices demanded by American distributors and falling box-office returns due to the numbers of patrons who had gone to the War. (As in the rest of the British Empire, the War was received very enthusiastically by young men.) In these conditions, Schlesinger decided to make 'South African films for South African audiences'. He founded African Film Productions, and built studios at Killarney, a Johannesburg suburb.

While the conditions for making films could not rival Hollywood, the Johannesburg area had its advantages. The sunlight and terrain were perfect for outdoor filming. There was a certain amount of capital available, and technicians and talent could easily be imported from Europe or America. Production costs were not high, and there was abundant cheap African labour for tasks like carpentry and sewing. Taking advantage of South Africa's adventurous past for stories, African Film Productions could hire savage hordes for a pittance. Since this was the era of silent films, there was no reason why South African productions could not compete in the international market.

DE VOORTREKKERS (WINNING A CONTINENT) (1916)

In 1916, Schlesinger hired an American film director, Harold Shaw, to make films in South Africa. Together with the Afrikaans historian Gustav Preller, Shaw wrote the script for the first South African epic film, *De Voortrekkers*. The filming of *De Voortrekkers* was undertaken a year after Griffith's *Birth of a Nation* opened, to unprecedented success, and was probably inspired by it.

The Boer word '*voortrekkers*' means 'pioneers' in the same sense as those who led the movement westward across America. The *voortrekkers* sought new lands to settle, often meeting armed resistance from the local inhabitants. Just as *Birth of a Nation* was a romantic interpretation of the creation of a new (and racist) South out of the ashes of the Civil War, so *De Voortrekkers* told the story of the forefathers of Afrikanerdom.

The English title of *De Voortrekkers* was *Winning a Continent*, a grandiose misnomer suggesting far more than the Boers ever achieved, or sought to achieve. Likewise, *Birth of a Nation* was more concerned with the postbellum agony of the South than with the nation as a whole.

Both films, whatever their intentions – and in neither case were these innocent – became highly politicised. In the case of *De Voortrekkers*, politics were there from the beginning. South Africa officially supported Britain in the Great War, but it was a divided nation. A large percentage of the Afrikaner people nursed bitter memories of the Anglo-Boer War, which had ended a little over a decade earlier. The Boers had seen thousands of their people perish at the hands of the same British army to which their country was now sending volunteers. Hatred of British imperialism would long remain a factor in South African politics, and motivated an early abortive rebellion during the Great War.

This was the atmosphere in which Schlesinger and Shaw set out to make *De Voortrekkers*, a paean to the Boer people's heroism. Director Harold Shaw wrote effusively:

> *The doings of the Dutch pioneers and their battles with Dingaan make distinctive history, and no other events now upon record can be compared with them ... (this is) a picture that will, for the first time, bring home to everybody with full force the hardships, sufferings, and stupendous difficulties that faced the early South African settlers. (**Stage and Cinema**, 30 December 1916)*

The production could not have been undertaken without the blessing of the government, which had full powers of censorship during wartime. Clearly, the government must have seen some advantage in having a film that could be a sop to Afrikaner Nationalist feelings without arousing anti-British sentiment.

In *De Voortrekkers*, the enemy is not a British army, but a Zulu one. In the sense that the Zulus represent the black masses, there is an unstated subtext to the film that it is not the British who are the Boers' enemy, but the blacks – the common enemy of Boers and Britons in their claim upon the land of South Africa. A reviewer in South Africa's *Stage and Cinema* of 1 September 1917, was to write:

> *(De Voortrekkers) has probably done more to bring Dutchmen (i.e. Boers) and Englishmen together and to help each other to a better understanding of the other's point of view, than anything that has ever previously happened. And it was solely due to the enterprise and initiative ... of the African Film Productions Ltd, that this great picture was produced, to form a lasting and glowing tribute to the heroism and self-sacrifice of the early Boers ...*

De Voortrekkers is based on the Great Trek of the Boers across southern Africa in search of a homeland in which to establish a free republic. The impetus for this migration was a desire to escape from British rule, which threatened the Boers' slave economy. However, this historical background is suppressed in the film – the opening caption to the silent movie reads:

> *Piet Retief, a farmer in Cape Colony has planned a great emigration to the Unknown for the purpose of buying territory from the natives upon which to establish a Free Dutch Republic.*

The British are conspicuously absent from *De Voortrekkers* – except in the credits, which among both the actors and the production team contain only one recognisably Afrikaans name. That name is significant: it is Gustav Preller, who is given credit for the scenario. Preller was a historian devoted to propagating Afrikaner Nationalism. He is acknowledged for his work in oral history, which included recollections from survivors of the Great Trek, and for his early recognition of the importance of film.

Depictions of the visual elements of the Great Trek – the clothes, the women's bonnets, the powder-horns, the muskets and canonry, the covered wagons – derive largely from Preller. In *De Voortrekkers*, he was able to indulge his own visual image of the Great Trek, which was one shaped by chauvinist ideology fully as much as by historical accuracy.

Coinciding with the period of the Great War, there was a resurgence of Boer nationalism after the terrible defeat of the Anglo-Boer War, which would continue and grow in strength. Preller was an important intellectual part of this movement. But his name on the script did not forestall Boer protests at least against the making of *De Voortrekkers*. These protests were not about the treatment of Boer history, but against the breaking of the Sabbath – many sequences were shot on a Sunday, because Shaw was using as white extras mineworkers from the mines around Johannesburg, and Sunday was the workers' only day off. However, the protests had no effect, possibly because Prime Minister Louis Botha took a personal interest in the production.

De Voortrekkers contains a number of scenes that required hundreds of African extras to play the part of Zulu warriors. African Film Productions drew these men from the mines also. There was an irony in this, since many of these men would have been descendants of those same Zulu soldiers who fought against the Boer intruders some eighty years earlier.

Since then, their rural economy and their social structure had been so savaged that they had been forced to leave their homes and families to seek work on the mines. And now they were being required to re-enact the trauma of the past. The insult implicit in this was lost on African Film Productions. The Department of Native Affairs, however, was aghast at the volatile situation that would be created with thousands of Africans being urged to attack whites in as lifelike a way as possible. A compromise was reached with an agreement to arm the natives with 'collapsible assegais' – spears that would bend on touching human flesh, instead of piercing.

The drama of *De Voortrekkers* was built on the clash between the migrating Boers and the Zulu *impis* under Dingaan. The only written accounts of this confrontation came from the Boer side, and this from the beginning was presented as a history of treachery and massacre on the part of the Zulus.

> *The grass was matted with the noble blood of women, girls, and tiny babes. The wagons were smashed and burned, the earth white with feathers from the bedding. Infants nursing at their mother's breast were pierced with tens of assegais – so that both bodies were fixed together. Children were seized by the legs and their heads smashed against wagon wheels. Women's breasts were severed, their bodies mutilated and ravished. Vultures circled over the laager of yesterday; among the dead and the still-smouldering ashes wild animals prowled around – presently to gorge themselves on human flesh.*

Thus wrote Preller in 1909, vividly describing the massacre at Weenen, the Place of Weeping. These images were in Preller's mind when he wrote the script for *De Voortrekkers*, and they were likely in the minds of the white miners who waited in the laager built for the re-enactment of the Zulu attack in 1916.

To an already fraught situation must be added current history, in the relationship between the white and the black miners. The first decades of the twentieth century saw the mass migration of increasingly impoverished Boers off the land and into the cities, where they had to seek work on the mines as unskilled labour. This meant that they were competing with black miners, over whom their skin should have given them superiority. The mine-owners became adept at playing the race game to keep wages down. For the Boers, this became a facet of the *swart gevaar* – the fear that Blacks would take away white jobs. So it was desperately urgent to the white miner, both for his economic well-being and for his badly battered sense of his own worth, that Africans be kept in their place.

So it is perhaps not altogether surprising that on that Sunday morning, some of the white miners allegedly took live ammunition with them into the laager prior to the attack. It is not clear whether the miner-voortrekkers inside the laager fired on the miner-warriors massed for attack before they were supposed to, or whether the miner-warriors anticipated Shaw's signal, and charged when their spirit was up. Whatever happened, the result was a battle more lifelike than Shaw had either anticipated or wanted.

> *While the natives were charging the laager, the Europeans within had fired shots. Harold Shaw had shouted to them to stop firing and when they had failed to do so, he had run among the natives in an attempt to stop it … when (Police) Major Trew saw a native pull a white man off his horse and jab at him with his improvised assegai, he realised the danger of serious disturbance. So far from co-operating in the dispersal of the natives, the Europeans in laager fired at close range even when the natives were withdrawing … The natives charged the laager furiously; but instead of recoiling and falling 'dead', continued into the laager itself where blows with Europeans were exchanged. Mounted police under the command of Major Trew were forced to intervene and to prevent the natives from attacking the laager in earnest. In moving them away from the scene of the 'battle', the police hustled the natives out of the laager and into the surrounding hills. Some escaped by swimming the river, and one was drowned …*[55]

This is South African film historian Thelma Gutsche's description of the battle scene. With the seething undertow of emotions that the battle forced to the surface, it seems miraculous that lives were not lost. That the harassed Police Major Trew, who was responsible for law and order on the day, later became a

---

[55] Thelma Gutsche, *The History and Social Significance of Motion Pictures in South Africa 1895-1940*, Howard Timmins, Cape Town, 1972, p. 314, n. 24.

member of the Cape Provincial and Union Censor Boards, seems no more than the act of a reasonable man.

Although this clash happened in the Transvaal, far from the original scene of battle, it might well be called the Second Battle of Blood River. The Battle of Blood River, which took place on 16 December 1838, established Boer military supremacy over the Zulus, and was endowed with mystical significance by Afrikaners thereafter. Fighting from a laager, a small force of voortrekkers repulsed a Zulu army with massive losses to the Zulus. Given the determination and discipline of the Boers, which were certainly considerable, it is more likely that their superior weapons technology, rather than the personal intervention of God, was the deciding factor. Nevertheless, prior to the battle, which the Boers knew would mean annihilation if they lost, they swore an oath to God that they would ever after devote that day to Him, if He gave them victory. The victory was so decisive that a nearby river ran red with the blood of slaughtered Zulus. The Day of the Covenant became for Afrikaners one of the holiest days of the calendar, a day which marked them out as God's Chosen People in Africa.

Absorbed into the canon of religious symbolism – a religion that strongly identified a god with one people – Blood River was no less than a massive blood sacrifice: the offering was black bodies. The mystical importance of this is not lessened by the fact that the Zulus had 'made themselves worthy of slaughter' by their own massacre of Piet Retief's party (which had gone to Dingaan's kraal for a peaceful parlay) and by the subsequent massacre of the Boer families at the Place of Weeping. Black bodies in abundance paid for this infamy. And it became most expedient to register and remember and intone, on 16 December every year after 1838, who the villains were, and to hold their descendants eternally responsible.

The Boers had come in peace – so the legend-as-history ran – and were met with violence. No room was left for the Zulu version – that the Boers were the vanguard of a large-scale invasion of their land which had to be discouraged in any way possible. The same clash took place in America, in the movement westward, with the same result: the destruction of the military power of the native peoples, followed by economic and cultural degradation. This process was justified by a vast campaign to turn the rightful owners of the invaded land into the Savage Other.

Gustav Preller had played his part in creating written legend-as-history, and he now turned to the cinema. *De Voortrekkers*, from his point of view, was intended to galvanise the process of nation-building that was taking place within the Afrikaner people at that time. It is even possible that the very title of D W Griffith's film, *Birth of a Nation*, inspired him in writing *De Voortrekkers*. Afrikanerdom, badly divided even at the time of the Anglo-Boer War, was embarking on a long quest for unity. In defining itself, Afrikaner Nationalism could not refer back to the Anglo-Boer War, so recent and so bitter in everyone's memory, and in any case a defeat. Instead, through *De Voortrekkers*, Preller enabled Afrikaners to look beyond the immediate past, into the roots of their history, to the time when they stood alone as a people, stood firm, and prevailed. The sense of Afrikaners as a people was defined and engraven as victory over the blacks, the Savage Other. And this is what is celebrated in *De Voortrekkers*.

Certain elements in *De Voortrekkers* are recognisable today as what would become standard fare in films about the clash of whites with 'primitive' peoples. The voortrekkers are sympathetically-drawn individuals, whereas the Zulus are for the most part an ant-like mass. The Zulu leader is not only treacherous towards the trusting Boers, but is guilty of infanticide – he orders the death of his own son and this is carried out in graphic detail. He is swayed by villainous whites, in this case Portuguese (Portugal was a rival to Britain for control of southern Africa). He is polygamous. In contrast, images of the nuclear family are important in depictions of the whites. But oddly enough, the underlying terror that permeates *Birth of a Nation* is completely absent from *De Voortrekkers*. That is the fear of miscegenation. *Birth of a Nation* depicts a South in turmoil after the Civil War because the natural order of things has been turned upside down – blacks rule over whites. And the most terrible feature of this anarchy is the vulnerability of white women to black men. The triumph celebrated in *Birth* lies in the re-establishment of white racial superiority through the vigilantism of the Ku Klux Klan and its ability to protect white womanhood. In his script, Preller never invokes the bogey of rape, even though it was present in his historical writings. In fact, this never seems to have been an important feature of South African films even in subliminal form.

Birth of a Nation had its good blacks, faithful servants who protect their masters and mistresses even against their own people. This was always part of the sentimental defence of slavery, that the slave loved the master he served. In *De Voortrekkers* there is also a Faithful Servant, who is given a major and revealing role. He is the Zulu warrior Sobuza. For reasons by no means clear, he is made the most interesting, taking precedence over the white characters, who are cyphers.

We are introduced to Sobuza when he is undergoing conversion to Christianity by missionaries. He is taught that killing is wrong:

> *Caption: And desiring that all men, white and black should live*
> *peaceably and without strife, God said: 'Thou shalt not kill!'*

His first test comes when he disobeys Dingaan's order to kill the king's baby son. He is shamed, and driven from the tribe. In his flight, he meets up with the missionary, who gives him a spear and a shield for his own protection. The missionary advises him:

> *Caption: Go South, to the White Man's country, where you may*
> *live without strife.*

Sobuza follows the advice, and staggers into Retief's laager, where he is given water and succour. Sobuza pledges allegiance to Retief:

> *Caption: Henceforth thou art my father and my Chief, and thy*
> *people shall be my people.*

Sobuza becomes part of the voortrekker family, but as a servant of a particular kind. Soon after his arrival at the camp, he is preparing to cook an evening meal – something normally done by women – and two boys come to watch. They have stolen a pipe and tobacco, and start smoking it. Sobuza watches them in the way of one who wishes to see them learn a lesson, as they cough and then run off to be sick. Sobuza returns the stolen pipe, and then tenderly covers them with a blanket as they fall asleep. Not only has the warrior Sobuza been domesticated, he has been emasculated – turned into a nanny.

Sobuza's devotion to whites, shown in this scene, is emphasised during the visit of Piet Retief's party to Dingaan's kraal. Sobuza survives the massacre of Retief and his followers, and returns to tell the tale to the Boers. He vows vengeance on Dingaan. After the defeat of the Zulu army, Sobuza tracks Dingaan down, and slays him in personal combat.

So, curiously, Sobuza becomes the central figure. His fidelity is absolute: he becomes the Faithful Servant who defeats the Savage Other. The final scenes are remarkable. The Boers have built a church dedicated to the Covenant of Blood River, and inside they are rendering thanks to the Almighty 'for the preservation of our race and country'. At the church porch sits Sobuza in Western clothing, staring with ecstasy at the cross. This scene holds a terrible irony, obviously quite unconscious for the film-makers. While he has devoted his life to serving whites, has fought for them, and has adopted their religion, his skin prevents him from taking part in their service – his greatest reward is to listen to it outside the white church.

The character of Sobuza, which is entirely fictitious, is not necessary in any way to the recounting of the exploits of the voortrekkers. The only way it can be understood is as an attempt to integrate black South Africans into a benevolent hierarchy, where they could be fully accepted providing they knew their place.

This is South African Zooluology. Beginning with *De Voortrekkers*, films on the Zulu show him in the wild state, to be brought down by white men's bullets. But the Zulus are also capable of domestication. Wild or domesticated, the film Zulu invariably served some political purpose for the white man, overtly or covertly.

The Second Battle of Blood River almost reversed the first. The Zulu charge was realistic but inauthentic; this time, if live bullets were used, they were not in such quantity as to deter the *impis* of miners, who swept into the laager. In 1838, the Zulus, who were encountering fire-power for the first time, did not manage in their three charges to get closer than 150 yards to the defensive circle. What Shaw had on film was great cinema, but atrocious history. The entire scene, with its thousands of extras, had to be reshot under tighter control. This time, Preller's vision remained inviolate. At home, it was welcomed by Afrikaners as their story. *De Voortrekkers*, almost two hours in length, entered into ritual, being shown on every Day of the Covenant down the years, to packed and enthusiastic audiences.

This silent film, undoubtedly powerful, was in no way shamed by comparison with the product of Europe and the United States, and it had some success on the world market. This encouraged Schlesinger to embark immediately on a second epic, *Symbol of Sacrifice*.

SYMBOL OF SACRIFICE (1918)

Having paid his dues to the Afrikaner people, Schlesinger now turned his attention to the British heritage in South Africa. The result was *Symbol of Sacrifice*. In its completed form, this work has unfortunately been lost, but a few thousand feet of out-takes remain in the National Archives in Pretoria, and these are sufficient to show the scope of the production. A copy of the script is also extant.

Symbol of Sacrifice was conceived and executed during the First World War, beginning at the end of 1917, when Britain was suffering appalling losses in France, and victory was far from certain. Although many Boers withheld support from Britain, and some were in open revolt, there was a strong emotional bond with the mother country among South Africans of British stock. *Symbol of Sacrifice* would give expression to this bond. The film's first image was of the Union Jack fluttering in the breeze, with these words superimposed:

> *I am the flag that braves the shock of war*
> *From continent to continent and shore to shore*
> *Come weal or woe, as turns the old earth round,*
> *Where hope and glory shine, there is the symbol found.*
> *Look! Sun and moon and glittering star,*
> *Faithful unto death, my children are!*
> *You who for duty live, and who for glory die,*
> *The symbol of your faith and sacrifice am I.*

It is an appeal to patriotism, to unquestioning obedience to a cause mystical in its power, the very emotions that made the Great War possible in the first place, and gave it the momentum to continue far beyond the bounds of sanity. *Symbol of Sacrifice*, in reviving past glories of the British Empire, exhorted to yet greater efforts. In this sense, it was certainly propagandistic in tone, but perhaps no more so than the many Hollywood films based on stories of empire, like *Gunga Din* (1936), *Soldiers Three* (1951) and *Charge of the Light Brigade* (1936), to name but a few. *Symbol of Sacrifice*, which was written by Schlesinger and South African writer F Horace Rose, takes place during the Zulu Wars of the 1880s. South Africa held a peculiar nemesis for the British Empire – it was there that it suffered some of its most devastating defeats, first at the hands of the Zulus, then the Boers. These defeats revealed what a dinosaur the British military machine was well before 1914 – the trenches simply confirmed the incapacity of the generals to learn the lessons of South Africa. But even defeats could be turned into propaganda victory, through the mystical appeal to blood sacrifice as an enobling experience – albeit for the survivors and the old men who did not have to fight, not for those who actually shed the blood.

The film deals with the crushing defeat of a substantial British force by the Zulus at Isandhlwana; the successful defence of Rorke's Drift by a company of British soldiers against overwhelming odds; and the vengeful destruction of the Zulu capital of Ulundi by the British, which effectively broke Zulu resistance for the next thirty years. This story had a bonus: the Prince Imperial of France, a descendant of Napoleon, happened to be serving with the British forces, and was killed. There was thus an appeal to the current Anglo-French alliance, and much was made of this in the film.

The symbol of sacrifice of the title is the Union Jack itself, and its deification constitutes the film's theme. Couplet quotations from the opening poem punctuate the action. The ethos of empire saturates *Symbol of Sacrifice*, and the strict human stratification upon which that empire depended is faithfully repeated in the film. The list of characters alone reveals this:

(*GERT MOXTER. A Dutch farmer.*)

(*MARIE MOXTER. His daughter.*)

PRESTON FANSHALL. A Young Englishman, owner of a farm. Affianced to Marie. About 30. A clean, well set up Young Britisher of the period.

PRIVATE TOMMY H'ATKINS of 'IGHGATE 'ILL. A decided type of Cockney soldier. About 30.

PRIVATE DENNIS DOGHERTY OF DUBLIN. About the same age, but of distinctive Irish type.

PRIVATE GEORDIE M'GLUSKIE o' GLASGIE AND EVERYWHERE. A typical raw-bones Scotch soldier of about 35.

GOBO. A faithful old Zulu servant who served the Moxter family since childhood. He wears the cast-off European clothing of old Moxter.

ALETTA. Marie's Cape girl maid. She is fat, forty and bare-footed, but in so far as possible apes her young mistress in the doing of her hair and trying to show a slender waist line.

DABOMBA. A witch doctor from Cetewayo's Kraal. A splendidly built Zulu of 35/40, who being one of Cetewayo's favourites proudly wears the full regalia of a leading witch doctor of the King.

TAMBOOKI. A finely built Zulu warrior, also favoured by Cetewayo. His attire and accoutrement would be of the finest Zulu type.

MELISSA. A finely set up Zulu girl of about 20. Not too black nor of too decided negro features.[56] She loves, and is beloved of Tambooki, and is also desired by Dabomba.

The delineations of class and race and sex are obvious. The middle class (the Moxters and Fanshall) are clearly the cream. The lower white classes, who appear as the Other Ranks of the army in Tommy H'Atkins (the 'H' added underlines Atkins's Cockney origin), Dogherty and M'Gluskie are denoted as *types*, a cross-section of the poor of the British Isles, whose loyalty is unquestioned, but who can be objects of light mockery. (This patronising depiction of 'the lower classes' was traditional in British theatre and cinema, and passed over later into television. It is not all that far removed from the Rastus-type of *Rastus In Zululand*, and seems to have fulfilled the same function, of keeping the lower orders in their place.)

The pretensions of Aletta, the Cape Coloured servant, may be suspect as much in her racial mixture as in her impossible attempt to be like her mistress. The scriptwriters Rose and Schlesinger were not middle class Englishmen, but there is no doubt that they carried the same prejudices against the lower classes and 'lesser breeds' of the empire. In a scene that is supposed to be humorous, Gobo takes his revenge on Aletta for an affront by pouring scalding water on her bare foot. This is followed by more slapstick:

Scene 38. On the stoep of Moxter's farm-house.

Action: Moxter, Marie and Fanshall seated, talking. Gobo enters with coffee pot, trying to restrain his laughter. Marie notices this, and asks him the cause. He explodes, and pointing towards the kitchen, begins to pantomime what had happened, in the doing of

---

56   This insistence on the undesirability of 'negro features' for young female leads is an enduring characteristic of cinema – even when the directors, like Spike Lee, are themselves black.

*which he burns old Moxter's hand with the coffee pot. The old
man yells, and jumping to his feet, shies a piece of jam-covered
bread to Gobo. He ducks, and the bread flies past him out
towards the corner of the house. Gobo quickly puts coffee pot
down, and jumps in time to miss a kick aimed at him by old
Moxter. The kick is not a vicious one, however, and old Moxter
joins Fanshall and Marie in a laugh at his own expense. Gobo
salutes and is sorry, but is forgiven and sent off.*

*Scene 39. (This scene is to be inserted into 38, just after the bread
which Moxter has shied at Gobo goes out of the picture.) (A black
child has been established as sleeping nearby.) A close up of the
piccaninn still sleeping, the bread strikes him, jam side to his
face. He wakens, looks at the bread, picks it up; rises; looks
towards the stoep, salutes, thanking his master, scrapes the jam
from his face with his fingers, which he proceeds to suck, then
crouching on his haunches, gets on with his meal.*

The presence of 'Dutchmen' in the film who fight on the side of the British
against the Zulus is clearly an appeal to Afrikaners to support the Empire in its hour
of need – when Gert Moxter is killed by the Zulus, his epitaph is the caption: '… a
brave and gallant Dutch farmer who fought for us'. As in *De Voortrekkers*, there is
a renegade white – not historically justified – with the distinctly German name of
Schneider.

What distinguishes *Symbol of Sacrifice* from its predecessor *Birth of a Nation* is
the value it gives to its black characters. The Zulus, while still featuring as the
obligatory massed warriors (5 000 of them this time), have a more personalised
presence than in the earlier epic *De Voortrekkers*, with diverse characters like
Cetewayo, Dabomba, Gobo, Tambooki and Melissa. Cetewayo appears as a
despotic leader, who in one scene lines up a row of women and children and has
them thrown off the top of a cliff in order to frighten a captive white woman. In
this, he is a replica of Dingaan in the previous film. Dabomba is the first
appearance on the screen of a witch doctor, but without the superstitious
dimensions that the figure would later acquire.

Once again, there is no underlying threat of rape, even though a white woman is
captured. On the contrary, a Zulu love story is written into the plot to parallel the
love story between Fanshall and Marie, and eventually is interwoven with it, when
Tambooki recognises their common humanity:

*Caption: LOVE. ONE TOUCH OF NATURE MAKES THE WHOLE WORLD
KIN*
And decides to help Marie escape.

From the point of view of the symbolic use to which it is put, the character of Gobo is the most interesting. The role of Gobo is played by the same actor who appeared in *De Voortrekkers* as the Zulu Sobuza, and the two roles have much in common.[57]

Gobo, the character in *Symbol of Sacrifice*, was formerly a Zulu warrior, but is now a servant on Moxter's farm. He exhibits a dog-like devotion to his white masters, rescuing Marie from the unwelcome attentions of Carl Schneider, but then being soundly whipped by the white bully.

> *Scene 15. By the gate.*
>
> *Action. Marie continues to struggle. Gobo hurriedly enters, and in answer to his mistress's appeal for help, throws Carl aside; then realising the enormity of his action in laying hostile hands on a white man, respectfully salutes Carl, but stands protectingly in front of Marie. Carl is furious, brushes his coat where the black hand fell upon it and raises his sjambok to strike Gobo. Marie intervenes and orders Carl away. With a threatening look at both, Carl exits through gate. Marie thanks Gobo who salutes and smiles his thanks. Marie exits towards house. Gobo looks over shoulder in direction Carl has gone, then looks regretfully after his mistress.*
>
> *Scene 18. By the gate.*
>
> *Action. Gobo looking after his mistress is about to go back to his work, when Carl sneaks through the gate behind him, and grabbing Gobo's arm, swings him around until they are face to face, then he soundly thrashes Gobo with a sjambok. Gobo, offering no further resistance, then appeals with outstretched arms.*

And Gobo, who cannot oppose a white man, has to be rescued by his mistress. (See also the rescue of 'the kaffir' by his master from the lion in *A Kaffir's Gratitude*.) Gobo's every gesture towards the whites is obsequious and fawning, grateful for every attention paid him. He demonstrates utter fidelity to his mistress when he rescues her from a Zulu kraal, and then sacrifices his life attempting to save her.

---

57 The name of the actor seems actually to have been Goba, and he appeared in a number of other films, including *A Zulu's Devotion* and *A Border Scourge*, both of which have been lost. In an early review in *Stage and Cinema* he was recognised as 'a natural born actor'. In the same publication, he is described as 'a picturesque old Zulu from one of the Native Missions in Natal, who has taken to "movie" work as a duck takes to water, and who, before long, will be a familiar figure on the world's bioscope screens ...' He can make a fair claim to being the first African star.

Much is made of the clothes Gobo wears: in the beginning, he is dressed in Moxter's cast-off clothing, showing him to be civilised, but not to such a degree that he can rival whites who can afford new clothing. He reverts to the dress of a Zulu warrior when he goes to Cetewayo's kraal to rescue Marie. Finally, ennobled by his sacrifice, his body is paid the ultimate honour, and covered with the Union Jack. This is perhaps a step further than the ending of *De Voortrekkers*, where Sobuza must still remain outside the church, and is an accidental comment on the difference between the British Empire, which at least in theory recognised the possibility of Africans being accepted within the pale, and the Dutch Reformed Church of South Africa, which could not conceive of any kind of equality between black and white.

This is not quite the end. Tambooki, the Zulu warrior who has turned renegade enough to help Marie escape, takes his love Melissa to Moxter's farm:

> *Scene 590. The stoep.*
>
> *Action: Marie starts up and draws Fanshall's attention. He looks and they nod recognition as Tambooki and Melissa come to the verandah steps. Tambooki salutes and says:*
>
> *Caption: 'WHITE CHIEF, THE WAR IS OVER, AND WE HAVE COME TO CLAIM A HOME WITH YOU AS YOU PROMISED'*
>
> *Action: Marie beckoning, Melissa mounts the steps. Aletta, with great disdain for a raw kaffir pokes her nose in air and exits into the house scornfully. Marie speaks to Melissa. Fanshall descending steps, Tambooki salutes and Fanshall beckoning him takes him away.*
>
> *Scene 592. Interior of Gobo's room.*
>
> *Action: Enter Fanshall and Tambooki. Fanshall points to Gobo's shield, spear, etc. on the wall, takes them and shows them to Tambooki and says:*
>
> *Caption: 'THESE BELONGED TO A BRAVE AND A FAITHFUL SERVANT. SEE THAT YOU ARE WORTHY TO FILL HIS PLACE'*
>
> *Action: Tambooki greatly impressed, says he will try to be, handles the articles, and replaces them. Fanshall shows him Gobo's European clothing and indicates that he must put them on.*

Thus *Symbol of Sacrifice* repeats an important element of *De Voortrekkers* – the taming and domesticating of the Zulu, the transformation of the Savage Other into the Faithful Servant. In this light, it would have been interesting to have had access to the first version of *King Solomon's Mines*, which was made in 1918.

But this, together with *Allan Quatermain, With Edged Tools, Prester John, The Gun-runner* and *Copper Mask* have all, alas, been lost. Fragments of *Copper Mask* remain, some in badly deteriorated condition. It is a South African attempt to copy the Western, complete with stage-coach hold-ups and gangs of horsemen galloping across the veld. But it also includes some intriguing scenes of witch doctor magic, so this may have been the first film to give shape to a more forceful witch doctor.

SILIWA THE ZULU (aka ZELIV) (1927)

Witchcraft featured as an important part of the story *Siliwa the Zulu*. This was a 'documentary' of a type common at the time – the phoney ethnographic film. It was a genre not far removed from the travelogue, and it took a 'primitive' people and imposed on them a Western-style story, usually a romance. In the case of *Siliwa*, an Italian team, led by Professor Lido Cipriani of the University of Florence, and Captain Attilio Gatti, a specialist in wild-life filming, journeyed to South Africa, and came back with *A Story of Love, Hate, Intrigue and Adventure in Zululand*, which sums up the film entirely accurately.

In keeping with Gatti's career, *Siliwa* deals with Zulus in their wild state, virtually untouched by white influence. The story is a hodge-podge of traditional ritual, folktale, European witchcraft practice, and made-up elements, revolving around Siliwa's desire to marry Mdabuli. He is frustrated by the actions of his friend Nomazindela, who unknown to him is also in love with Mdabuli. Siliwa loses his bride-price when his cattle are poisoned. Seeking help, he goes to a witch doctor. She casts bones and reads them, and tells him that Nomazindela is to blame, that he will go through many hardships, but will eventually overcome to win Mdabuli. (One positive element of the film is that the witchdoctor is not demonised, and actually prophesies accurately.)

The film includes many war dances and dances of maidens. (After the Dance of the Virgins comes a classic comment: 'And then the virgins rest their weary loins.') Gatti is clearly delighted with the unabashed nudity of the women, and there are a few salacious images, notably Mdabuli at the stream. The film-maker seems to have gone to Zululand with well-established preconceptions about what constituted Zulu behaviour, and reproduced them in his film. The film was apparently quite successful in Europe; in South Africa, it was distributed under the title of *Witchcraft*, but even this was not enough to arouse interest in a film with an African subject.

MY SONG GOES FORTH
(aka AFRICA LOOKS UP and AFRICA SINGS) (1936)

Apart from the travelogue and ethnographic film, there was little interest in documenting black life in South Africa. Judging from the existing early films, you would have the impression that black life was still 'tribal', with all the connotations of the primitive, the backward, the unspoiled and the picturesque that that word conjures up. In fact, many Africans were highly urbanised, and already influenced by Western cinema and American jazz, as well as by mission schools.

It is not clear what motivated him, but a British film-maker, Joseph Best, came to South Africa around 1935, and shot what may have started as a travelogue, but ended as a documentary on African life, largely urban, of a kind that had not hitherto been attempted. There are invaluable images of location life, schools and colleges, and a cross-section of occupations, from mine-workers to road-gangs to school-teachers to house-servants to waiters to cane-cutters. There are scenes of men queuing up outside a pass office and a native court, of convicts.

While made from a perspective that we would nowadays call 'liberal', for its time the film was quite radical, since it maintained that, with good education and opportunities, Africans are fully capable of advancement. The film is shaped by the values of the enlightened vanguard of the British middle class. Showing two natives swathed in blankets, Best's narration intones:

> *This is a couple who have tramped in from a reserve some 200 miles away. Their intelligent bearing is due to the fact that they are educated natives who have been to a mission school on the reserve ...*

This is certainly more than can be read from the neutral shot of two people staring at the camera. This forcing of an interpretation upon the viewer reaches a climax at the end of the film, when Best presents us with a series of before-and-after contrasts. (Most of Best's images of the 'primitive' are borrowed from *Siliwa the Zulu*.) The text amply describes the pictures we are being shown:

> *The Zulu of former times, a picturesque figure in his warrior array, whose chief occupation was warring with rival tribes, has given place to the smartly dressed gentleman, perfectly groomed in the European fashion, possibly a graduate of a university, driving a car, attending education conferences, and taking part in native social welfare work.*
>
> *Whereas in former times grievances would be aired by a chief*

calling together his warriors round a hut in the kraal, and inveighing against the neighbouring tribes and calling for war – this has given place to this businesslike meeting in the location.

The educated native is becoming socially and politically minded, and in the different locations, meetings are held at which the speakers discuss native conditions in the best parliamentary style, suggest reforms, and generally air their grievances. They are not unfriendly in their attitude towards whites, but urge that the native has now grown up, and should not be treated as a child any longer, and should be given some responsibility with regard to native interests.

Another contrast, the witch-doctor, in this case a female one, who by throwing the bones foretold coming events, or explained tribal calamities, and diagnosed troubles generally, who have exercised great power and terror over the simple superstitious primitive natives – she has given place to the cultured native lady educated at a native high school or college, with a university degree, such as this, who is a native teacher at the Adams Institute. And these gentlemen with her, also university graduates, might have been witch-doctors too, but for the coming of the white man ...

The implications of the possibilities of betterment overstress the reality, but the feeling that Africans had gone through a period of tutelage under European rule and were now poised to assume more responsibility was certainly a force in the African community. The image of men on the march that filled so many movies of the 1930s from America (see most obviously the logo for the *March of Time* series), Britain, Italy and Germany could be interpreted as nationalistic, fascistic, or democratic – it may have been any of these, but it invoked a sense of discipline, of purpose, of organisation towards a common goal. Best does not have any powerful image of marchers in South Africa to draw upon, so he is reduced to showing the passers-by in a Durban street scene, characteristically using the text to point us in a direction the picture does not suggest:

And so Africa marches on, from the jungles, the kraal, and the hut
to towns and cities and the ways of civilisation.

Best's 'civilisation' is in the direct line of descent from the missionary conviction that the European way is the right way, and that what is 'primitive' must be jettisoned. White education, and the emulation of white dress and customs, will produce an 'intelligent native' who can take his or her place alongside whites.

By itself, the film seems more appropriate to the lecture hall than to a London West End cinema. But Best brought off a coup: he somehow persuaded Paul Robeson to supply a wrap-around – an on-camera piece to go at the beginning and end of the film. Robeson was by that time at the height of his fame, an actor and singer of international standing. His presence in the film could bring it the boost that would make all the difference. Robeson himself obviously felt that the film was a positive contribution, as he reads in the prologue:

> *When you are shown pictures of Africans doing their ancient war dances or other traditional picturesque ceremonials, you may be inclined to think, not understanding their culture, that such people are still very primitive, not capable of education, and unable to appreciate all the blessings of civilisation. Such a wrong idea this film will help to correct ...*

The words Robeson reads are a plea for *acceptance* and an attempt to overcome racial prejudice. However, Robeson did make some amendments to the prologue, which included the following condemnation:

> *Every foot of Africa is now parceled out among the white races. Why has this happened? What has prompted them to go there? If you listen to men like Mussolini[58] they will tell you it is to civilise – a divine task, entrusted to the enlightened peoples to carry the torch of light and learning, and to benefit the African people ... Africa was opened up by the white man for the benefit of himself – to obtain the wealth it contained ...*

But this text does not appear in the version of the film still extant. What we have is a shorter version that Best put out under the title *Africa Sings* when the original did not do well. It is easy to see that *My Song Goes Forth*, lacking in art, artifice, exoticism and glamour of any kind, would not have strong popular appeal; but Best attributed the failure to a strong reaction against the film from South Africa House, which protected South African affairs in Britain, and was very powerful. The shorter version, omitting Robeson's incendiary lines, may have been Best's attempt to placate South Africa House.[59]

The short version at least contains no criticism of the South African government. This was a decade before the word 'apartheid' came into usage, a

---

58   This is a reference to Italy's invasion of Abyssinia.

59   Paul Robeson had the opportunity of going to South Africa in 1936, but work, and the opposition of both the British and the South African governments, decided him against going. Later, because of his opposition to apartheid, Robeson's records were banned on South African radio. (I am indebted to Martin Duberman and his book *Paul Robeson* for much of this information.)

period when the condition of blacks in South Africa did not show up so badly in comparison with colonial practice in the rest of Africa, a period when, as the film stresses, it was possible for 'the poor African' to aspire to 'the light of knowledge and education, and the higher and finer things of life' (Prologue as read by Robeson). However, Best was guilty of one egregious and unpardonable error – in the film, he made derogatory remarks about whites. Specifically, on a number of occasions, Best shows 'poor whites':

> *Among the diggings around Kimberley are many of the class known as 'poor whites', one of the minor problems of South Africa. They are of a low mental standard, only able to do the most menial kind of work.*
> *The home of those poor whites is a corrugated iron shanty. Here they scratch about for diamonds and exist in the most squalid conditions. There are about a quarter of a million poor whites in South Africa, the result mainly of former poverty-stricken conditions, and the acquired habits of indolence through the slave labour of early days.*

The existence of white poverty was an extremely sensitive issue. This was in the middle of the Depression, which hit South Africa's mines, industries and farms hard. The American Carnegie Commission inquiring into white poverty at that time estimated that 300 000 whites lived at the lowest level. The problem of 'poor whites' started with the destruction of the Anglo-Boer War and was almost exclusively an Afrikaner phenomenon. Therefore, for Best to make the following comparison, in his usual blithe fashion, was to question the racial superiority on which the superstructure of South African society depended:

> *An intelligent-looking native is followed by an unintelligent-looking white, one of the poor white class. Placed side by side with these keen, alert-looking natives, this poor white shows up badly. The government is doing its best to raise these poor whites.*

Throughout the film, Best is at pains not to condemn authority, as his last sentence shows. *Africa Sings* is in no sense a revolutionary film, but the temper of the times must be remembered. The British Empire could not exist without the ideology that held everything together, the conviction of racial superiority. The censored words of Paul Robeson and Best's images of poor whites alongside prosperous natives might well have been offensive not only to South Africa House, but to the vast majority of Britons also. *Africa Sings* brought no return on Robeson's investment, and Best claimed that he barely broke even on the film, which is not unlikely. Today, the film is invaluable as a unique document.

KING SOLOMON'S MINES (1936)

Paul Robeson appeared in a number of films with African settings, although he never set foot in Africa. Films like *Sanders of the River*, from 1935, and *King Solomon's Mines*, made in the same year as *My Song Goes Forth*, were made by British companies and had colonialist themes. The Gaumont British production *King Solomon's Mines* (see earlier plot description) leans heavily on the traditional image of the Zulu nurtured by the cinema.

All the elements are there – the despotic king, the obedient warriors, the witch doctor, the threat to whites. All of these come together in a climactic scene, where a small group of white characters is surrounded by an armed black mass. Gagool, the witch doctor, is sniffing out enemies, whom Twala, the king, then orders to be killed on the spot – the obligatory arbitrary killing scene (see also *De Voortrekkers*, Dingaan's murder of his baby son; *Symbol of Sacrifice*, the women and children thrown off the cliff). The whites know that it is only a matter of time before the evil Gagool sniffs them out.

Then comes their discovery of an amazing coincidence: there will shortly be an eclipse over southern Africa; this enables them to demonstrate that their magic is superior to Gagool's – the subtext being that scientific knowledge (a white monopoly) defeats superstition. The tribe cowers at the withdrawal of the sun, just as the tribe is terrified by the anger of the gods demonstrated in the last scenes of *Dingaka*, and with the same final outcome – Umbopa (Paul Robeson) defeats Twala and takes over the leadership of the tribe. Once more, the tribe is a will-less mass, ready to follow any leader. Umbopa – who has befriended the whites – turns out to be the true king. The true, the good and the benevolent are thus seen to be the virtues of those who help whites, while the cruel and tyrannical are attributes of those who threaten them.

In this film, the witch doctor Gagool (her very name resonates with 'ghoul' and 'gargoyle') comes into full sinister form. She is the personification of superstition, the evil influence, the guardian of the mine, the one who wants to thwart the whites from gaining access to its riches. I am indebted to Mbulelo Mzamane for pointing out the full significance of the Gagool figure. The 'witch doctor' (more properly, *sangoma*, these days often translated as 'traditional healer') was the keeper of the religion and of the culture, and as such, *sangomas* were among the most determined in the resistance to white rule. Added to this was the anti-Christian nature of the *sangoma* – perforce, since the *sangoma* represented traditional religion.[60] This accounts for the particular malevolence with which colonial literature painted the *sangoma* (not only in South Africa, of course).

---

60   Nowadays, most *sangomas* seem to be Christians.

The *sangoma*, from the point of view of the colonisers, was the quintessence of Africa, the one who wanted to keep the continent 'dark', that is, free from white influence. In the solar eclipse scene, the whites have power over both darkness and light, both literally and figuratively. That their victory also allows them to gain access to the mineral wealth underlines that this is a telling in mythical form of the story of the conquest of Africa.

When we compare this version of the film with the original adventure yarn written by H Rider Haggard in 1885, it is unsettling to see what has become of it. In both film and novel, the despotic king and evil witch are firmly established, as is the insistence on the Zulus as a warrior nation (the Kukuanas are related to the Zulu.) There is also the fact that the Kukuanas do not value the diamonds. (Umbopa: 'the diamonds are surely there, and you shall have them since you white men are so fond of toys and money.') But the incipient love affair between the white man Good and the black woman Foulata has been dropped entirely (admittedly, in the novel the love is doomed – 'the sun cannot mate with the darkness, nor the white with the black' – but it does exist)[61] and replaced with a white-white romance. Most significant is the shift in emphasis from a quest for a missing brother in the novel to the itch for diamonds in the film.

DIE BOU VAN 'N NASIE (THEY BUILT A NATION) (1938)

King Solomon's Mines was unconscious propaganda for white supremacy. In 1937 and 1938, a film was made with a deliberately propagandistic agenda. This was *They Built a Nation*, a film showing the history of the Afrikaner people. It was made to be used as part of the celebration of the centenary of the Great Trek (and Battle of Blood River) that was planned for 1938. The centenary included a re-enactment of the Great Trek, with ox-wagons starting out from Cape Town on the 800 mile journey to Pretoria, and gathering force along the way. The journey was dedicated with these words:

> *We place our trek in the service of the People of South Africa …*
> *We bring praise to those who won for us a land and a future and*
> *we give honour to the Almighty, in the firm belief that He will*
> *make us a powerful People before His countenance … This*
> *movement is born from the People; may the People carry it in their*
> *hearts all the way to Pretoria and Blood River. Let us build up a*
> *monument for Afrikaner hearts. May this simple trek bind together*
> *in love those Afrikaner hearts which do not yet beat together …*

---

61   In an earlier, lost version (African Film Productions, 1919) Foulata was not suppressed – but was played by a white woman.

The trek inspired the unity it sought. As was intended, it was a great outpouring of patriotic sentiment, with a political goal. It culminated in a mass gathering at the foundation stone of the yet-to-be-built Voortrekker Monument outside Pretoria, where the movement's stormtroopers, the *Ossewa Brandwag* (the Ox-Wagon Sentinels) were prominent.

That it was reminiscent of the Nuremberg Rallies was, as they say, no accident – many Afrikaner intellectuals were adherents of Nazism. Their nationalism appealed to the mystique of blood and soil and to a racism that included hatred of the British, Jews, and, it goes without saying, 'kaffirs'. The film was to be shown in conjunction with the celebrations, and to demonstrate to Afrikaners their own greatness as a people.

The nationalism that drove Preller to write *De Voortrekkers* two decades earlier also inspired *They Built a Nation*, which was the fruit of the new Afrikaans film industry, which dated from the 1930s, and was itself part of the Afrikaner Nationalist movement. *They Built a Nation* included, as any national mythology must, triumph over adversity. For the Boers, this was the struggle against the British and the clash with Dingaan, the Zulu. (In the film, Dingaan's villainy seems to be most acutely expressed in his habit of spitting.)

More so than in the earlier films of Zulu wars, the Zulu warriors are depersonalised. There are no attempts to create characters. The film is as cavalier towards English-speaking South Africans as towards blacks. There were two versions, one in Afrikaans and one in English. The Afrikaans version was shown to a rapturous audience shortly before the Day of the Covenant, 1938. This was a closed screening for Afrikaners. It was not released until six months later, when it enraged English-speaking audiences.

The English-language press was especially incensed because public money was used on a film that was blatantly propagandistic in tone. While naturally most of the resentment was inspired by the portrayal of the British, the *Cape Times* objected: 'There is something distasteful about the Blood River scenes and their revival of old unhappiness. Too much space is given up to battles and massacres ...' The protests continued until well after the outbreak of war with Germany (South Africa declared war immediately after Britain), and the disruptive film was withdrawn from exhibition. But the chauvinistic sentiments displayed in the film would reveal their power a decade later.

In this regard, it is worth referring back to Joseph Best and his poor whites of *My Song Goes Forth*. During the Depression, Afrikaners had seen thousands of their volk reduced in their standard of living to the level of blacks. During the Second World War, with the surge in agricultural and industrial output together with the absence of many Afrikaners on military service, Africans made inroads into jobs that had formerly been protected by a colour bar. (This is well recorded in newsreels and documentary films from the period.)

Working class Afrikaners felt vitally threatened by the *swart gevaar*, the fear of black competition. The National Party, which was overwhelmingly Afrikaner, promised to protect them, and was voted into power in the so-called 'apartheid election' of 1948. The impact of apartheid on all parts of the film industry had a staggeringly negative effect, and led to such absurdities as dividing the industry into streams – films for an Afrikaans, an English or an African audience, the latter further subdivided ethnically. Such a structure for an already small industry could be maintained only by government subsidy; in consequence, the government poured in funds that seldom produced a profit, the major portion going to Afrikaans producers.

UNTAMED (1955)

Perhaps because of the dangers of rousing the kinds of atavistic passions present at the shooting of *De Voortrekkers*, the domestic film industry during the apartheid period kept well clear of the Zulu Wars. Overseas, there were no such inhibitions. Twentieth Century Fox, when it purchased the rights to a raunchy novel by the South African writer Helga Moray, saw in it an exotic locale for what was essentially a Western. Twentieth Century Fox had in the 1950s sunk a lot of money into Cinemascope, and was looking for tales with wide horizons.

The novel *Untamed* had some of the elements of *Gone with the Wind* – a tumultuous historical background and a spunky heroine who did not recognise convention, and fought and schemed for what she wanted. Add to this an intrepid hero, who for reasons best known to himself, loves, but rejects, the heroine; a bold villain, who lusts after the heroine; covered wagons; and – Zulus.

The plot links a passionate Irish beauty, Katie O'Neill (Susan Hayward), with the leader of a Boer commando, Paul van Riebeck (Tyrone Power). They meet first at Katie's ancestral home in Ireland, where, after the ball, Paul

> *... ambushes her in a darkened hall and convulsively kisses her, murmuring: 'You're a beautiful murderous killer, Katie.' (Press release synopsis)*

Accepting the compliment (even though her lover is spastically 'convulsive' rather than 'impulsive'), Katie returns his passion. They meet next in the South Africa of the voortrekkers, when Paul and his commando ride to the rescue of a wagon train attacked by Zulus. Riding into the laager, Paul is astonished to find Katie, who has just killed her first Zulu. He stammers incredulously: 'You – here – in Africa – fighting Zulus.' This being southern Africa, diamonds and gold are thrown into the plot – even though the events occur in the 1840s, some twenty years before the discovery of diamonds, and forty before the discovery of gold. What does it matter? This is adventure and romance.

The film does nothing to dispel the old stereotypes. The wagon train and its hardy pioneers are white and good, while the Zulus are a faceless, threatening mass. The only good Africans are the servants, especially Paul's faithful sidekick Tshaka (read Tonto to the Lone Ranger), who ultimately delivers the *coup de grâce* to the baddie threatening his master, skewering him with a spear. The ideology of the film is best revealed in a scene between Paul and Katie. They ride out into a beautiful valley which they have decided to make their own. Katie surveys the panorama and asks breathlessly: 'How much is mine?' When Paul replies, 'As much as you can ride around in one day,' Katie's eyes widen in covetous astonishment, and she whips her horse into a gallop.

The underlying assumption is, of course, that this is virgin land, belonging to no-one, and therefore it is fitting that the beautiful and the glamorous take possession. Without being in any sense intentionally propagandistic, but no less opinion-forming for that, it strengthens the impression given by this and other films on Africa that whites have every right to be there, indeed, to own it.

The director of *Untamed*, Henry King, was a veteran of Hollywood who had been in films since silent movies. Cinemascope was new to him, but this was clearly a Western set in Africa, and presented no real problems, other than dealing with Zulus.

Variety carried the following article on the making of *Untamed*:

HENRY KING FINDS BEER BEST WEAPON AGAINST 'UNTAMED' ZULUS IN DARKEST ZANUCKVILLE[62]

The maps will never show it, but for several months earlier this year South Africa had a thriving little tent community called Zanuckville, inhabited by some white film-makers and a couple of thousand hot-tempered Zulus doubling as extras.

Story deals with the Boers' legendary 'great trek' from Johannesburg (sic), an event that preceded the Boer War and which cost thousands of the settlers' lives in battles with the Zulus... King confides that it was the 'most strenuous job' he'd undertaken in his long film career.

Rule number one in making a film with Zulus ... is to be sure of a plentiful supply of beer, King relates. 'They drink the stuff as part of their regular diet,' he said. 'We almost got into an awful lot of trouble at the start because we didn't provide enough of the local Kaffir brew. Later we knew better, and Zanuckville had a regular brewery along with the rest of the facilities.'

King used about 2 500 Zulus who would come drifting into camp in tribal strength when they heard of the project. But having them

---

62   Named after producer Darryl F Zanuck.

there and getting them to perform properly before the cameras were two different matters. 'They're a proud people,' King said. 'At first we had to have something like "get together" parties for them where they could get acquainted and get to know the various chiefs. Finally, we formed three different "regiments" of about 750 Zulus each and they made out fine.'

However, his troubles didn't stop there. The Zulus are trained as warriors from early childhood, and while the government doesn't permit them to carry their traditional spears, they are armed with sharp sticks and protective shields. At one point, while staging a battle between Zulus and the Boers, one of the tribal chiefs approached King in great agitation.

'My men say they'll not play this game any longer unless you change the rules,' he declared. King, who had assigned certain of the attacking Zulus to fall dead in the face of the Boer fire, expressed his surprise.

'Our history tells us that the white men died also,' the chief pouted. 'So why do you have only our Zulu warriors falling dead. It isn't fair.'

There were other difficulties. Half-dressed Zulu women would frequently stray within camera range and had to be removed. And some of the extras, getting bored with the routine, would just pack up and leave, their curiosity satisfied. King said he ran into no racial trouble and got fine co-operation from the South African government ...

The *Variety* article displays the same cavalier attitude towards historical and geographical accuracy as does the film itself. This is not to be wondered at, since most Americans' knowledge of Africa came from the cinema. What is most disturbing is the description of the Zulus.

Even allowing for hype – it was good publicity to have it believed that filming the Zulus was about as difficult as fighting them – the interview is drenched in racial prejudice. The Zulus are depicted as both shiftless drunkards and childlike. Their lives are aimless – they 'come drifting into the camp'. They have a short attention span ('would just pack up and leave'). The chief 'pouts' and complains that 'it isn't fair', like any kid when things aren't going his way, and the Zulus 'won't play this game any longer'. At the same time, they can turn dangerous – they are 'hot-tempered', they get truculent when deprived of their beer, and they carry sharp sticks. There is the insistence on the Zulu as warrior ('trained from early childhood'), as if they had no other occupation.

The need for a protective weapon invoked by the title, however much it appears to be jocular, together with the use of 'untamed' and 'darkest', all conjure up the direst images of Africa and perpetuate the stereotypes – stereotypes that in 1954 seemed to be in no way in Hollywood's interest to expunge, even if it could recognise their existence. Do not misread the meaning of 'King said he ran into no racial trouble ...' The meaning is perhaps not so obvious today, but at that time, and in the context of the tone of *swart gevaar* in the article, it can only mean 'blacks attacking whites'. King is anxious to put in a word on behalf of the South African government, and this was expedient.

South Africa was one of Twentieth Century Fox's best distribution territories, and the Hollywood company had even developed a relationship with the government. In the late 1950s, in the words of an African Mirror Newsreel:

> *Twentieth Century Fox signed a contract with the South African Department of Information to give worldwide release to information films made in South Africa ... and State Information Office films, which reached an estimated 100 million last year, will take a tremendous step to being viewed by a potential 400 million in numerous countries. And so the true story of South Africa will be brought to vast audiences throughout the world.*

That is to say, Twentieth Century Fox undertook the task of distributing South African propaganda to cinemas and television worldwide.[63]

The material disseminated may have appeared to be harmless enough, mere travelogue in nature; but it invariably propagated the view that South Africa was White Man's Country. If blacks appeared at all, they appeared as servants or as part of the fauna. Zulus were invariably picturesque, but the threat was there that they could readily revert to their warlike state. (The narration of the travelogue *Zululand*, from 1947, for example, says '... the Zulus who once fought the British empire in violent wars are little changed as they dance in old barbaric rituals ...') The fiction film *Untamed*, which masquerades as South African history, was in harmony with the South African government's white supremacist ideology.

---

63   *South Africa Today,* a Twentieth Century Fox travelogue in Cinemascope from 1962 (only two years after Sharpeville), contains the line '... this bright new republic ... stands as a bulwark against Communism on these shores and across the earth'. But this was not unique. Even non-Twentieth Century Fox travelogues on South Africa carried the same messages. The Encyclopedia Britannica Films educational film, *Union of South Africa: The Land and its People* (1956) preaches that 'It is a land where light- and dark-skinned races work side by side to build a secure and prosperous way of life. South Africa is one of our good neighbours in the world family of nations ...'

THE FIERCEST HEART (1961)

The historical distortions of *Untamed* are as nothing compared to those of *The Fiercest Heart*. This was another acquisition from a South African writer by Twentieth Century Fox, this time Stuart Cloete. Although *The Fiercest Heart* (whose title echoes the wildness of *Untamed*) was given the full cinemascope-and-colour treatment, its stars are not of the quality of Tyrone Power and Susan Hayward; they are Stuart Whitman, whose muscles far outweighed his acting ability, and Juliet Prowse, a pouting South African who had made her way to Hollywood. Raymond Massey, who had seen better days, is there, as a crusty Boer patriarch. Goodness knows what Geraldine Fitzgerald was doing in this movie.

It is the veld meets *Oklahoma!*, with hoe-dances, tumbling in the hay, lovable farmers, bodice-bound cleavage. All of this as they march into Zulu-infested country. *The Fiercest Heart* was another variation on the Great Trek, but one that would have made Piet Retief turn in his grave. As the most deadly, yet blissfully unconscious, insult to the voortrekkers, the film has the Great Trek led by a renegade from the British Army, whose sidekick is a black deserter! Also present in the wagon train is the Jew Bauman, who acts as the conscience-figure. There is even a scene where Bauman and Prinsloo, the Boer patriarch, pray together. (It would be going too far to suggest that this is a subtext on South African–Israeli co-operation.) The film includes a villainous white slave-trader, but in none of these films is there ever any suggestion that the Boers might be slave-owners, even though blacks drive the Boers' oxen. Nzobo, the black deserter, behaves, and is treated by the Boers, as an equal.

There is much talk of 'the Promised Land', especially by Prinsloo. By the time they find it, Prinsloo is dead, and with totally unintended irony, it is Nzobo, the African, who points to it and says, 'the Promised Land!' Unfortunately, the Zulus think otherwise, and there is the obligatory laager-circled-by-Zulus battle. As with *Untamed*, this is resolved by the faithful black, Nzobo, killing the enemy leader with a spear. Oh, and yes – it wouldn't be South Africa without a glitter of gold in the story, this time a barrel of the stuff, the Boers' treasure.

ZULU (1964)

Earlier on in the 1960s, the British actor Stanley Baker had visited South Africa to play in Jamie Uys's film *Dingaka*. He appears to have been taken with the country, because he returned in 1963 to produce and act in a film of his own, *Zulu*.[64]

---

64   As a point of interest, the director of this film was Cy Endfield. Endfield had been raised in the United States, but left that country as a fugitive from the anti-communist witch-hunts of the 1950s, settling in England.

This was standard British colonial war, stiff-upper-lip stuff, and apart from a nagging need to boost British morale in a period of declining power, there seems to have been no good reason to make the film. The fact that it was a story of *Welsh*, as opposed to English, heroism had something to do with it – the heroic soldiers are from a Welsh regiment, and Baker was a Welshman. The battle commemorated in the film is that of Rorke's Drift, which came shortly after the Zulu victory at Isandhlwana. The Welshmen's repulse of the attacking Zulus came as a kind of consolation prize for a country appalled by the Isandhlwana shambles, and the little band of soldiers was showered with the highest British military award, the Victoria Cross, by a pathetically grateful War Office.

Like *De Voortrekkers* and *Symbol of Sacrifice*, *Zulu* includes scenes from the kraal of the Zulu king, in this case Cetewayo. These include the mandatory dancing – a war-dance and a Dance of the Maidens. An observer of these dances is the film's amateur anthropologist, the Swedish missionary Wits (Jack Hawkins), who carefully explains to his daughter that the little spears carried by the dancing virgins are 'a symbol of their chastity'. (He does not elaborate.) Margareta is horrified that these young girls are being married to much older warriors, but her sage father compares it to the European custom of young women marrying older men for their money. As with the earlier mock-anthropological production *Siliwa the Zulu*, the chief interest in showing such scenes lies not so much in the opportunity to make cross-cultural connections, but in the salacious advantage to be gained from displaying the bare breasts of the maidens.[65]

---

65 'I once read somewhere that modesty is a matter of geography, and there was one big scene in *Zulu* that proved this beyond all doubt. It was a big celebration scene in which a couple of hundred girls do a traditional tribal dance. Some of the dancers were from the tribal lands and a few of them were Zulu girls... who lived and worked in Johannesburg. When it came to filming, Cy (Endfield) discovered that the correct costume for this dance was a tiny bead apron and nothing else. No underwear. Nothing. He asked the wardrobe department to run up a couple of hundred pairs of tiny black panties what would retain some modesty and prevent an apopleptic censor but would still give the impression of the correct historical costume. This compromise was eventually accepted by even the most ardent traditionalists among the tribal dancers. Cy thought his troubles were over until he was informed that the Zulu girls from the city would not dance barebreasted and wanted to wear brassieres. This of course was completely out of the question for the tribal girls, they had already given way in the knicker department and they were not about to concede any further. There was an almighty row between the two sets of girls, with Cy in the middle trying to get the pants on one side and the brassieres off the other lot. Peace was finally restored and we shot the sequence once, but had to shoot it again because as the camera tracked along the line of dancing girls, the camera operator suddenly shouted "Cut!" He pointed at one of the girls and said, "That one's got no drawers on," and indeed she hadn't. Her reply was translated back to Cy: "I am sorry," she had said. "I'm not used to them and I just forgot."' (Michael Caine, in his autobiography *What's it all About?*, p 153.)

Tediously, once again, the Zulus are a faceless mass of warriors, with Cetewayo as absolute leader. In *Zulu*, his power over life and death is demonstrated in somewhat ambiguous fashion: when Wits and his daughter try to leave Cetewayo's kraal after a messenger has brought word of the defeat of the British at Isandhlwana, a warrior intervenes to prevent them. For this act, Cetewayo orders him killed on the spot. So the Zulu king is at the same time merciful to the foreign missionaries, and merciless towards his own followers.

As always, the focus of interest is on the white characters, on the relationship between the two untried British officers who are in charge, and characters who make up the Other Ranks – the hard-bitten sergeant, the raw recruits, the malingerers who in the end give of their best. The script is familiar. The Zulus are there to charge, repeatedly, and to die, although there is just a suggestion of something more when the Zulus sing a war-song and the Welsh reply with their own battle-song, *Men of Harlech*. The final song of the Zulus comes with their admission of defeat, when they salute the brave Welshmen prior to their withdrawal.

Although the film does not caricature the Zulus, half a century after Goba appeared in *De Voortrekkers* and *Symbol of Sacrifice* there is no attempt to personalise them either. Even though a soldier pays them the compliment of 'I think they've got more guts than we have, boyo', they are still the savage mass. The most memorable scene in the film comes near the end, with a crane shot over piles of Zulu corpses, up onto the band of white soldiers standing on the barricade above them. It is an image that could have come straight out of the *Illustrated London News* of eighty years before.

It would be fine if one could dismiss *Zulu* as simply an adventure story, irrelevant to our times. But I am haunted by another series of film images from a few years before *Zulu*. These were again the result of a black and white clash, where the whites were outnumbered, and undoubtedly felt themselves threatened by the hordes surrounding them, and fired to defend themselves – only the hordes were unarmed, and they were not marauding, they were demonstrating. It was a massacre, perpetrated by the police, at a township called Sharpeville.

Sharpeville attained the place it holds in popular memory largely because of the visual images it left. The newsreel cameraman arrived there shortly after the shooting, and filmed some of the dead bodies on the ground, others being carried away, people helping the wounded. What has been captured is the post-climactic moment, and in this sense, it is analogous to the fictional scene at Rorke's Drift after the last charge. In both scenes, the rifles of the whites have prevailed; and I strongly suspect that the image bank inside the head of every Afrikaner policeman who stood and fired at Sharpeville contained visual paradigms for what had become imprinted behaviour – that is, to fire on blacks when threatened by them.

This was a laager situation all over again, and ineluctably produced its own river of blood.

And so Stanley Baker's homage to warrior ancestors, in the post-Sharpeville climate of the early 1960s, seems a dangerous indulgence, echoing, as it does, to the clash of other battles and other ancestors, whose descendants lay bleeding on the field of Sharpeville. The extent to which life and cinema imitate each other, with infinite variations of lockstep, is terrifying.

Stanley Baker probably produced *Zulu* with no thought to the recent history of South Africa, and he would have rejected accusations of racial aggrandisement.[66] Baker was clearly not a white liberal, but he was working in times sensitised by Sharpeville and the paroxysms that succeeded it. His distorted view of South Africa and life there was gleefully reported by a reporter of the South African *Sunday Express*:

US TOLD *ZULU* WAS FILMED IN EAST AFRICA

Film star Stanley Baker is busy rewriting the world's history and geography books – for, in the advance publicity campaign for **Zulu***, he has said that the Battle of Rorke's Drift occurred in the Zulu-occupied part of EAST Africa.*

Baker made this statement to leading entertainment columnist Sheila Graham – and it was published recently under her name in the **New York Mirror***.*

Any mention of South Africa, where the film was actually made, was completely omitted by Baker – who stars in the film with Jack

---

66   Michael Caine relates this story about the making of the film: 'This was my first visit to South Africa and I had no preconceived notions about their politics or racial policy – nobody had. However as I worked and watched what was going on around me I was uncomfortable, then concerned and finally downright angry. Most of the workers on the set were black, but they were not tribal – simple ordinary carpenters and electricians from the city, just like anybody else. But all the foremen were white Afrikaans and they treated the black workers with incredible rudeness the like of which I had never seen before. They literally talked to them as though they were dogs.
    'One day I saw a black worker make a mistake and I stopped to watch him get a real telling off, just as any worker would in the same situation. To my astonishment, the foreman didn't reprimand him; he smashed a fist into his face instead. I was so shocked at this I couldn't move, and then suddenly I started running towards the man, screaming at him, but Stanley (Baker) got there first. I had never seen him so angry. He fired the man on the spot and then gathered all the white gang bosses together and laid down the law on how everyone was going to be treated on this film set from then on. He was in absolute fury and so were the rest of the British contingent. It brought home for the first time what this word "apartheid" really meant.' (Michael Caine, *What's it all About?*, p. 154.)

Hawkins. The omission was motivated, apparently, by the mounting world-wide hostility to this country.

Other Baker observations are:

* That the men used in the film wore necklaces of claws from wild animals.

* That they don't use money, and wouldn't know what to do with it.

* That women start bearing children at 13, and they work hard so that their husbands can earn more cattle to replace them (the lobola system).

Miss Graham continued quoting Baker: 'The Native in his own surroundings, is a wonderfully happy man. They are mostly vegetarians. When we roasted a couple of oxen for a special meal, they went crazy with joy. Meat is only eaten at a feast, and they sing and dance around the meat before eating it.'

African expert Stanley Baker's assessment of the Zulu people is: 'The women do all the work, tilling and sowing, while the men do absolutely nothing except singing and dancing.'

*Footnote: **Zulu** is expected to be the Royal Command film in London next February.*

The insistence on the feckless nature of the Zulu character resembles the remarks of Henry King a decade earlier regarding the making of *Untamed*. It conjures up a Hollywood that clings to its myths, even when contrary evidence is at hand. King and Baker were there, in place, but shunned direct experience. Apart from Baker's cavalier sense of geography, the remarks of the two directors could have been made by the average purblind white South African. Exploitation of the Zulu image for hype occurred, lamentably, even in conjunction with *Jim Comes to Jo'burg*. As one of its press-blurbs, the producers in 1949 gave out the following misinformation:

ZULUS BAFFLED BY MOTION PICTURES

*The Zulu in Africa is one of the few natives who refuse to become urbanised. Even when they do come to the towns they still wear earrings and live together isolated from other tribes. Cinemas are something magic and forbidding to them and they stay away from such white man's Spirits. For the all-native film **Jim Comes to Jo'burg**, the producers decided to show a part of all the aspects of native life and incorporate a Zulu dance. The Zulus, well disciplined, did as they were told during the shooting of the scene and went home without a query. Later the producers decided the*

> *Zulus must see themselves on the screen. They were shepherded unprotestingly into the darkness of the cinema and the film began. Murmurs of wonder and cries of fear broke from them when they saw themselves on the screen. An interpreter explained the strange reaction. None of them had seen a moving picture before and they had thought the film unit were just another lot of tourists taking their snaps with a specially big camera.*

This certainly apocryphal scene was pulled out of publicity files, dusted off, and regurgitated on location with *Zulu*:

> *None of the Zulus had ever seen a movie so Cy (Endfield, the director) set up a screen and a 16mm projector and they all gathered to watch and see what they were supposed to be doing. The film was an old Roy Rogers western, and when it first came on there was a gasp from everyone at the wonder of it ... The biggest laugh came when Roy Rogers sang as he rode along. They obviously could not understand why a man would want to sing riding a horse alone on a prairie, and were puzzled about where the music was coming from ...*[67]

What is frightening about Hollywood is that it is able to impose its fantasy view of the world upon millions of people. It is impossible to chart the impact of *Zulu*, an accomplished film, upon the mass psyche, but it undeniably perpetuates the mythology of empire, and of white supremacy.

Nevertheless, there was indignation in the Zulu community when the South African censors banned *Zulu* to Africans. The Johannesburg *Star* (21 January 1965) quoted from an African newspaper, *Umthunywa*, published in Umtata:

> *There is widespread concern among African cinema fans throughout the Republic of the decision taken by the Publications Board to ban Africans of all ages from seeing the much talked about film **Zulu**, the cast of which includes thousands of Africans ... The picture, we are told, depicts scenes of violence and bloodshed involving Whites and Africans.*
>
> *If the ban has been placed only because there is fear that such scenes might cause racial friction, these assumptions must be dismissed as nonsensical.*
>
> *Our African folk, we maintain, have as much decency as theatre-goers of other racial groups. With their many years as theatre patrons there is nothing to justify any assumption that they*

---

67 *What's it all About?*, p. 148.

*will suddenly turn savage and allow their feelings to run high at
the sight of war scenes to which one is much accustomed on the
silver screen.*

*If Africans in the rest of the Republic are prepared to tolerate
this ban, those in the Transkei should not.*

*At least the Republican Government has considered them mature
enough to merit self-government. It is inconceivable that at that
stage of their development they must not be allowed to see a film
which adults of other racial groups are entitled to see, and thus be
treated as non-African children under 18 years of age.*

Although in the film it is the guns of the white soldiers that shed the most blood, typically the film was not banned to mature white audiences. What the censors feared, apparently, was the power of the film to stir up African passions.[68]

On the African side, there was a natural and long-lasting resentment at being treated like children; but there was probably also a desire to participate in an experience of their own history – the film was called *Zulu*, and was about the last period of power experienced by the Zulu nation. The educational system of South Africa had been deliberately structured to deprive Africans of a sense of continuity, of a past in which they could take pride, and a movie offered, in a graphic way, some access to their own history, however inaccurately presented. Never mind that the film glorified white heroism and conquest, there were images of African warriors on the screen. As contemporary cinema in America has revealed, black people would rather have images of black villains than no images of themselves at all.

---

68   Almost 30 years later, in 1993 the film was acquired for airing on SABC TV.
     It was withdrawn after protests. 'We received numerous calls from concerned
     viewers saying it would be insensitive to screen the movie with so much violence
     going on,' said Mariaan Esterhuysen, the television spokesperson.
     Barry Ronge, then film critic for South Africa's *Sunday Times*, dismissed this
     explanation as 'daft'. 'We're not talking *Terminator II* here. It's a level of violence
     passed by the British and South African censors in the mid-1960s,' he pointed out.
     Ronge claimed the film was withdrawn for 'politically correct' reasons, since it
     depicted black-on-white violence, 'the massacre of a small number of white people
     by an overwhelming black majority'. But this is precisely what the film does *not*
     portray. It is difficult to see how Ronge could read the film in this way other than
     by taking a laager viewpoint, for it palpably shows how a small number of whites
     were able to mow down a considerable number of Africans. But the question of
     who massacred whom in the film seems to me of less importance than that the
     racial warfare portrayed in the film had to be viewed in the context of the massive
     letting of blood in contemporary South African society, and in that context, the
     decision to run the film in the first place seems criminally myopic. As it transpired,
     the SABC proved to be sensitive to criticism, and rescinded its decision to cancel the
     film, and it was shown later in 1993.

In all these films, the apparently willing accomplice was the faceless mass itself – the Zulu horde. Where films of the conquest of the American West were concerned, from the beginning native Americans were supplanted by Hollywood extras, and are only now beginning to be given leading roles. In South Africa, the situation was quite different. The historical films were often shot in the locales where the original battles had taken place, where there were still Zulu people living close by, but in any case, there was no pool of extras to draw on, and particularly no black pool.

While a Hollywood extra could pass for an Indian, especially in a Sioux headdress, this was not the case for a race as different from white as the indigenous peoples of South Africa. During the salad days of film-making, a D W Griffith could get away with having white actors play Zulus, but in more sophisticated times this became no longer acceptable. Besides, in South Africa, it was far cheaper to hire black extras than white. The scenes of massed battle of *De Voortrekkers*, *Symbol of Sacrifice*, *Untamed* and *Zulu* were cheap in terms of costs for actors, which is partly what made them so attractive to make.

Why has it always been so easy to find masses of extras willing to re-enact the defeats of the Zulu nation, preserving past humiliations and thereby contributing to the continuance of white hegemony? Not least must be counted the attraction of play-acting itself, of appearing before the camera in a role that offers escape from the humdrum. It is not hard to imagine the glee of mineworkers offered the recreation of play, even at the sacrifice of a day off, to be part of the glamour of cinema. To this must be added the strong sense among Zulus of belonging to a warrior nation, and the pride and social bonding this entails; the traditional dances are still alive, and were often incorporated into the films. It was only a short step from there to fall into the part of the charging warrior, thus reliving the glories of the past – ignoring that on the screen these became the humbling of the Zulu *impis*. In a society that keeps wages low for Africans, even the pittance paid to extras must also be a consideration.

That participation in such films was not necessarily in the best political interests of Zulus, in a society controlled by whites, does not appear to have been considered, or, if it was, to count for anything. From the point of view of the white film-makers, it was always of course essential to have control over the warrior extras; certain passions were being roused which had to be exploited for the camera, but never allowed to get out of hand.

As we have noted, at the time of *De Voortrekkers*, ancient animosities were sufficiently revived to threaten that the attacking Zulus would burst through the constricting frame of cinema into the dimension of real life; at the time of *Untamed*, the suggestion was that this dangerous ardour had to be doused with beer. But what was critical to the participation of Zulu people in these film versions of white history was the collaboration in some form of the leadership of the Zulu nation.

Where this leadership stood can be seen very precisely in images from *Zulu*, for among the leaders of the impis attacking the white garrison can be discerned the face and figure of Chief Mangosuthu Buthelezi, who plays the Zulu leader, Cetewayo. His presence in the frame signifies his approval of the project, and this approval would have been essential not only for the film to be shot in Zululand, but for the Zulu people to take part in it. Depending on where you stand, this can be seen as seizing an opportunity to bring cash and jobs to the homeland, on whatever ephemeral basis location filming brings; or it can be seen as a cynical selling-out of Zulu heritage and history.

For Buthelezi, there was a bonus both from the filming and from his role-playing in some of those films in that through his on-screen persona, the historical figures he portrayed fused with his image as a legitimate modern leader, in much the same way as the panoply and ritual of royalty give a mystical legitimacy to the individual holding the office.

As a postscript to *Zulu* and its political comae, here is what Bill Keller, the *New York Times* correspondent, wrote in his despatch from South Africa of 25 November 1993:

> By uncanny coincidence the Friday night movie on television last week, after South Africa's political rivals had signed a constitution, was **Zulu**, a 1964 film ·about the Zulu struggle against British colonialists in the last century.

(To describe the film in this way is to turn it upside-down. There is no doubt that it is the British soldiers who are the heroes.)

> Viewers who paid close attention may have recognised the man portraying Cetshwayo, the Zulu king who led his people in a valiant but calamitous war that ended the Zulus' hopes of independence. The amateur actor was Cetshwayo's great-grandson, Chief Mangosuthu G Buthelezi.
>
> Three decades after his cinematic turn, Chief Buthelezi is now the most formidable figure in an alliance of holdouts, white and black, who reject the new order embodied in the constitutional pact last week.

In bringing notice to the film in these terms, Keller is plainly implying that Buthelezi's current actions may be as calamitous as those of his forefather. However, even if Buthelezi and Inkatha would like to present their actions, like those of Cetshwayo in the last century, as a defence of Zululand, the comparison is faulty. Cetshwayo was mounting a fully justified defence against invasion; he could not be blamed for the outcome, however calamitous it proved for the Zulu people.

ZULU DAWN (1980)

I knew little about Africa, and virtually nothing about Zulus; I had optioned the screenplay only weeks before. What knowledge I had about the dark continent came to me by way of Tarzan movies, television programs like **Wild Kingdom**, *and a dim recollection of the film* **Zulu** *which I had seen when it first came out in 1964. In short, if I was expecting anything, it was jungle, apes, elephants, lions and natives. I was prepared for adventure, and wild fantasies filled my head.*

In this fashion does Nate Kohn (in his admirably frank essay 'Glancing off a Postmodern Wall: A Visit to the Making of *Zulu Dawn*', written in 1991) describe the frame of mind he was in when he embarked on producing *Zulu Dawn*. It bears witness to how the screen has moulded our image of Africa – note how Kohn can still refer to it as 'the dark continent' – and how the tenaciousness of this image tends to overwhelm all other evidence.

At another point in his essay Kohn acutely observes that 'movies deliver up other times and other places better than other times and other places do on their own'; although he does not attempt to explain what he means by 'better' here, we can take it to mean 'more excitingly'.

As he describes it, Nate Kohn was in something of a time warp when he arrived in Africa. Like Lionel Rogosin almost twenty years earlier, Kohn found in South Africa something he recognised, something he calls 'Memphis 1955' – that is to say, a place of privileged whites and repressed blacks, but also a place where change could not be postponed indefinitely. What had happened in the American South, he felt, would inevitably happen in South Africa.

But he was trapped inside another time warp, the time warp of the nineteenth century. He has already revealed as much by his ready reference to 'the dark continent'. The story he was there to film emphasises it. Here is how he describes it:

The movie we were about to make told the story of the events leading up to the Battle of Isandhlwana on January 22, 1879, and of the battle itself. Natal was a crown colony on the Indian Ocean. Zululand surrounded most of it. Borders were contested. The British, ever expansionist, sent an Imperial Army under the command of Lord Chelmsford to tame the Zulus. Encamped on the slope of a large hill named Isandhlwana deep in Zululand, half the British expeditionary forces, about 1 500 Welsh and English redcoats plus some native contingents, were attacked by about 30 000 Zulu warriors. The British, a powerful modern army, had cannons, rockets, rifles, pistols, bayonets. The Zulus had spears. The battle lasted 45 minutes. At the end of it, the British were all dead, except for about 20 who managed to escape. It was the worst defeat ever suffered by British forces at the hands of a native army to that date. Back in England the word Zulu suddenly became synonymous with Bloodcurdling Terror.

Yet another twist to the warp: *Zulu Dawn* was written by Cy Endfield, who twelve years earlier had written and directed *Zulu*. Had Hollywood's view of the Zulus changed in that time? Scarcely. In hindsight, Nate Kohn recognised this:

Our concern ... was with creating a dramatic look, a visual strength that catered to our Anglo-American sensibilities and expectations. The tradition we were following was a filmic one, not a Zulu one, not even an African one ... We were confident we knew best how to represent the Zulus and make them come alive in performance for our First World audiences ...

Again, this was Hollywood perpetuating the imperial mythology of the last century. Somewhat ruefully, Kohn commented, 'Although we didn't know it at the time we were probably participating in the colonial discourse.'

Nate Kohn approached Chief Buthelezi for his permission in making the film:

(Chief Buthelezi) wanted to make sure that we did not pay the Zulu extras more per day than they were making in the sugar cane fields or factories, so that the normal work patterns would not be disrupted ... He insisted that we cast only Zulus to play Zulus ... Zulu actors needed work.

However, Chief Buthelezi declined to do a reprise of the part of Cetshwayo that he had played in *Zulu* for his friend Cy Endfield.

According to Kohn's estimate, this feature film was going to bring an injection of a significant portion of the 12 million dollar budget into the economy of KwaZulu, at that time and place a not inconsiderable sum, yet neither Chief Buthelezi nor King Goodwill Zwelithini took much interest in the project, and did not try to control it or draw personal profit from it.

The screen image of the Zulu nation has always been in the hands of white film-makers, until recently with no oversight by Zulus themselves.[69] Commonly, these film-makers would have had little, if any, direct contact with Zulus, simply

---

69   Nate Kohn also held much the same opinion of the truculent nature of the Zulu extras as Henry King before him.

taking a received story and turning it into a film script. For Kohn, the perspective was (as with Rod Amateau and Harold Nebenzal and *The Wilby Conspiracy*) Hollywood's Wild West: '(The) concept was: Custer's last stand in Africa ... We were making a western.' But curiously (because not fully explained), Kohn goes on: 'A revisionist pseudo western with a major black victory as its central element couldn't lose at the box office.' In what sense is *Zulu Dawn* revisionist, and why was it timely to portray a black victory?

Nate Kohn's first visit to Africa, to South Africa, occurred in the fateful year of 1976. He places it as at the very time of Soweto, but writes that he was not fully aware of what was going on because of the efficacy of government control of the press and television, and did not appreciate its importance until he had left South Africa. But the film was not shot for another two years, and there was ample time for the meaning of the Soweto uprising to be absorbed.

Cy Endfield was of course primarily responsible for authorship of the film, and Kohn writes that the script was actually written in the early 1970s, and that 'it is as much an African western as *Zulu* is';[70] there were certainly rewrites, and these rewrites may well have introduced the element of revisionist history that distinguishes the film. And such rewrites may have been, consciously or unconsciously, influenced by what began as the Soweto uprising, which enforced respect worldwide for the courage of black South Africans.

Fifteen years earlier, Cy Endfield's *Zulu* had presented a not disrespectful depiction of Cetshwayo and his armies, and this was repeated in *Zulu Dawn*; but the latter film differs significantly from Endfield's earlier film in its depiction of the white characters:

> The idea of **Zulu Dawn** (the Movie Project) was to make a film of epic scale that glorified the British common soldier in defeat, vilified the generals and politicians, and portrayed the Zulus and their chief as men of honor, courage, and cunning who achieved a magnificent victory through superior military strategies and tactics. The fact that they were fighting in defence of their homeland also helped. (Nate Kohn, 'Glancing off a Postmodern Wall')

Zulu was a celebration of white warriors from which the politics were completely absent. *Zulu Dawn*, on the other hand, is anxious to set the record straight with regard to the invasion of Zululand. The governor sends an ultimatum to Cetewayo which he knows will be rejected. An early scene is set at a garden party, with ladies and gentlemen playing croquet on the governor's lawn. But this appears as a veneer of civilisation, when the governor, Sir Bartle

---

70   Personal letter dated 20 August 1994.

Frere (played by John Mills), makes a public declaration of war against the Zulus: 'Let us hope this will be a final solution to the Zulu problem.' Lord Chelmsford, the British general (Peter O'Toole), remarks: 'For a savage as for a child, chastisement is sometimes kindness.'

A callous indifference towards African life is depicted in ways not seen in earlier films: at the fording of the river separating Natal from Zululand, when a native bearer is swept away by the current, more concern is expressed by the quartermaster-sergeant for the loss of the ammunition box he was carrying than for the life of the African; an elderly Zulu scout is lanced to a tree by a soldier, as if he were hunting down a boar; and a twelve-year-old herdboy is cut down. Such images of white behaviour in Africa are quite uncommon for the screen.

The Zulu dawn of the title refers at one level to the surprise early morning attack on the British army at Isandhlwana – the dramatic defeat that preceded the compensation prize 'victory' at Rorke's Drift depicted in *Zulu*; at another level, the title implies the ascendancy of the Zulu army, which had shamed the world's foremost military power – albeit for too brief a time. Once again, however, the focus is on the white protagonists, who are individualised, even while we recognise a number of stereotypes, dating back at least to *Symbol of Sacrifice*. The story is really about the machinations of empire, and the incompetence of the leader of the expeditionary force, Lord Chelmsford. Against the machiavellian governor and the arrogant Chelmsford is balanced the bravery of the soldiers – an overworked theme of war films, which allows a film to condemn war while at the same time glorying in it.

Producer Kohn recognised the imbalance:

> ... *Things were askew. The star power of our white cast members combined with their studied and evident acting power tilted the balance, forced the focus in their favor, making the film much more conservative and predictable than it should have been. Here we were, in the middle of Zululand, ten thousand miles from Hollywood, five thousand from London, among a magnificent native people in a wilderness of immense proportion, and we could do little to keep the camera from involuntarily swinging toward a (Burt) Lancaster close-up with five hundred out-of-focus Zulus charging in the background. Economics also came into it. If you are paying Lancaster $750 000, as we were doing, you want to get your money's worth. Each Zulu extra cost only $7 a day, figuratively about a dime a dozen ... We constantly filled the foreground with the high drama of white faces acting. ('Glancing off a Postmodern Wall: A Visit to the Making of **Zulu Dawn**')*

On the one hand, Kohn imbues the camera with a will of its own; on the other, he invokes the very real force that directed the camera – money. Both tend to obfuscate the fact that virtually every image was very precisely set down on paper long before shooting began, and there was no way to shift emphasis on to the Zulus.

Even with the respect that both Cy Endfield and Nate Kohn undoubtedly had for the Zulu people, the established cinema image of them persists. The film opens with the stereotypical attributes that supposedly make up the 'tribe' – dances by bare-breasted maidens and warriors, the bellicose mass ruled by an all-powerful chief. Single combat is taking place before Cetewayo, who is being served food. One man falls, and Cetewayo casually gives the sign for him to be dispatched. This scene of an absolute monarch's power of life and death over his people is obligatory for all films depicting the Zulu – Endfield's *Zulu* has it, even the 'anthropological' *Siliwa the Zulu*.

Much is also made of the power of the assegai; the British quartermaster-sergeant strikes fear into the heart of a raw recruit with the words: 'The black wave of death in the thousands. Them assegais – stabbing!' Not unique to this film is the suggestion that the weapons of the Savage Other are themselves somehow more fearsome and barbaric – even though all the historical evidence is that it was the death-dealing efficiency of the 'civilised' weapons that made the conquest of Africa possible. And guns were of course most effective against an enemy who, like the Zulu, relied upon massed charges to overcome, and whose favoured weapon, the stabbing assegai, was effective only at arm's length. At Isandhlwana, by means of a forced march and a surprise attack, the Zulus were able to fight on their own terms – hand-to-hand combat. At Rorke's Drift, the British could make effective use of their rifles. In *Zulu*, Lieutenant Chard expresses indignation that the Zulus are able to fire upon them with rifles captured at Isandhlwana – this was definitely not cricket, and was a serious threat to racial order.

In spite of *Zulu Dawn*'s apparent willingness to deal more objectively with history, the film ends with a curious throwback to *Symbol of Sacrifice*. The earlier film, which was made during the period of empire, had as its theme a sentimental attachment to the British flag and an engulfing mystique of mindless patriotism. Separated by over sixty years in time from *Symbol of Sacrifice*, with all the miasma of racism that pervades those years, *Zulu Dawn* yet perversely insists on harking back to the chauvinism of that earlier period. In the closing scenes of the film, a group of British officers escapes across a river with the colours. The colours are captured by the pursuing Zulus, and taken back across the river. But one of the officers, mortally wounded, has been overlooked. In a final effort, he fires his carbine at the Zulu bearing the colours. The Zulu is hit, and the colours fall into the river, and are swept away. Having saved the colours – the honour of the regiment –

from the enemy, the British officer dies. In a fashion not untypical of cinema, *Zulu Dawn* tries to have it both ways; in our supposed enlightened times, the film aspires to undermine the conqueror's version of history, and to reveal the double-dealing, brutality and incompetence of Britain's takeover of southern Africa. Simultaneously, there is a clinging nostalgia for the glory days. But the doublethink of *Zulu Dawn* is mild when compared with the tortured convolutions of the epic series *Shaka Zulu*.

SHAKA ZULU (1986)

Most of the fiction films dealing with the Zulus are based on historical events, however warped. The films dwell on the bellicose nature of the Zulus because these are adventure films, dazzled by the glory of white conquest. All the films lay claim to historical accuracy, albeit modified by dramatic imperatives. But it is, of course, history according to the conquerors.

Until William Faure's *Shaka Zulu*, no-one had attempted a screen Shaka, although he had been much written about in history books and in literature, including Zulu literature. There are a number of reasons for this neglect. Shaka, unlike Dingaan and Cetshwayo, had never fought the white invaders. The portrait painted by white men's history was certainly of a man bloodthirsty enough to make a screen villain, but without whites as heroes, there was no game.

So Hollywood was incapable of making *Shaka Zulu*. It would be no exaggeration to say that it needed the intersection of a number of complex political circumstances – the Soweto uprising of 1976 and the watershed that that created, the Nationalist government's need to establish the Zulu nation as a political player, re-evaluations of South African history – to propel Shaka onto the screen. At all stages, in development up to distribution, the project was controversial.

Although *Shaka Zulu* was intended for television rather than the cinema, it was filmed as a movie epic. It was the South African Broadcasting Corporation's (and the South African movie industry's) most ambitious project to date, by far (it cost 24 million dollars). Even though it was a co-production with overseas investors (chiefly German and American), it represented a major commitment of funds on the SABC's part. At this time, in the 1980s, the SABC was not merely financed by monies allocated by the government, it was still virtually an arm of the South African government's propaganda machine.

Inside the country, its task was, by selective reporting, to lull the population into a sense of security, and to maintain a negative image of the liberation movement. The SABC's external service was devoted to convincing the rest of the world that South Africa was in responsible hands, and that whatever problems existed were the result of plotting by international communism.

By the early 1980s, however, there was a growing recognition among influential sections of Afrikanerdom that the dismantling of apartheid was as inevitable as it was desirable, and that some accommodation had to be reached with the black majority. The public relations banner that was unfurled at that time was no longer that of a country of distinct but somehow equal ethnic groups, but of a country that, for all its faults, was being built through the efforts of blacks and whites moving towards a common goal.

In the latter part of the decade, under the rubric of the South African Office of Tourism, a very accomplished 15-minute film was made. In video form, it was distributed free of charge by South African consulates overseas. Its title, as audacious in its sentimentality as in its hypocrisy, was *Love Changes People*.

Distributed as a tourist film, it contains the inescapable images of a game-packed country. But beyond that, it sets out to depict a country that gives equal ranking to black and to white. By dint of selective editing, blacks appear to be sitting in the same classrooms as whites, and competing in the same sports. Black and white interviewees testify to having friends of a different race. Major anti-apartheid breakthroughs, like the Comrades Marathon and an interracial concert, are presented as evidence of the non-racist character of South African society, and even offered as the norm; this despite the fact that they were the end result of years of defiance of government bans on racial social mixing.

In the final scene of this deceitful film, a candid camera watches two naked toddlers, one black, one white, romping together in a mud puddle. The white child falls, and when he picks himself up, appears, zebra-like, to be striped black-and-white. The film freezes on this outrageous image.

This government film reveals the mindset of Afrikanerdom at that juncture. If the Nationalists could not bring themselves actually to call for a democratic society, *Love Changes People* at least indicates that they might be beginning to think about the unthinkable, even if in a perverse and hypocritical fashion. But the machiavellian habit is a hard one to kick. Nationalist conspirators had spent millions of dollars in buying friends and influencing people. They had secretly bought into foreign newspapers and television. They had seduced politicians abroad with junkets and favours.

This had gone on for decades, and was part of a massive public relations war between the South African government and the anti-apartheid forces overseas. *Love Changes People* offered the vision of a South Africa not divided by ethnic hatreds. At the same time, Nationalist strategists were playing for all it was worth their trump card – the Zulu ace. And this was no more than the ancient strategy of 'divide and rule'.

When Bill Faure came along with the *Shaka Zulu* project, the subject was pregnant with interpretations and nuances that could serve the purposes of Nationalist machinations without being overtly propagandistic, infinitely more subtle than a *Love Changes People*. So, deflecting Opposition questions in Parliament about the cost, the government blessed the 24 million dollars the SABC shelled out to realise Faure's grandiose project. It took five years, was aired in South Africa in 1986, and has not been off world television screens since then.

Shaka Zulu really has two plots, and the clumsiness with which they are entwined reflects the failure of the scriptwriters (Joshua Sinclair and Bill Faure) to resolve the conflict between the historical and the fabulous elements. One concerns the interaction of three main characters: Shaka, king of the Zulu nation that he has single-handedly created; Lt Farewell, an emissary of the British crown, whose task it is to win the confidence of Shaka and bend him to ends beneficial to Britain; and Fynn, an Irish doctor whose integrity is compromised by working with Farewell.

The second plot, which makes liberal use of flashbacks, magic and fantasy, is a gothic romance woven around the life of Shaka. There is a serious gulf between the sheer silliness of the attempt to embellish a Shaka myth, and the far more interesting interplay of *realpolitik* between men from different worlds, that prevents the story from achieving its full potential. This does not handicap *Shaka Zulu* from being a fascinating study of the hopes, fears and contradictions that tortured Afrikanerdom at a time when it was having to face up to new racial realities.

Playing with time, *Shaka Zulu* begins with an Epilogue, 'The Death of an Empire'. Queen Victoria receives Cetswayo, king of the Zulus. The Zulus, who had briefly challenged the British in South Africa, have been massively defeated, and Cetswayo, who has been exiled, is suing for the return of his country.

This scene is a device for a lesson in Zulu history concerning the importance of Shaka. During his reign from 1816 to 1828, we are told, Shaka created an empire comparable to that of Napoleon. He turned his warriors into a spartan army of '80 000 highly trained ruthless warriors', and the 'war-machine created by Shaka Zulu was so monolithic it has survived his death by almost half a century'. This 'war-machine' is clearly still a potential threat to the interests of the British crown. The Queen's counsellor gives her the following advice: 'if the Zulus won't bend – break 'em!' The Queen is heedful, and declines to reinstate Cetswayo. Cetswayo points out the gulf between the Zulus and the British: 'We have so little in common – especially our concepts of human respect.'

This Epilogue/Prologue ends with an intonation by the Narrator:

> *And so it was that the empire created by Shaka Zulu some six*
> *decades earlier was disbanded, the king's territory subdivided,*
> *and placed under British supervision. The resulting political*
> *mismanagement, continual white interference in the ensuing strife*
> *would effectively destroy the House of Shaka. From this time on,*
> *the Zulu people would only be able to dream of the dignity and*
> *the glory given them by their legendary king. This then is his story.*

At this point, we are thrown into the introductory images that precede each episode of *Shaka Zulu*, a montage of warriors, faces of individual characters who will appear, Zulu pomp, an explosion, a helicopter shot of Shaka cavorting with shield and assegai on a hilltop, sinister witch-like figures, and a zoom in to a close-up of Shaka.

The story proper begins once again at the English court, but this time it is the court of King George IV, sixty years earlier. The lascivious king is depicted as more interested in his doxies than in affairs of state, airily dismissive of 'a tribe of savages running around in their birthday suits'. The king's counsellor, Lord Bathurst, is less easily dissuaded from regarding the Zulus as a threat to Cape Colony, but believes that they can be outwitted:

> *(Guns) are not our only superior weapons. We have one other,*
> *gentlemen. Civilisation – years of tried and tested double talk. If*
> *we cannot soothe the savage beast, we can at least confuse him,*
> *whilst we mount an effective military defence.*

The man chosen to double talk the Zulus is Lt Farewell. Farewell is unorthodox in manner and thought – he unceremoniously receives the royal envoys in his bath-tub, and demurs from Bathurst's point of view regarding the superiority of the 'civilised man' over the 'savage':

> *Centuries of enlightenment do not necessarily make a country or*
> *its people militarily stronger – indeed, as Attila the Hun proved,*
> *domestication is usually a weakening factor.*

Despite his scepticism, Farewell signs on, lured by the prospect of a fortune in ivory. Although he dutifully carries out the designs of his employers, he does so without illusions, and even with an anachronistic sense of racial equality. He scandalises Lord Somerset, Governor of the Cape Colony, when he remarks:

> *Lord Charles, the only chance the Crown has of preserving its*
> *territories in Africa, America, or Asia is if it finally sheds its*
> *hypocrisies and starts treating others as equals.*

Fynn, who carries most of the burden of the film's Voice Over narration, is first seen tending sick Africans in what is either a prison or slave quarters – it is not clear which. This scene is intended to put him on the side of the enlightened, a man without racial prejudice, like Farewell himself, but without Farewell's deviousness.

When they reach him, Shaka is intrigued by these visitors, and they are impressed by his intellect. Early on, there is a confrontation that establishes Shaka's power. Fynn and Farewell come across a funeral party, but Fynn notices that the hand of the corpse, a young girl, is moving slightly. Fynn intervenes, and with a few slaps to the girl's wrist, brings her back to life. To the natives, this endows him with supernatural power. When Shaka learns of this, he has the girl killed, and invites Fynn to bring her back to life again. But even though Fynn of course cannot do this, the Zulus still believe that he and Farewell have magical power.

We are introduced to Shaka's mother, Nandi, his aunt Mkabayi, and 'the grotesquely old and frail chief witch doctor of the realm', Sitayi, about whom Fynn archly comments:

> *I suppose the best way to describe her was that she constituted the*
> *spiritual arm of his court, a bit like the Archbishop of Canterbury,*
> *I suppose, although I'm not sure he would appreciate the*
> *comparison.*

With Sitayi, the film enters the realm of 'supernatural forces, great prophecies and magical witchcraft', with gloomy forests, lightning flashes, hellish jackals. We go into flashback, beyond the time when Shaka was born – in fact, dealing with his conception. We are given the time and place, South-East Africa, 1786.

Nandi, bathing in a stream, is espied by Prince Senzangakona. He is smitten by her, gets her pregnant, but through the influence of his sister, Mkabayi, marries another woman. When Nandi confronts the prince, he says he does not know her. The pregnant Nandi is attacked in the forest, but rescued by Sitayi's jackals. Sitayi is involved with some prophecy regarding Nandi.

Senzangakona becomes king, and his illegitimate child is born to Nandi. This is a primitive childbirth, with a rope around Nandi's ankles to assist the delivery. Shaka is born in a storm, in darkness illuminated by flashes of lightning striking trees. Sitayi seems to preside over it all in the forest. Fynn's commentary expounds:

> *History had cast its die. And in Africa, a force had been generated*
> *that in time would rock the very foundations of the African*
> *subcontinent.*

Nandi brings the child to Senzangakona's kraal. By sheer force of personality, she negotiates a lobola for herself of 55 cattle. Rivalry between Nandi and Senzangakona's sister Mkabayi. Nandi taunts her with 'What do you know about being a woman?' which suggests either that she has no man, or no children. Senzangakona insults Nandi in front of Shaka as 'the queen of whores', and the boy Shaka threatens to kill him. Senzangakona is warned that Shaka is the child of a prophecy, and must be killed.

The boy Shaka is subjected to a test by three dwarf witch doctors. His ankle is cut to draw blood, which is heated over a fire, and drunk by the leading dwarf. At this, Sitayi in the forest casts a spell, and the witch doctor falls down dead. Shaka faints. His mother flees with him by night from the king's kraal. The small group wanders through the wilderness, and Shaka's grandmother dies. Nandi finds her way to a former suitor, Gendeyana, who takes her in and treats her well.

After some time, Mkabayi tells Senzangakona that Shaka has a brother now, and suggests that Shaka be taken away from Nandi, and brought to the royal kraal. Senzangakona presides over the circumcision ceremony for Shaka, who is now a young man. The king publicly accepts Shaka as his heir, and offers him the symbol of manhood. But Shaka defiantly taunts him, and rejects the symbol. Shaka is ordered to leave the kingdom on pain of death. He flees to the forest, where he stumbles upon people slaughtered in an ambush. He rescues a wounded man, Dingiswayo. The two part, but are destined to meet later.

At the Zulu royal kraal, Senzangakona is warned to act against Shaka. Learning of this threat, Shaka and Nandi leave Gendeyana's kraal. The kraal is raided by Senzangakona's men, and Gendeyana is slain. In the forest, in order to save them, Shaka separates himself from his mother and the others, is speared in the leg, and falls into a river. Despite his wounded leg, he manages to climb a sheer cliff face and elude his pursuers. He is discovered by bare-breasted maidens cavorting in a stream. The maidens bear him away, the pursuers arrive and claim him. But this turns out to be the land of Dingiswayo, whom Shaka had earlier saved from death, and Shaka is rescued by Dingiswayo's men.

Shaka is billeted with Dingiswayo's warriors, and shows promise as a soldier. His independent mind leads him to question the traditional military tactics. He suggests larger shields for protection, and close-in fighting. The Zulu general is incompetent, but when Shaka tries to change the battle tactics, he becomes a laughing stock.

With the assistance of Sitayi, Shaka goes to the forest to have a magical weapon forged. When he finally has his assegai (a short stabbing spear), he performs a spear-dance, prancing on a hill-top. At the Mtetwa military kraal, Shaka asserts himself. He defies the general to kill him. The general complains to Dingiswayo. But another general suggests that Shaka's tactics should be tried. Shaka is given his own brigade. When Dingiswayo is attacked by Senzangakona, Shaka overcomes with his new tactics while his father, Senzangakona, looks on. In revenge for his grandmother's death when they were fleeing from Senzangakona, two captives are impaled on stakes.

Senzangakona dies. A successor is chosen, but Shaka plans to take over the throne. He confronts the selected heir, and kills him. Nandi comes into her own as the royal mother, and shows mercy towards Senzangakona's sister Mkabayi, who had plotted against her.

At this juncture, we are thrown back once more into the present, with Farewell and Fynn at Shaka's kraal. During a dance ceremony, there is an attempt on Shaka's life. Nandi begs the white men to save his life. Sceptical of being successful, Fynn nevertheless makes the attempt. Shaka begins to recover, and

Farewell touches up Shaka's greying hair with Rowlands Macassar Oil Hair Dye, while Nandi looks on in amazement at this 'rejuvenation'. He is carried outside his dwelling to be shown to the people. With a great effort he raises himself up and salutes with his spear. He accepts the homage of the crowd, including his aunt Mkabayi, who is disappointed at his survival. The crowd greets him with '*Bayete!*' ('Hail!').

To deflect suspicion from herself, Mkabayi points to others as the culprits for the attempt on Shaka's life. Shaka says he knows that it is Dingane who is to blame. He impales ten of his bodyguard for failing to protect him.

Shaka honours the white men who he believes have saved his life. He signs a document ceding much land to Farewell, and he elevates the whites to kingly respect. He invites them to participate in the war against his enemy Zwide. With the help of the cannon and muskets of the white men, Zwide is defeated, and Fynn is ordered to execute him by cannon. Fynn reluctantly complies to prevent harm to the whites.

Wishing to return to the Cape, Farewell builds a ship. Shaka holds his men as hostage for his return. Because he refuses to contemplate a future without his own existence, Shaka has his own child killed. Nandi falls sick, and Shaka summons Fynn to help her recover but Fynn is powerless to do so. In grief at her death, Shaka proclaims a Year of Wailing, and orders a number of people to be put to death.

Farewell and his Zulu emissaries are received by Lord Charles Somerset at the Cape. Word is brought that Shaka is marching on the Cape. Farewell returns to a Zululand devastated by Shaka's decree of mourning. He passes through a landscape filled with impalements. He goes to Shaka, who accuses him of failing him. Shaka is assassinated, and the royal kraal goes up in flames ...

William Faure, the film's director, has said that the cornerstone of his impassioned interest in the figure of Shaka was his desire to do historical justice to the African people:

> *I think it goes back to when I was at school ... Our white textbooks primarily dealt with white history, and white history was always seen from a white perspective. And I felt that there was a big gap in the market in terms of interpreting black history both in our history books but definitely on the screen ... And I felt that it was time to give black history an entirely new perspective, give it the dignity and the respect that it deserved in terms of cinematic interpretation. So that was really the driving force behind it ...*
> *(Interview, 1990)*

Faure's freewheeling invocation of history and the market forces of cinema in the same breath is certainly in the tradition of Hollywood arrogance, swept along by a mudslide of ignorance. Faure was of course not wrong in perceiving the wilful and contemptuous neglect with which African history had been mistreated. But what kind of service does Faure do to Africans and to history with his grandiose ballad *Shaka Zulu*?

In staking his claim as a champion of black history, Faure realised that he was at a disadvantage:

> *... We're dealing here with a white director (i.e. himself) and immediately we're faced with the same problems again of white interpretation of a black history. OK. So that is a problem we've had to overcome. What I did right from the onset, I liaised very closely with the Zulu royal family, as well as the Zulu government, only in so much as I needed Zulu approval ... We felt that it was in our interest to see to it that at all times we were being advised by the proper people, and what the king then did, he delegated Prince Gideon Zulu, who, I think, is a relation to the king, his uncle, he's the king's uncle. And he, plus the Prime Minister's grandmother, were asked to be our cultural advisers on the project. So everything we did was subject to their approval. But having said that, they also understood that we were creating an entertainment piece ... So there had to be a marriage between what was absolutely culturally historically correct and what would be needed to make the thing an entertaining adventure piece as well, we had to meet those two requirements, obviously, especially for the American market, as you can imagine. And they understood that, and were perfectly happy. (Interview, 1990)*

In order to get their co-operation, Faure felt that he had to appease the jealous guardians of some kind of traditional Zulu history. Yet Faure was well aware of the difficulties surrounding interpretations of Zulu history:

> *... Up to a point, you know, there is no written history, because the Zulus never had a written history ... So any stories that we have pertaining to Shaka, and especially the early period, before the whites arrived, is the verbal history, the history passed down... from generation to generation. (Interview, 1990)*

Having admitted this, Faure then went on to reveal his real infatuation:

> *... Certainly from our point of view, the mythology, the legends, the stories of the influences of the sangomas, the witchdoctors, and the traditional adherence to that kind of mythology was very much in line with what we were looking for, it gave it colour, it gave it interest, so we added all that in ...*

What Faure gives us is closer to the Arthurian legend than a serious attempt to present a moment in the history of the Zulu people. I suspect that John Boorman's *Excalibur* exerted an influence on Faure. Indeed, the character Fynn actually invites the comparison:

> *Fynn: Tales of supernatural forces, great prophecies and magical witchcraft, surrounding the king's power in the making of his spear ... almost an Excalibur, as it were ...*

The pyrotechnics of Sitayi's sorcery – lightning flashes, reddened eyes, figures looming through the half-light of the forest, vicious houndlike creatures – all derive from hundreds of horror films, themselves based on gothic literature. They have nothing to do with Zulu mythology.

Although Faure could not conceive of Shaka as anything other than a made-for-Hollywood character, he nevertheless believed that he was making a contribution to black liberation:

> *Shaka Zulu is, as far as I am concerned, a powerful political statement ... What I needed to do, I felt, as a white South African, is to say to white South Africans, Look at your fellow South Africans, look at them in a new light ... and see that their history is every bit as valid, in some cases even more valid, and more important than your own. Look at, for instance, with Shaka Zulu, the Zulu history, their traditions, look at it and you will find something of worth, something of value, to be studied, looked at, and respected. So that when you meet a Zulu again, or you meet a black man, you understand that he's not just some, you know, faceless, you know, man who comes from some township somewhere, because we've never bothered to make contact with him, understand that when you look at a black man, he also has an extraordinary, dynamic and very interesting history à la Shaka Zulu. (Interview, 1990)*

This is an utterance that could probably only emanate from the hubris generated by the fantasy world of cinema. Faure creates a cheap mythology, calls it history, and then uses this fabrication to legitimise black people in the eyes of whites. How can any history, of a people or of an individual, be any more or less *valid* than that of another? All that counts is that it be explored with respect and understanding, and above all, accuracy.

What has become clear over the last decade, with the emergence of revisionist studies that look critically at the image of Shaka passed down over the last century and a half is that it is just that – an image, with very little solid historical foundation. The Europeans who met and described Shaka all wanted to exploit him in one way or another, like Farewell, who wanted chunks of his territory. Nathaniel Isaacs, who had close contact with Shaka at the same time as Farewell, later wrote *Travels and Adventures in Eastern Africa* (1836), which Dan Wylie, of Rhodes University, claims 'disintegrates as a credible source' upon close examination. Yet this work formed the basis for most subsequent accounts, and is a prime source for *Shaka Zulu*. The histories were suspect because the historians accepted uncritically the view of Shaka as a bloodthirsty tyrant ruling a nation he had forged for war.

It is not that there was some kind of conspiracy among historians. If you share an ideology, you do not need a conspiracy. The image of the Zulus that was passed down justified white rule. The fact that the Zulu people tended to regard themselves as a nation of warriors, and nursed a nostalgia for a lost greatness, does not legitimise white historians with a one-sided view of history. One passage of the foreword to John Selby's *Shaka's Heirs* (1971) reads:

> *It was the settled conviction of every Zulu that his manhood was not complete nor his tribal standing established until he had 'washed his spears' in the blood of a foe.*

The fact that this was written by Commandant S Bourquin of the Department of Bantu Administration suggests how self-serving the image was. On the Zulu side, the image of the proud warrior helped to salve the shame of being a defeated people. The same image served a different purpose for each side.

The popular white image of Shaka began conventionally enough. He was an African leader, and therefore despotic, arbitrary, ruthless, with judgment bordering on the psychotic. This was the stereotype handed down to cinema in say Dingaan and the fictitious Haqeba from Uys's *Dingaka*. The overwhelming political purpose – more or less unconscious – was to perpetuate an awareness of the Savage Other who is out there, not too far away, poised to overwhelm the whites, and as a reminder of the nature of black rule, which has fortunately been displaced by white. (The grotesque figure of Idi Amin was an overwhelming bonus for Afrophobes during the 1970s and early 1980s.) This quotation from Isaacs's *Travels* (as cited by Wylie) could equally have been applied to Amin as to Shaka:

> *When once he had determined on a sanguinary display of his power, nothing could restrain his ferocity; his eyes evinced his pleasure, his iron heart exulted, his whole frame seemed as if it felt a joyous impulse at seeing the blood of innocent creatures flowing at his feet; his hands grasped, his Herculean and muscular limbs exhibiting by their motion a desire to aid in the execution of the victims of his vengeance ...*[71]

---

71   Dan Wylie, '*Who's afraid of Shaka Zulu?*', *Southern African Review of Books*, May 1991.

The more threatening the depiction of black rule, the more humane must appear white rule.

Africans held a different concept of Shaka, and Jordan Ngubane[72] lays out the opposing views:

> *One cannot readily think of an African who rose from greater adversity to write across time for all men to read, a bolder and more enduring epic of human achievement than of Shaka the Great, founder and emperor of the Greater Zulu nation ... Shaka has been hailed as a military genius and a symbol of African excellence.*
>
> *He has also been denounced as a vindictive, insensitive and bloodthirsty tyrant.*
>
> *The chorus of praise has come mainly from African historians, authors, journalists and poets while the calumniation has flowed generally from white explorers, scholars and writers. While the conflicting assessments might reveal Shaka's complex character, they need to be seen in the contexts provided by history as viewed from different angles by Africans and Whites and the different perspectives from which the two races see reality, society and the person.*

Ngubane goes on to claim that Shaka was an early Pan-Africanist who wanted to draw the peoples of southern Africa into one nation. It was this interpretation of the Shaka legend that came to serve a nefarious political purpose during the 1970s, 1980s and 1990s.

At the time when the film was still in its formative stage, another highly charged element was well entrenched to vex the ghost of Shaka. This was the figure of Mangosuthu Buthelezi, the Zulu leader, who had long ago emerged as a player of weight on the uneven playing field of South African politics.

Buthelezi has long fused his name and associated his policies with Shaka, 'that magnificent forefather of the Zulu nation', and claims: 'I trace my ancestry back to the very founders of KwaZulu.'[73] Buthelezi deliberately invites comparison with Shaka.

While claiming that his work was 'a powerful political statement' directed at whites, Faure vehemently rejected any accusation that in making *Shaka Zulu* he was covertly supporting the Zulu nationalist movement – 'we weren't in this to produce a political statement'. But he did become incensed when he perceived the

---

72   In his essay 'Shaka's Social, Political and Military Ideas', in *Shaka, King of the Zulus in African Literature* (edited by Burness, 1976).

73   Speech by Buthelezi of 18 January 1992.

Zulu nation to be under attack, as in a negative review of *Shaka Zulu* in the *Los Angeles Times* written by Howard Rosenberg ('gory, foolish and demeaning').

Most damaging, in two articles, written in November 1986 and in October 1989, Rosenberg cannily queried the murky origins of this series. Although press releases in America publicised *Shaka Zulu* as a Harmony Gold production, Rosenberg found publicity from other countries that listed it as a South African Broadcasting Corporation production.

> *And **Shaka Zulu** is identified as 'the greatest project yet undertaken by the SABC' – and important for the nation's 'image abroad' – in the public record of a 1984 South African parliamentary debate held in advance of shooting. (**Los Angeles Times**, 21 November 1986)*

Rosenberg reasonably concluded that the involvement of the South African Broadcasting Corporation had been deliberately hidden:

> *Given the strong anti-apartheid feeling in America, you can guess why South African involvement had been concealed.*

The *Los Angeles Times* reviewer challenged Frank Agrama, of Harmony Gold, the American company that was publicised as producer in the US, with this.

> *Agrama said that **Shaka Zulu** is a co-production with Germany's Tele-Munchen, Italy's RAI, Australia's Nine Television Network and SABC. He maintained that in such cases, it is the practice of each co-producing company to list itself as sole producer in its own nation.*
>
> *Actually, that's not the typical practice in the United States, where international co-productions list each producer separately.*

Rosenberg went on to ask Agrama why Harmony Gold omitted from its publicity the credit for the South African Broadcasting Corporation while listing the other co-producers.

> *'Well, you know,' Agrama said, 'we were a little bit, you know, after the override of (President Reagan's) veto (of limited economic sanctions against South Africa), we didn't want to make the controversy bigger.'*

When TBS (Turner Broadcasting Service) acquired the mini-series for national airing three years later (an indication of its perdurability and popularity), Rosenberg questioned TBS executive vice president Bob Levi about the programme's genesis:

> *Levi characterised the South African Broadcasting Corp's*
> *financial involvement ... as nothing more than a routine 'pre-buy'*
> *for South African broadcast rights. 'The key is that they had no*
> *script approval,' he said. (**Los Angeles Times**, 9 October 1989)*

Levi of TBS also so grossly misrepresents the content of *Shaka Zulu* that one has to assume that he has either not seen the series, or is deliberately falsifying. He is quoted by Howard Rosenberg as saying that the mini-series shows 'African resistance to English colonialism', which it palpably does not. He adds that 'It's relevant and it's good television.' Relevant it certainly was, although in a way Levi may have been too ingenuous to recognise. Millions around the world did apparently take it for good television.

Director Faure launched a massive counter-attack on Howard Rosenberg. Since the production was undeniably South African, Faure carefully chose not to involve himself in that matter; instead, he accused Rosenberg of ethnic prejudice, a distortion for which there is absolutely no evidence.

> *He'd obviously been fed all this unadulterated crap by various*
> *interested people who were determined to see that the Zulus got no*
> *exposure whatsoever, because there's a vendetta against the Zulu*
> *people ... (Bill Faure, interview 1990)*

It is difficult to imagine that Howard Rosenberg, or even ANC supporters who Faure implies may have put pressure on him, could have any vendetta against the Zulu people. It shouldn't be forgotten that the Zulu nation, like almost all polities active in South Africa at that time, was divided within itself; no-one could justly claim to speak for 'the Zulu nation'. But it was the conservative element, the Inkatha-supporting royal family, with which Faure had had to deal in order to get the film made. And it was the Nationalist Government, whose purposes Inkatha served at that time, that was financially supporting Faure's production, through the middleman of the South African Broadcasting Corporation.

There was political capital to be made through the film. For a domestic audience, it could be expected to feed breakaway Zulu nationalism, while at the same time appearing to demonstrate that the SABC could deliver black subjects with black heroes. The impact of such a film overseas was much less predictable, but it could be calculated to win some goodwill. The SABC could claim to be showing an interest in African history, and few would have the political savvy to draw attention to the Inkatha parallels.

Faure claimed that he wanted to pass on a positive message. But, despite its being built around a black personality, the film's most obvious message is a negative one, and one that employs all the clichés of narrative films on Africa: Shaka is a tyrant who kills and tortures at will, and whose obsessive interest is in warfare. To the extent that the portrait of such a leader – bloodthirsty, impetuous, wilful – strengthens deeply-ingrained prejudices, it is a political film that served well the aims of the National-Party at that juncture. And all Faure's protestations to the contrary were disingenuous.

Faure waxed indignant at the suggestion that his film could be interpreted as being in some way supportive of apartheid:

> *Bullshit. Bullshit. Absolutely bloody bullshit. And it's the kind of crap we've had to cope with, you know, throughout the last two or three decades where there are people who are genuinely working inside the country against the system, but are being victimised because they happen to be South Africans, OK. And I think there has to be a distinction drawn between people who are blatantly working to support and prop up what is a totally immoral, you know, totally fascist apartheid system, and people who are working within the system to try and change the system.*

The ANC-led cultural boycott, which was a form of pressure on the apartheid regime, often had ludicrous and questionable consequences, but, like the sports boycott, it had an undeniable impact, not least in drawing attention to the influence of apartheid in areas often presumed to be politically neutral. It was part of the propaganda campaign against the odious system, and criticism of the role of *Shaka Zulu*, as much as the role of *The Gods Must Be Crazy*, was a legitimate part of the debate.[74]

Claiming that denunciations of the programme were losing him sales, Faure counter-attacked: '... We decided on a strategy, and we flew in Henry (Cele), who plays Shaka, and we systematically worked round the United States, telling the truth, telling the people why we'd made this production.' The deployment of an African actor was a masterly tactic, deflecting accusations of racism, and the

---

74 In Britain, *Shaka Zulu* coincided with a particularly acrimonious feud within Equity, the actors' union, over relations with South Africa. The actors Edward Fox and Robert Powell were vigorously denounced; Fox defended his participation by saying in an interview with the *Independent* newspaper that 'The only thing that keeps South Africa from becoming a Third World country is the wealth generated by the White influence there.' The Association of Cinematograph Television and Allied Technicians lobbied to secure a ban for the film on British television. The Anti-Apartheid Movement called *Shaka Zulu* 'a laundering operation to enable violation of the cultural boycott', to which Faure deceptively countered that it should be remembered that *Shaka Zulu* was produced by an American company, Harmony Gold. The pious hope expressed by *Shaka Zulu*'s scriptwriter, Joshua Sinclair, back in 1984, that the film could be 'a vehicle to bring the world closer to the problems of South Africa' and that it would be 'a bridge between (England and South Africa). Shaka, the Man of War, can be a vehicle of peace ...' becomes, in hindsight, pathetic.

appearance of Cele and Faure in tandem on talk-shows around the country, together with clips from the film, was all good publicity. Cele was capable of remarks such as:

> *... I went through the ... script. Oh, the first thing that impressed me was that Shaka didn't kill not even one white person ... That's why I loved the script, because this time it was Shaka wanting the black and whites together,*

which must have thrilled the South African Embassy. Whether Faure's *blitzkrieg* had an effect or not, far from being wounded by criticism, *Shaka Zulu* turned out to be a huge success, especially with black Americans. Even in South Africa, where government and SABC critics could see exactly what was going on, the image of Cele/Shaka hung over the beds of thousands of young boys.

> *People look upon me and say, 'This is Shaka Zulu,' and they think I'm the King. And I always tell people, 'Please I'm just as human as you are.' (Interview with Henry Cele, 1990)*

As with *The Gods Must be Crazy, Shaka Zulu* reveals the stresses caused within white society by the tension between imprinted prejudices and a sincere desire to see Africans anew. Shaka may be an African hero, but he is still one who relies upon the scientific knowledge of whites in applying their medicine, and upon their technological advantage in fighting his battles. Shaka confesses that he seeks 'the power of their knowledge' – but at the moment he is saying this, he is sighting along the barrel of a musket, which plainly implies that he intends to use this fatal 'knowledge' to kill and conquer, just like all the other African despots.

It is beyond coincidence that Shaka's dream of the future, expressed to the white man Fynn, echoes a National Party game-plan:

> *Perhaps a nation could be built where the whites and the Zulus could live in harmony. A council of elders would be formed, with the wisest elders of each kingdom ...*

These sentiments, put into the mouth of an African leader, carried a different message to different constituencies. For an overseas audience, it could be read as a plea for blacks and whites to work together to build a new South Africa. For a domestic audience, the appeal could be to form a Zulu/white axis that would shut out the ANC.

Nevertheless, the worn image of African politics, posing as history, takes over. Shaka's reign collapses in wanton savagery, for which Shaka blames the 'swallows' – the whites. Farewell returns, uttering the plea 'Hating my people is not the answer. We must search for a solution together,' reiterating what Shaka had himself said earlier. But Shaka rejects him, and the black-on-black violence culminates in the assassination of Shaka himself. For viewers in South Africa, the lesson to be drawn from this might have been that South Africa still needed white law and order to stop the country from falling apart.

History According to the Conquerors

Piet Retief and his men arrive at Dingaan's Kraal,...

...they sign a pact with the Boers...

...and they are slaughtered. *De Voortrekkers*, 1916.

The Imperial Imperative

Symbol of Sacrifice, 1918.

A *Gone With the Wind* set in South Africa.

Hollywood's distortion of 'white history' – the Great Trek led by white and black deserters from the British army!

Nate Kohn

Clichéd images of Zulus: as dancers in *Zulu Dawn*, 1980 (above)
and as warriors in *Zulu*, 1964 (below).

Jürgen Schadeberg

Revisionist history: the British shown for the first time as invaders of
Zulu territory. *Zulu Dawn*, 1980.

Demonisation of African Leaders

The evil witchdoctor terrorises his own people. *Dingaka*, 1964.

Cetewayo, the Zulu king (Simon Sabela) has absolute power of life and death over his subjects. *Zulu Dawn*, 1980.

Nate Kohn

Henry Cele

Above: Revisionist history: an ambiguous approach to a black king as hero – but still a tyrant.

Below: Fiction into themepark – the Shaka legend lives on!

Peter Davis

The Body Politic

Early European writers on Africa saw the unclothed human form as an expression of the uncivilised state, of savagery. Films on Africa, fiction and travelogues, have always delighted in presenting the African body in a primal condition, that is to say half-naked, and executing wanton movement, typically performing tribal dances or engaged in warfare, suggesting an analogy with Africa's wildlife – the exotic shapes call for admiration, but also demand to be shot down. Beyond its habitat in primal Africa, the naked black form, male or female, inevitably invokes memories of slavery – the unadorned human form as a commodity for exploitation.

Shaka Zulu made ample use of this tradition in displaying both men and women. Its presentation of the love affair between Senzangakona and Nandi went further than the SABC would have dared to go with a white couple. But it is Faure's display of Henry Cele's body, and what happens to it, that reveals most about the meaning of power in South Africa. Henry Cele, before acting the part of Shaka, was famous as a soccer star. He is a superb physical specimen, with the spare body of an athlete, not the bombast of a body-builder. His muscles are etched, not swollen.

Faure claimed that Cele bears an uncanny physical resemblance to Shaka; an odd claim, because we have only one illustration of Shaka, in which the features could look like Henry Cele – or ten thousand other Zulus. At the time Cele was selected to play Shaka, he had had very little acting experience, and it is hard not to conjecture that he was selected more for his torso than for anything else. (This is not to suggest that Cele does not acquit himself well in the film.) In the charged atmosphere of South Africa, this became a case of the body beautiful intervening in the body politic.

For the politics of *Shaka Zulu* do not lie alone in the covert messages with which the series is suffused. If our first level of understanding is of the story itself, and a second is of the parallels with contemporary politics, there is another level of cinema as psychodrama. This involves the communication of messages absorbed by the audience at a subconscious level. This information may reinforce the overt message of the film; it may be distinct from it; or it may even subvert it.

Shaka Zulu is far from a great film, but it is an accomplished work of cinema.[75] It is epic, and epic is the least subtle of cinematic genres. Despite this, *Shaka Zulu* does offer interpretations that can help us to understand the human psyche and human behaviour in the context of the clash and interflux of race and power, not only in South Africa. While the film operates at the levels of adventure story and of propaganda, the central image that informs the film is of the naked body of Shaka/Cele. It is an image that fuses power and sexuality – the quintessential Hollywood formula.

---

75 Unfortunately Bill Faure died at an early age in 1994.

There are of course other naked bodies in the film, played for soft porn value, as in the begetting of Shaka, or impaled on stakes, in by no means the worst examples of sadism in cinema. But it is the body of Shaka that dominates the film, from the ludicrous solo war-dance he executes on a hilltop, to the final *Götterdämmerung*. Every opportunity is seized for ritual annointing and bedecking of Shaka's torso. At the ceremony of Shaka's circumcision, we are offered a view of the adolescent Shaka's tight buttocks. (It is worth noting that, perhaps out of some SABC sense of delicacy, the true rigours of the circumcision ceremony are avoided.) His pectorals routinely glisten with sweat. It is a body that is frequently gashed with wounds, and in one instance, when Shaka has fainted from pain and exhaustion, is borne by naked maidens, in a South African version of a Burne Jones painting of a dying knight.

In preparation for the takeover of his father's realm, Shaka presents himself against a backdrop of a waterfall and assembled warriors, to have his nude body lovingly annointed by a maiden.[76] (For added impact, this scene is intercut with the preparations for his estranged father's burial, juxtaposing the quick and the dead.) While performing a dance – that is, while displaying the naked body in motion – Shaka is stabbed in an assassination attempt. His body is cared for, and cured, by the ministrations of Fynn, the white doctor, who succeeds in restoring the wounded body to health.

Up to this point, the body of Shaka has been admired by the camera as the image of kingly authority, and as a celebration of maleness. Tended by Fynn, Shaka seeks the source of Fynn's magical power, and finds it while rummaging through his doctor's Gladstone bag. It is a Bible. This Bible contains its own image of nakedness – a picture of Christ on the cross. Fynn's subsequent explanation to Shaka of the meaning of Christ introduces an element concerning the nature of power and of sacrifice, specifically of sacrifice of the body of the king for the good of the people. What follows from this has, I believe, as much to do with being brought up in South Africa as it does with the labyrinths of Faure's own psyche.

Fynn imparts to Shaka the meaning of the dying god, the Christian concept of strength through weakness:

> *Fynn: Christ is the lord of the whites, he is lord of all men, he is the son of the heavens.*

> *Shaka: Do you derive your powers from him? (Shaka is referring here to Fynn's curative powers.)*

> *Fynn: He is Power. With Christ at your heart, you're stronger than all the regiments on earth.*

---

76   For the original description of Shaka's public bathing, see the account by Henry Fynn.

Sitayi (Shaka's priest): If Christ is power, why did he not save himself? (Fynn remains silent.)

*Shaka: Christ had to die so that the heavens would pass on that power to me. The youth you've given me (Fynn has blackened Shaka's greying hair with macassar oil) is proof that I've inherited that power. Heavens belong to Zulu,[77] and Shaka is their son. If the Swallows (the whites) wish to be my friends, they must remember that. In this land, there is only one **Nkosi amaNkosi**. Only one King of Kings – Shaka.*

*Fynn: (diplomatically acquiescing) **Yebo, Nkosi.***

Fynn, showing some remorse at the manipulation of Shaka through the figure of Christ, remarks to Farewell: 'We've even turned the sanctity of Christ into a political device.'

The hubris is of course Shaka's, and it would be both shocking and amusing for a Christian audience to hear Shaka claim the mantle of Christ, perverting the nature of Christian power by subjecting it to his own interpretation. However, the confusion of the naked Christ with the naked Shaka that follows is an invention of Faure. During the Prologue/Epilogue, there is a specific reference to 'a messiah, a god-figure, like a messiah ...'

Through most of the film, Shaka is depicted as having minimal interest in the opposite sex. After his victory over Zwide – a demonstration of both his power and his cruelty – Shaka distances himself from the celebrations to retire to his hut, where he toys with a musket belonging to the white men. The musket is a symbol of power (specifically, white power) and, not unrelated, the cliché symbol *ad nauseam* of male potency. While holding the musket, Shaka is approached by a maiden who offers herself:

Pampata: Let me love you, Shaka, let me help you find love.

Shaka: For what purpose, little one? Perhaps through that love, you'll show me how to better rule my people?

Pampata: No, your people have nothing to do with it. I merely want to help take away the loneliness.

Shaka: A man who builds a road to the heavens must travel alone.

If we want to find a cinematic ancestor to Shaka at this point, we need look no further than the Western. The traditional cowboy hero is a loner (*Shane, High Noon, Unforgiven*), who intuitively understands that duty precludes sex, insisting

---

77   This is a reference to the word 'Zulu' meaning 'people of the sky'.

that 'a man's gotta do what a man's gotta do', and what a man's gotta do is bestride a horse, not a woman. Women are a threat to male freedom, corralling him with domesticity, impeding his duty. In *Shaka Zulu*, the hero, tempted by a naked woman, can see no point in succumbing, because to do so is an irrelevance. Christ too remained chaste. This comparison is invited by Shaka's 'A man who builds a road to the heavens must travel alone.'

But Pampata puts aside Shaka's musket, and since manhood is nowadays confused with potency, Shaka succumbs, with as much grace as reluctance can muster. Their lovemaking is spied through the flames of an open fire – not an original image for the passion of love, but in this case portentous: the flames will recur at Shaka's assassination. In the final scene, Shaka walks through a burning kraal, where the bodies of those he has ordered killed are impaled on stakes. His people, including his bare-breasted lover (whose baby he has slain, though this apparently does not daunt her affection), bow before him, acknowledging his kingly status.

Assassins close in behind him, but Shaka is unperturbed. He flings off his cloak, leaving himself almost naked. Those who will betray him, including his aunt, Mkabayi, gather behind him. He appears almost to welcome slaughter, as he asks, 'And now, Mkabayi, what now? For the good of the nation, you already said,' and he turns towards the assassins. 'I am once more in your hands.' He is stabbed repeatedly. As his kraal is put to the torch, we see again the naked body of Shaka through the flames, not this time in the act of love, but dead, cradled in the arms of his weeping lover. A Zulu *pietà*. Thus, at the end, Shaka presents himself, like Christ, as a suffering yet willing sacrifice.

Earlier on, after the assassination attempt, at the moment when Fynn appears to have resuscitated Shaka, Farewell remarks to him: 'Well, you've saved his skin, old boy. So now let's deal with his imagination.' While Faure has spoken much about Shaka's formidable intellect, and while this does represent an innovation for an African screen hero, in the film the struggle is more about possession of Shaka's body than of his mind. The tradition in cinema is to express white power over other races in pseudo-scientific terms, especially of medicine as fetish. In *King Solomon's Mines* the whites, at a desperate juncture, orchestrate an eclipse of the sun. In *The Gods Must be Crazy*, the zoologist employs a sleeping potion. There is usually a polarity – white science overcomes 'black magic'.

The device appears early on in *Shaka Zulu* when the 'doctor' Fynn brings back to life a 'dead' girl. Fynn's act is of course benevolent. But Shaka interprets it as a challenge to his absolute power over the lives of his subjects. He orders the girl killed, and defies Fynn to resurrect her once more. Shaka's cruel act is the obligatory arbitrary execution – as in *Zulu Dawn, Symbol of Sacrifice, De Voortrekkers, King Solomon's Mines* – which proves the African leader to be a despot. But here, the latent meaning – that whites do not treat blacks as badly as the blacks' own leaders do – is closer to the surface. It is a direct confrontation between black and white over black life. The life wantonly destroyed by Shaka has already been saved by the white man. (This point is underlined by our first view of Fynn, when we see him tending to African slaves.)

Although the historical Fynn was a trader and not a doctor, he did, according to his own account, tend to Shaka after the assassination attempt, and Shaka did recover. Metamorphosed for the sake of the film into a professional doctor, Fynn narrates and comments on much of the action. In the context of the film, he has an inflated integrity: he is the voice of history, doubly authoritative because the cinema traditionally grants unimpeachable status to doctors.

Although he cannot resurrect the dead girl, he does seem to succeed with Shaka. And by so doing the Swallows incur Shaka's gratitude. The 'owing' of a life-debt has a long history. In colonialism we need go no further back than *Robinson Crusoe*, in which Friday is saved by Crusoe from cannibals. Thereafter he belongs in a very real way to Crusoe. In South African cinema, it manifests itself in the character of Sobuza in *De Voortrekkers*, Sobuza being succoured by whites when forced into the wilderness by Dingaan. Similarly, in the American-made *The Kaffir's Gratitude*, where the African servant is rescued from a lion, by this act the master gains an added claim to the body of his servant. The body 'belongs' to the white man. It is the black body as commodity. And precisely as with *The Kaffir's Gratitude*, the apparently benign act of salvation has the effect of concealing a bitter and contrary truth – that whites in Africa, far from shielding black lives, often wantonly destroyed them, either through direct slaughter or callous neglect. The white impact was generally not to succour, but to subjugate.

A parting of the ways

What happens in *Shaka Zulu* to the division, as old as the century itself, of Africans into the two cinematic stereotypes of the Savage Other and the Faithful Servant? Shaka does not hesitate to threaten the white party – at a whim, he can destroy them. But he is not entirely alien. He is a magnificent ferocious beast, yet one that can be manipulated, if not entirely tamed. While he never becomes the servant of the white men, he can be tricked into doing their will when, for example, he signs over lands to Farewell.

As with the Bushman Xi, there seems to be a serious attempt to endow Shaka with a personality, as opposed to making him a cypher. A kind of intimacy is established between Shaka and Farewell and Fynn which hovers on the buddy relationship; but Shaka's ascendancy is established when it is the Swallows who are co-opted into fighting Shaka's war. In the end, Shaka asserts his individuality by rejecting the kind of united endeavour that Farewell offers, preferring instead to choose his own destiny, cataclysmic as that may be.

The Gods Must be Crazy and *Mapantsula* contain their own versions of rejection of what whites have to offer. Xi is prevailed upon to accept the money offered for his assistance, but he does it simply to placate the white man. And then, instead of returning to the Kalahari, he gets on with his self-appointed task, which involves rejection of the white materialist world in the shape of the Coca-Cola bottle. Like Shaka, he walks away from the white man. In *Mapantsula*, Panic, too, rejects the way out offered by a white policeman, which is the way of collaboration, albeit as an informer. Panic clearly cannot physically walk away, because he is a captive, but his moral rejection of the white offer is also the assertion of a black will which challenges the white.

All three films end with choices, and the ways taken are not those that the whites in the films would prefer. The simple recognition of this fact – which is also an acknowledgement that South Africa itself was at a figurative crossroads – marks an advance in the way South Africa and its black inhabitants were perceived, at least by white South African film-makers.

Filmography

Adventures of a Diamond (1919)

Africa Looks Up (aka *My Song Goes Forth* and *Africa Sings*) (1937)
    Producer/Director: Joseph Best
    with Paul Robeson

Africa Sings (aka *My Song Goes Forth* and *Africa Looks Up*) (1937)

African Jim (*aka Jim Comes to Jo'burg*) (1949)
    Production company: Warrior Films
    Producer: Eric Rutherford
    Director: Donald Swanson
    with Daniel Adnewmah, Dolly Rathebe, Dan Twala

African Mirror (Newsreel series) (began 1913)
    Production company: African Film Productions

Allan Quatermain (1919)
    Production company: African Film Productions
    Producer: I.W. Schlesinger
    with Mabel May

Amok (1983)
    Production company: Interfilms
    Director: Souheil Ben Barka
    with Robert Liensol, Miriam Makeba, Douta Seck

Beautiful People (1974)
    Producer/Director: Jamie Uys

Birth of a Nation (1915)
    Production company: Epoch
    Producer: D.W. Griffith
    Director: D.W. Griffith
    with Lillian Gish, Mae Marsh, Wallace Reid, Raoul Walsh

Black and White in South Africa (1957)
    Production company: National Film Board of Canada
    Producer: Ronald Dick

Die Bou van 'n Nasie (They Built a Nation) (1938)
    Production company: African Film Productions/
    South African Railways and Harbours
    Producer: D.M. Robertze
    Director: Joseph Albrecht

Cabin in the Sky (1943)
    Production company: MGM
    Producer: Arthur Freed
    Director: Vincente Minelli
    with Eddie 'Rochester' Anderson, Ethel Waters,
    Lena Horne, Louis Armstrong
Chicken Thief (circa 1910)
    Production company: Pathé Frères
    Producer: Siegmund Lubin
Come Back, Africa (1960)
    Producer: Lionel Rogosin
    Director: Lionel Rogosin
    with Zachariah Mgabi, Vinah Bendile, Bloke Modisane,
    Can Themba, Lewis Nkosi
The Condemned Are Happy
    Production company: Jamie Uys Productions
    Producer: Jamie Uys
    Director: Jamie Uys
Copper Mask (1919)
    Production company: African Film Productions
    Producer: I.W. Schlesinger
    Director: Joseph Albrecht
    with Holger Petersen, Adele Fillis
Cry Freedom (1987)
    Production company: Marble Arch Productions
    Producer and director: Richard Attenborough
    with Kevin Kline, Denzel Washington, Penelope Wilton,
    Zakes Mokae, Timothy West, John Thaw
Cry, the Beloved Country (1951)
    Production company: London Films
    Producer: Zoltan Korda and Alan Paton
    Director: Zoltan Korda
    with Canada Lee, Sidney Poitier, Lionel Ngakane
The Defiant Ones (1958)
    Production company: United Artists/Stanley Kramer
    Producer: Stanley Kramer
    Director: Stanley Kramer
    with Sidney Poitier, Tony Curtis
Desert Nights (1929)
    Production company: MGM
    Producer/Director: William Nigh

with John Gilbert, Mary Nolan, Ernest Torrence

Diamond City (1949)

Production company: GFD/Gainsborough Pictures

Producer: A. Frank Bundy

Director: David MacDonald

with David Farrar, Honor Blackman, Diana Dors,
Mervyn Johns

Diamond Safari (1958)

Production company: Twentieth Century Fox

Producer/Director: Gerald Mayer

with Kevin McCarthy, André Morell

Dingaka (1964)

Production company: Embassy

Producer: Jamie Uys

Director: Jamie Uys

with Ken Gampu, Stanley Baker, Paul Makgoba, Juliet Prowse

Dry White Season (1989)

Production company: UIP/MGM/Star Partners II

Producer: Paula Weinstein

Director: Euzhan Palcy

with Donald Sutherland, Zakes Mokae, Janet Suzman,
Marlon Brando, Jurgen Prochnow

The Fiercest Heart (1961)

Production company: Twentieth Century Fox

Producer: George Sherman

Director: George Sherman

with Stuart Whitman, Juliet Prowse, Raymond Massey,
Rafer Johnson

The Fox Has Four Eyes (1959)

Production company: Jamie Uys Film Productions

Producer/Director: Jamie Uys

Friends (1993)

Production company: Friends Productions Ltd/ Rio SA/
Chrysalide Films/ Channel 4/ British Screen.

Director: Elaine Proctor

with Kerry Fox, Dambisa Kente, Michelle Burgers

Gandhi (1982)

Columbia/Goldcrest/Indo-British/International
Film Investors/National Film Development
Corporation of India

Production company: Marble Arch Productions

Producer: Richard Attenborough
Director: Richard Attenborough
Gloria (1916)
Production company: African Film Productions
Producer: Harold Shaw
Director: Lorrimer Johnston
with Mabel May, M.A. Wetherell, Frank Cellier
The Gods Must Be Crazy (1980)
Production Company: New Realm/Mimosa/CAT
Producer: Jamie Uys
Director: Jamie Uys
with N!Xau, Marius Weyers, Sandra Prinsloo
The Gods Must Be Crazy II (1989)
Producer: Boet Troskie
Director: Jamie Uys
with N!Xau, Lena Farugia, Hans Strydom
Gold! (1974)
Production company: Hemdale/Avton
Producer: Michael Klinger
Director: Peter Hunt
with Roger Moore, Susannah York, Simon Sabela,
John Gielgud, Bradford Dillman
The Great Kimberley Diamond Robbery (1910) (aka *Star of the South*)
Production company: Springbok Film Company
The Gun Runner (1916)
How Long? (1976)
Producer: Gibson Kente
How Rastus Got His Pork-Chop (1908)
Production company: Pathé Frères
Producer: Siegmund Lubin
How Rastus Got His Turkey (1910)
Production company: Pathé Frères
Producer: Siegmund Lubin
Jim Comes to Jo'burg (aka *African Jim*) (1949)
(see *African Jim*)
The Kaffir's Gratitude (1916)
Production company: Centaur
Producer: David Horsly
with William Clifford, Fred Montague, Margaret Gibson
King Solomon's Mines (1937)
Production company: Gainsborough

Producer: Geoffrey Barkas
Director: Robert Stevenson
with Cedric Hardwicke, Paul Robeson, John Loder
Lost in the Stars (1974)
Production company: Ely Landau Organization
Producer: Ely Landau
Director: Daniel Mann
with Brock Peters, Raymond St. Jacques, Clifton Davis, Paul Rogers
Love Changes People
Produced for Satour
The Magic Garden (1951)
Production company: Swan Film Productions
Producer and director: Donald Swanson
with Ralph Trewhela, Matome Tommy Ramokgopa,
Dolly Rathebe, Tommy Mchaka
Les Maîtres Fous (1955)
Production company: Films de la Pléiade and CNRS
Producer/Director: Jean Rouch
Mapantsula (1988)
Production company: Haverbeam and Hannay
Producer: Max Montocchio
Director: Oliver Schmitz and Thomas Mogotlane
with Thomas Mogotlane, Marcel van Heerden,
Thembi Mtshali, Dolly Rathebe, Peter Sephuma,
Darlington Michaels, Eugene Majola
Missionaries in Darkest Africa (1912)
Production company: Kalem
Director: Sidney Olcott
with Robert Vignola, Jack Clark, Gene Gauntier
My Country, My Hat (1983)
Production company: Bensusan Films
Producer/Director: David Bensusan
with Aletta Bezuidenhout, Peter Se-Puma, Regardt van den Berg
My Song Goes Forth (aka *Africa Sings* and *Africa Looks Up*) (1937)
Producer/Director: Joseph Best
with Paul Robeson
N!Ai, the Story of a !Kung Woman (1980)
Production Company: Documentary Educational Resources
Producer: John Marshall and Sue Marshall-Cabezas
Director: John Marshall and Adrienne Miesmer
with N!ai Short Face, /Gunda, Gao Lame, /Wi Crooked

On the Bowery (1956)
    Producer/Director: Lionel Rogosin
Out of Africa (1985)
    Production company: Mirage/Sidney Pollack
    Producer: Sidney Pollack
    Director: Sidney Pollack
    with Meryl Streep, Robert Redford, Klaus Maria
    Brandauer
The Piccanin's Christmas (1917)
    Production company: African Film Productions
    with Mabel May
Power of One (1991)
    Production company: Warner
    Producer: Roger Hall
    Director: John Avildsen
    with Stephen Dorff, Morgan Freeman, Winston Ntshona,
    Marius Weyers, Armin Mueller-Stahl, John Gielgud
Prester John (1920)
    Production company: African Film Productions
    with Ernest Groves, Dick Cruickshanks, Masoja,
    Adele Fillis
Pull Ourselves Up Or Die (1985)
    Production Company: Documentary Educational Resources
    Producer: Claire Ritchie
Queen for a Day (1913)
    Production company: Vitagraph
    with Bridget McSweeney
Rastus in Zululand (1910)
    Production company: Pathé Frères
    Producer: Siegmund Lubin
    Director: Arthur Hotaling and Epes Winthrup Sargeant
    with John and Mattie Edwards
Rhodes of Africa (1936)
    Production company: Gaumont - British
    Producer: Geoffrey Barkas
    Director: Berthold Viertel
    with Walter Huston, Oscar Homolka, Basil Sydney, Ndanisa Kumalo
Round-up Time in Texas (1936)
    Production company: Republic Studios
    Producer: Nat Levine
    Director: Joseph Kane

with Gene Autry, Smiley Burnette
Sanders of the River (1935)
> Production company: London
> Producer: Alexander Korda
> Director: Zoltan Korda
> with Leslie Banks, Paul Robeson

The Search for Sandra Laing (1978)
> Production company: ITC Entertainment
> Producer/Director: Antony Thomas

Shaka Zulu (1986)
> Production company: SABC/Harmony Gold
> Producer: Ed Harper
> Director: William C. Faure
> with Henry Cele, Edward Fox, Robert Powell, Dudu Mkhize

Siliwa the Zulu (aka *Zeliv* and *Witchcraft*) (1927)
> Production Company: Exploration Ltd.
> Producer: Prof. Lidio Cipriani
> Director: Attilio Gatti

Sins of Rosanne (1920)
> Production company: Paramount
> Director: Jack Noble
> with Ethel Clayton, Jack Holt, Fred Malatesta,
> James Smith

Six Days of Soweto (1978)
> Production company: Associated Television
> Producer/Director: Antony Thomas

Song of Africa (1951)
> Production company: African Film Productions
> Director: Emil Nofal
> with Joseph Muso, Maybel Magada, George Mabuza

South Africa Today (1962)
> Production company: Twentieth Century Fox

Stanley and Livingstone (1939)
> Production company: Twentieth Century Fox
> Producer: Kenneth MacGowan
> Director: Henry King
> with Spencer Tracy, Cedric Hardwicke

Story of the Rand (1916)
> Production company: African Film Productions
> Producer: Lorrimer Johnston
> with Caroline Frances Cook, H.B. Waring, Julius Royston

Symbol of Sacrifice (1918)
>   Production company: African Film Productions
>   Producer: I.W. Schlesinger
>   Directors: I.W. Schlesinger, Dick Cruickshanks,
>   and Joseph Albrecht
>   with Goba

There's a Zulu on my Stoep (1993)
>   Production company: Toron Films
>   Producer: Edgar Bold
>   Director: Gray Hofmeyer with Leon Schuster
>   and John Matshikiza

They Built a Nation (*Die Bou van 'n Nasie*) (1938)
>   (see *Die Bou van 'n Nasie*)

Trader Horn (1930)
>   Production company: MGM
>   Producer: Irving Thalberg
>   Director: W.S. Van Dyke
>   with Harry Carey, Edwina Booth, C. Aubrey Smith

The Union of South Africa: The Land and its People (1956)
>   Production company: Encyclopedia Britannica,
>   in affiliation with Clifford J. Kamen Productions

Untamed (1955)
>   Production company: Twentieth Century Fox
>   Producer: William Bacher
>   Director: Henry King
>   with Tyrone Power, Susan Hayward, Richard Egan

De Voortrekkers (aka *Winning a Continent*) (1916)
>   Production Company: African Film Productions
>   Producer: I.W. Schlesinger
>   Director: Harold Shaw
>   with Goba, Dick Cruickshanks, Edna Flugrath,
>   Caroline Cook, Tom Zulu, M.A. Wetherell

The Wilby Conspiracy (1975)
>   Production company: United Artists/Optimus/Baum-Dantine
>   Producer: Martin Baum
>   Director: Ralph Nelson
>   with Sidney Poitier, Michael Caine, Nicol Williamson,
>   Saeed Jaffrey, Prunella Gee, Joseph De Graf

A Wild Ride (1913)
>   Production company: Selig
>   with Bessie Eyton

Winning a Continent (aka *De Voortrekkers*) (1916)
    (see *De Voortrekkers*)
With Edged Tools (1919)
    Production company: African Film Productions
    Producer: I.W. Schlesinger
    with Edward Vincent, Mabel May
Working for Britain (1978)
    Production company: ITC Entertainment
    Producer/Director: Antony Thomas
A World Apart (1987)
    Production company: Palace/British Screen/Atlantic/
    Working Title
    Producer: Sarah Radclyffe
    Director: Chris Menges
    with Johdi May, Barbara Hershey, David Suchet
Zeliv (aka *Siliwa the Zulu* and *Witchcraft*) (1927)
    (see *Siliwa the Zulu*)
    Producer: Prof. Lidio Cipriani
    Director: Attilio Gatti
Zonk (1950)
    Production company: African Film Productions
    Producer: Ike Brooks Baruch
    Director: Hyman Kirstein
    with Sylvester Phahlane, Daniel Lekoape,
    Timothy Zwane, Fiver Kelly, The Manhattan Stars,
    Samuel Maile
Zulu (1964)
    Production company: Diamond Films Ltd.
    Producer: Stanley Baker, Cy Endfield
    Director: Cy Endfield
    with Stanley Baker, Michael Caine, Chief Buthelezi,
    Jack Hawkins
Zulu Dawn (1980)
    Production company: Samarkand/Zulu Dawn
    Producer: Barrie St. Clair, Nate Kohn
    Director: Douglas Hickox
    with Burt Lancaster, Denholm Elliot, Peter O'Toole,
    John Mills, Ken Gampu, Simon Sabela
The Zulu King (1913)
    Production company: Lubin Films

Zululand (1947)
>   Production company: Twentieth Century Fox

Zulu-Land (1911)
>   Production company: Selig

A Zulu's Devotion (1916)
>   Production company: African Film Productions
>   Producer: Lorrimer Johnston
>   Director: Joseph Albrecht
>   with Goba, Mabel May, Dick Cruickshanks

The Zulu's Heart (1908)
>   Production company: American Mutoscope and Biograph
>   Company
>   Director: D.W. Griffith
>   with Mack Sennett, Florence Lawrence

Bibliography

Alexander, P.F.: *Alan Paton*. Oxford University Press, Cape Town, 1994.

Attenborough, R.: *Richard Attenborough's Cry Freedom*. Alfred A. Knopf, New York, 1987.

Ballard, C: *The House of Shaka*. Emoyeni Books, Marine Parade, 1988.

Biko, S.: *I Write What I Like*. Harper & Row, San Francisco, 1978.

Billson, A.: *My Name is Michael Caine*. Muller, London, 1991.

Breitenbach, J.J.(editor): *South Africa in the Modern World*. Shuter and Shooter, Pietermaritzburg,1974.

Brink, A.: *A Dry White Season*. W.H. Allen & Co., London, 1979.

Buchan, J.: *Prester John*. Penguin Books, London, 1987. (First published 1910.)

Bunting, B.: *The Rise of the South African Reich*. Penguin African Library, Harmondsworth, 1969.

Burness, D. (editor): *Shaka, King of the Zulus in African Literature*. Three Continents Press, Washington, DC, 1976.

Caine, M.: *What's it all About?* Ballantine Books, New York, 1992.

Cinémathèque Française, La: *Afrique du Sud: Cinéma sous Influence*. Les Ecrans de la Liberté, 1990.

Conrad, J.: *Heart of Darkness*, 1902.

Cripps, T.: *Slow Fade to Black*. Oxford University Press, Oxford and New York, 1993.

Diawara, M.: *African Cinema: Politics and Culture*. Indiana University Press, Bloomington 1992.

Du Buisson, L.: *The White Man Cometh*. Jonathan Ball, Johannesburg, 1987.

Duberman, M.B.: *Paul Robeson*. Alfred Knopf, New York, 1988.

Eckhardt, J.P. and Kowall, L.: *Peddler of Dreams: Siegmund Lubin and the Creation of the Motion Picture Industry 1896-1916*. National Museum of American Jewish History, Philadelphia, 1984.

Ewers, C.H.: *Sidney Poitier: the Long Journey*. Signet Books, New York, 1969.

Gibson, J.Y.: *The Story of the Zulus*. Negro Universities Press, New York, 1911.

Golan, D.: *Inventing Shaka*. Lynne Rienner Publishers, London, Boulder, 1994.

Gray, S.: *John Ross, the True Story*. Penguin, Harmondsworth, Middlesex, 1987.

Gutsche, T.: *The History and Social Significance of Motion Pictures in South Africa 1895-1940*. Howard Timmins, Cape Town, 1972.

Haggard, H.R.: *King Solomon's Mines*. Puffin Books, London, 1958. (First published 1885.)

Henderson, R.M.: *D.W. Griffith: the Years at Biograph*. Secker & Warburg, London, 1971.

IDERA Films and Carrefour International: *Africa on Film and Videotape*. Montreal, 1990.

Korda, M.: *Charmed Lives*. Random House, New York, 1979.

Kuli, K.: *Alexander Korda*. W.H. Allen, London, 1975.

Le Roux, A.I. and Fourie, L.: *Filmverlede: Geskiedenis van die Suid-Afrikaanse Speelfilm*. Universiteit van Suid-Afrika, Pretoria, 1982.

Leab, D.J.: *From Sambo to Superspade*. Houghton Mifflin, New York, 1975.

Leonard, Richard: *Apartheid Whitewash: South African Propaganda in the United States*. Richard Leonard and the Africa Fund, 1989.

Low, R.: *History of the British Film, 1914-1918*. George Allen & Unwin, London, 1950.

Maré, G.: *Brothers Born of Warrior Blood: Politics and Ethnicity in South Africa*. Ravan Press, Johannesburg 1992.

Marquard, L.: *The Story of South Africa*. Faber & Faber, London, 1966.

Marquard, L.: *The Peoples and Policies of South Africa*. Oxford University Press, London, 1969.

Martin, A. (editor): *African Films: the Context of Production* (BFI Dossier No 6). British Film Institute, London, 1982.

Maynard, R.A.: *Africa on Film: Myth and Reality*. Hayden Book Co., Rochelle, New York, 1974.

Moodie, T.D.: *The Rise of Afrikanerdom*. University of California Press, Berkeley and Los Angeles, 1975.

Morris, D.R.: *The Washing of the Spears*. Simon & Schuster, New York, 1965.

Nesteby, J.R.: *Black Images in American Film, 1986-1954*. University Press of America, Washington, DC, 1982.

Niver, K.R. (edited by B. Bergson): *Motion Pictures from the Library of Congress Paper Print Collection, 1894-1912*. University of California Press, Berkeley and Los Angeles, 1967.

Ozynski, J. (editor): *Film: What the Censors Think*. Anti-Censorship Action Group for the 1989 *Weekly Mail* Film Festival, Johannesburg.

Paton, A.: *Cry, the Beloved Country*. Penguin Books, London, 1970.

Paton, A.: *Journey Continued* (autobiography). Charles Scribner and Sons, New York, 1988.

Phillips, R.E.: *The Bantu in the City*. The Lovedale Press, Alice, 1938.

Pines, J.: *Blacks in Film*. Cassell and Collier MacMillan Publishing, London, 1975.

Poitier, S.: *This Life*. Alfred A. Knopf, New York, 1980.

Ritter, E.A.: *Shaka Zulu*. Penguin Books, London, 1978.

Roux, E.: *Time Longer Than Rope*. University of Wisconsin Press, Madison, 1978.

Rutherford, E.: *Nine Lives*. Ragweed, Prince Edward Island, 1993.

Schmitz, O. and Mogotlane, T.: *Mapantsula*. COSAW, Fordsburg, 1991.

Selby, J.: *Shaka's Heirs*. George Allen & Unwin, London, 1971.

Slovo, S.: *A World Apart*. Faber & Faber, London, 1988.

Stanley, H.M: *In Darkest Africa*. Charles Scribner and Sons, New York, 1890.

Stultz, N.M.: *Afrikaner Politics in South Africa, 1934-1948*. University of California Press, Berkeley and Los Angeles, 1974.

Thomson, D.: *A Biographical Dictionary of the Cinema*. Secker & Warburg, London, 1975.

Tomaselli, K.G.: *The Cinema of Apartheid*. Smyrna/Lake View Press, Chicago, 1988.

Tomaselli, K.G.: *The South African Film Industry*. African Studies Institute, University of the Witwatersrand, 1980.

Tomaselli, K.G., Steenfeld, L., Tomaselli, R., Williams, A.: *Myth, Race and Power: South Africans Imaged on Film and TV*. Anthropos, Bellville, 1986.

Tomaselli, K.G. and van Zyl, John, editors: *Critical Arts, Special Issue on Anthropology*, March 1981, Vol.1, No.4.

Ukadike, N.F.: *Black African Cinema*, University of California Press, Berkeley and Los Angeles,1994.

Volkman, T.A.: *The San in Transition. Vol.1: A Guide to N!ai, the Story of a !Kung Woman*. Documentary Educational Resources and Cultural Survival, 9, 1982.

Woods, D.: *Asking for Trouble*. Beacon Press, Boston, 1982.

Woods, D.: *Biko*. H. Holt & Co., New York, 1983.

Articles & Reviews

Beittel, M.: *'Mapantsula*: Cinema, Crime and Politics on the Witwatersrand.' *Journal of Southern African Studies*, Vol.16, No. 4, December 1990, pp. 751-760.

Black, G.: 'Silencing the Dissenters.' *The Nation*, 18 June 1988, pp. 854-856.

Canby, V.: 'Is *The Gods Must Be Crazy* Only A Comedy?' *New York Times*, 28 October 1984.

Carchidi, V.: 'Representing South Africa: Apartheid from Print to Film.' *Film & History*, Vol. XXI, No.1, February. 1991, pp. 20-27.

Cooper, M.: 'Hollywood Acts?' *American Film*, Vol.11, No. 2, 1985, p. 35.

De Kock, B.: 'Film Production'. *Standard Encyclopedia of South Africa,* Vol. 4, pp. 503-507.

Etherington, N.: 'Shrinking the Zulu.' *Southern African Review of Books*, September-October 1992, p. 23.

Evans, G.: 'Arm's Length and the National Film Board: Black and White in South Africa.' *Department of History*, Dawson College, Montreal, Canada. June 1986.

Gallagher, J.T.: 'Henry Morton Stanley, I Presume.' *Film & History,* Vol. XVI, No.1, February 1986, pp. 9-17.

Gavshon, H.: '"Bearing Witness": Ten Years Towards an Opposition Film Movement in South Africa.' *Radical History Review*, 1990, pp. 1-14.

Gutsche, T.: 'Fifty Years of South African Cinema.' *Cape Times Week-end Magazine*, 11 May 1946, pp. 2-3.

Gutsche, T.: 'Film Production.' *Standard Encyclopedia of Southern Africa*, Vol. 4, pp. 498-503.

Hamilton, C.A.: 'A Positional Gambit: *Shaka Zulu* and the Conflict in South Africa.' *Radical History Review,* No. 44, 1989, pp. 5-31.

Hochschild, A.: 'Hollywood Discovers South Africa.' *Mother Jones*, December 1987, pp. 34-37, 42.

Kowall, L.: 'Siegmund Lubin, the Forgotten Filmmaker.' *Pennsylvania Heritage*, Winter 1986, pp. 18-27.

Laurence, P.: 'To Tell the Truth.' *Africa Report*, March-April 1987, pp. 9-13.

Moore, C.: 'African Films in America'. *Africa Film & TV*, 1994, p. 56.

Rogin, M.: 'Blackface, White Noise.' *Critical Inquiry,* No.18, Spring 1992, pp. 417-453.

Rogosin, L.: 'Interpreting Reality.' *Film Culture*, No. 21, Summer 1960, pp. 20-28.

Shute, J.: 'South Africa on Screen.' *The Boston Review*, February 1990, pp. 7-9.

Van Wijk, S.L.: 'Film Services, Educational'. *Standard Encyclopedia of Southern Africa*, Vol. 4, p. 508.

Walker, J.: 'Sacred location for *Shaka Zulu.*' *South African Digest*, 30 November 1984, p. 2.

Wylie, D.: 'Who's Afraid of *Shaka Zulu?*' *Southern African Review of Books*, May-June 1991, pp. 8-9.

Zolberg, A.R.: 'Tribalism Through Corrective Lenses.' *Foreign Affairs*, July 1973, pp. 728-739.

References

Index